MATHS FOR YOU

Book 2

Duncan and Christine Graham

Hutchinson

London Melbourne Sydney Auckland Johannesburg

Contents

To the teacher

Maths for You 1 and 2 is a two-year CSE course. Every CSE mathematics syllabus has been closely studied and the topics in these books written to cover the common core syllabus.
Book 2 starts with 5 sections, each containing about 10 topics, a calculator page and a Recap. The topics are classified into mathematical areas on page 231. Other mathematical activities, called Sidetracks, provide short breaks from the main topics.
It continues with a basic revision programme containing:

  advice on revision and examination technique,

  explanations of common 'exam words',

  revision summary pages and past examination questions organized in mathematical areas (see p. 231) and sample examination papers.

Book 2

Duncan and Christine Graham

About this book

This book was written to help you to study mathematics. Your CSE syllabus has been split into short topics. This page shows you how the topics are set out in this book.

Topics often start with these instructions:

'You need:' tells you the extra equipment you need for the topic. You always need a pen, pencil, rubber and an exercise book.

'You should have done:' tells you the topics you should have done in this book before starting.

You will see these signs in the margin.

reminds you of work you have done before and need in the topic.

tells you where a calculator would be useful.

shows you how to set down your answer to a question. Some working is explained in the margin.

tells you the important points in the topic. It is very useful when revising.

There are three kinds of exercises in this book.

A You do these as you work through the topic. They will help you to understand the work. You can check your answers with those at the back of the book. It is no use cheating: you will be caught out by the EXERCISE.

Only your teacher has the answers to these. You can both check whether you have understood the work.

Recap This has questions from all the topics in a section. It will help you to revise your work.

Calculator magic

80	1	3	4	5		70	71	66
15			20	21	56		54	
14	63	52		31	47	46	19	68
10	60	34	44		42	48	22	72
9	25	33	39	41	43	49		73
	24	50	40	45		32	58	8
75	23	36	53	51	35	30		7
	28	65	62		26	27	18	6
16		79	78	77	13	12	11	2

This is a magic square.
If you:

← add across each row ⎫
↓ add down each column ⎬ you get the same magic number.
⤢ add diagonally ⎭

What is its magic number?

Hint: Find a complete line. Add the numbers.

Copy the square. Fill in the missing numbers.

Hint: Look for lines with only one number missing first.

Take away the outside numbers. You should have a 7 by 7 square.
Is it magic?
See how many more magic squares you can find.

24	2	36
18	12	8
4	72	6

Is this a magic square?

It is. But it is no use adding!
You have to multiply this time.

What is its magic product?

Copy and complete these 'multiplying' squares.

36		48
	12	
3		4

18	4	3
		36
12		2

9	81	729
		3

60	5	90
	30	

108		
48	36	
9		

Pick your own

You need: a ruler and centimetre graph paper.

Jackie and Tina worked at a fruit farm in the summer.
They kept records of the sales.

Strawberries		
Weight	Tally	Frequency
1 lb	⊦⊦⊦ ⊦⊦⊦ ⊦⊦⊦ ⊦⊦⊦ ⊦⊦⊦ ⊦⊦⊦ ⊦⊦⊦ ⊦⊦⊦ ⊦⊦⊦ llll	49
2 lb	⊦⊦⊦ ⊦⊦⊦ ⊦⊦⊦ ⊦⊦⊦ ⊦⊦⊦	25
3 lb	⊦⊦⊦ ⊦⊦⊦ ll	12
4 lb	⊦⊦⊦ ⊦⊦⊦ l	11
5 lb	⊦⊦⊦ ⊦⊦⊦ ⊦⊦⊦ ⊦⊦⊦ ⊦⊦⊦ ⊦⊦⊦ l	31

Raspberries		
Weight	Tally	Frequency
1 lb	⊦⊦⊦ ⊦⊦⊦ ⊦⊦⊦ ⊦⊦⊦ ⊦⊦⊦ ll	27
2 lb	⊦⊦⊦ ⊦⊦⊦ ⊦⊦⊦ ⊦⊦⊦ ⊦⊦⊦ ⊦⊦⊦ ⊦⊦⊦ ⊦⊦⊦ ⊦⊦⊦	45
3 lb	⊦⊦⊦ ⊦⊦⊦ llll	14
4 lb	⊦⊦⊦ ⊦⊦⊦ ⊦⊦⊦ ⊦⊦⊦ ll	22
5 lb	⊦⊦⊦ ⊦⊦⊦ ⊦⊦⊦ llll	19

Loganberries		
Weight	Tally	Frequency
1 lb	⊦⊦⊦ ⊦⊦⊦ ⊦⊦⊦ ⊦⊦⊦ ⊦⊦⊦ ll	27
2 lb	⊦⊦⊦ ⊦⊦⊦ ll	12
3 lb	⊦⊦⊦ lll	8
4 lb		0
5 lb	⊦⊦⊦ ⊦⊦⊦ ⊦⊦⊦ ⊦⊦⊦ ⊦⊦⊦ ⊦⊦⊦ lll	33

Jackie drew histograms to show their data.

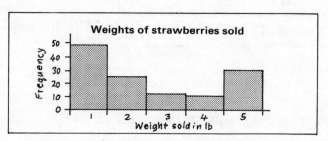

Weights of strawberries sold

 Draw histograms for the other fruits.

The farmer had different punnets for each weight.

 A Which size did he need most for strawberries?

 **Memo** Mode: the item which occurs most often in a tally.

 B What is the mode for each fruit?

The farmer wanted to know the mean weights.

Strawberries

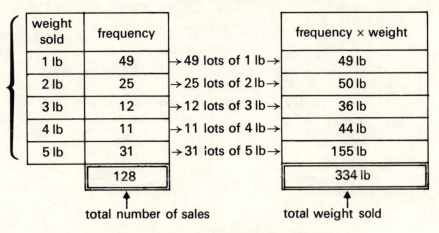

frequency
table
or
distribution

weight sold	frequency		frequency × weight
1 lb	49	→ 49 lots of 1 lb →	49 lb
2 lb	25	→ 25 lots of 2 lb →	50 lb
3 lb	12	→ 12 lots of 3 lb →	36 lb
4 lb	11	→ 11 lots of 4 lb →	44 lb
5 lb	31	→ 31 lots of 5 lb →	155 lb
	128		334 lb

total number of sales   total weight sold

$$\text{mean weight sold} = \frac{\text{total weight sold}}{\text{total number of sales}}$$

$$= \frac{334}{128} \text{ lb}$$

$$= \underline{2.6 \text{ lb}} \quad \text{(to 1 d.p.)}$$

For each fruit:
(a) make a frequency table,
(b) work out the total number of sales, total weight sold and the mean weight sold (to 1 d.p.).

A frequency table or distribution can be made from a tally chart. It lists values and their frequencies.

The mode is the value which occurs most.

Mean value from a frequency table:

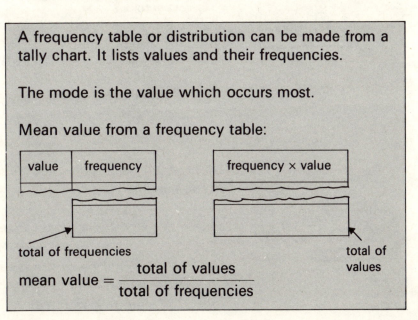

value	frequency		frequency × value

total of frequencies   total of values

$$\text{mean value} = \frac{\text{total of values}}{\text{total of frequencies}}$$

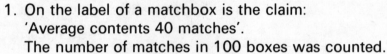

1. On the label of a matchbox is the claim:
   'Average contents 40 matches'.
   The number of matches in 100 boxes was counted.

38	39	40	40	41	40	38	41	41	39
40	40	40	39	40	40	40	40	40	40
39	42	38	41	40	41	41	41	41	40
42	40	40	42	42	39	40	40	39	40
40	40	40	40	40	40	40	40	40	40
41	39	40	40	40	40	41	39	41	41
40	40	41	40	41	41	40	40	40	40
41	40	38	42	40	40	42	41	42	41
41	39	40	40	42	39	40	38	40	40
40	40	40	42	40	40	41	40	41	42

(a) Draw up a frequency table for this data.
(b) What is the mode of the number of matches?
(c) Use your frequency table to calculate the mean.
(d) Is the match maker's claim justified?

2. A secretary noted the number of phone calls she made each day.

3	9	5	6	7	5	6	13	14	10
5	7	7	7	4	5	12	6	10	3
5	6	2	4	6	2	6	9	6	7
4	3	5	9	11	9	8	12	6	15
6	11	10	8	11	5	8	7	3	5
8	6	6	8	7	3	6	11	2	10

(a) Tabulate the data in a frequency distribution table.
(b) What is the mode of the number of calls?
(c) Using the frequency distribution, calculate the mean number of calls.

3. In a penalty kick competition, each boy takes ten penalties against an international goalkeeper.

No. of goals	0	1	2	3	4	5	6	7	8
No. of boys	2	5	7	5	5	3	1	1	1

(a) How many boys were there in the competition?
(b) Write down the mode of this distribution.
(c) Calculate the arithmetic mean of this distribution.

Sines and cosines

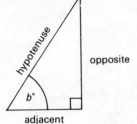

hypotenuse
opposite
$b°$
adjacent

You need: 3 figure tables and a ruler.

Here is a right-angled triangle.
Its base angle is $b°$.

What have we called the side:
(a) across from the right angle?
(b) across from the base angle?
(c) next to the base angle?

This is a very small right-angled triangle.
We can hardly see it.

It can be enlarged using a powerful magnifying glass.
Now we can see:

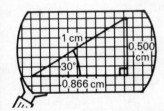

base angle: 30°
hypotenuse: 1 cm
opposite: 0.500 cm
adjacent: 0.866 cm

Exercise 1

Here are some more magnified right-angled triangles.
1. Copy and complete the table.
2. What do you notice about the hypotenuses in your
   table?

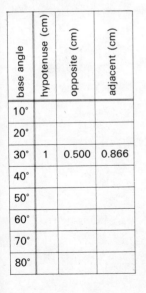

base angle	hypotenuse (cm)	opposite (cm)	adjacent (cm)
10°			
20°			
30°	1	0.500	0.866
40°			
50°			
60°			
70°			
80°			

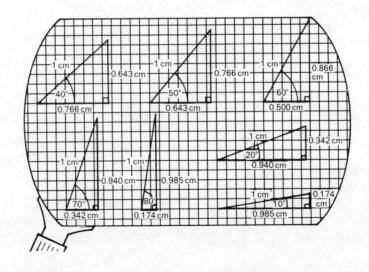

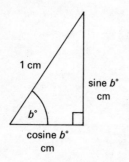

When the hypotenuse is 1 cm long:

(a) the opposite is **sine $b°$** cm long,

(b) the adjacent is **cosine $b°$** cm long.

Look at your table from Exercise 1.
All the hypotenuses are 1 cm long. So your table gives the sines and cosines of the angles.

sin means sine
cos means cosine

Use your table to find:

1. sin 30°	3. cos 40°	5. sin 50°	7. cos 80°
2. cos 10°	4. sin 70°	6. cos 60°	8. sin 20°

We could find other sines and cosines by drawing triangles. But we do not have to.
Tables of them have been worked out for us.

Use your sine and cosine tables to find:

1. sin 32°	6. cos 47°	11. sin 46°	16. cos 69°
2. sin 74°	7. cos 15°	12. cos 21°	17. sin 5°
3. sin 90°	8. cos 84°	13. cos 90°	18. cos 72°
4. sin 17°	9. cos 53°	14. sin 51°	19. cos 38°
5. sin 25°	10. cos 9°	15. sin 83°	20. sin 68°

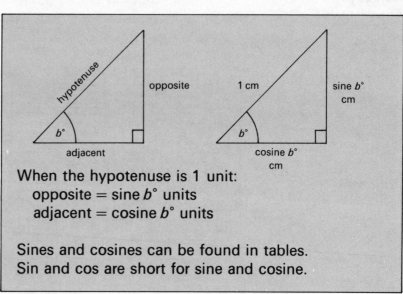

When the hypotenuse is 1 unit:
    opposite = sine $b°$ units
    adjacent = cosine $b°$ units

Sines and cosines can be found in tables.
Sin and cos are short for sine and cosine.

**Exercise 3** Copy these triangles. They are not drawn accurately. Use your tables of sines and cosines to fill in the missing lengths.

1.
1 cm
54°

4.
1 cm
76°

7.
1 cm
42°

10.
1 cm
11°

2.
1 cm
35°

5.
1 cm
23°

8.
1 cm
7°

11.
1 cm
32°

3.
1 cm
19°

6.
1 cm
81°

9.
1 cm
65°

12.
1 cm
48°

Tessellations

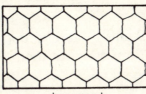
honeycomb

patchwork quilt

In each tessellation (tiling pattern): the tiles are congruent (same shape and size), there are no gaps between tiles, the pattern could go on forever if you had room.

Creating new tessellations is easy. Start with a tile you know tessellates.

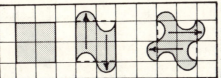

And a little imagination can give:

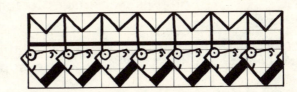

Try some yourself. Look in the library for some by an artist called Escher.

Subject	mark	total marks
Maths	54	60
TD	60	80
History	20	80
English	51	75
Woodwork	49	70
RE	15	45
Physics	45	75

Comparing

Paul got most marks in TD in his mocks.
But is it his best subject?

Percentages make it easier to find out.

write as a fraction

$$\text{TD mark} = \frac{60}{80}$$

multiply by 100

$$\text{TD percentage mark} = \frac{60}{80} \times 100\%$$

work it out

$$= \frac{\cancel{60}^{3}}{\cancel{80}_{\cancel{4}1}} \times \cancel{100}^{25}\% = \underline{75\%}$$

 Change all of Paul's results to percentages.
Which is his best subject?

Paul's mum and dad have just bought a garden shop.
He works out their profits (and losses).

item	cost price	selling price	profit (loss)
seeds	40p	46p	6p
shears	£8	£10	
spade	£12	£15	
chair	£15	£16.50	
heater	£22	£27.50	
mower	£45	£63	

difference between selling price and cost price

 Work out their profit (or loss) on each item.

He uses percentages to compare their 'profits'.

Seeds:

$$\text{percentage 'profit'} = \frac{\text{'profit'}}{\text{cost price}} \times 100\%$$

$$= \frac{\cancel{6}^{3}}{\cancel{40}_{\cancel{2}1}} \times \cancel{100}^{5}\% = \underline{15\%}$$

 Work out their percentage profit (or loss) on each item.

Percentages make it easy to compare other things too.

write the fraction

multiply by 100%

Express 24 cm as a percentage of 1.5 m.

$$\frac{24\,cm}{1.5\,m} \quad \xrightarrow{\text{same unit}} \quad \frac{24\,cm}{150\,cm}$$

$$\frac{\cancel{24}^{\,8}}{\cancel{150}_{\,31}} \times \cancel{100\%}^{\,2} = \underline{16\%}$$

Express the first quantity as a percentage of the second:
1. 36 cm, 1.2 m   3. 540 ml, 2.7 l   5. 48 min, 2 h
2. 375 g, 1.5 kg   4. 126 m, 1.4 km   6. 581 mm, 7 m

Percentages make comparing easy.
To change a fraction to a percentage, multiply by 100%.

$$\text{percentage profit (or loss)} = \frac{\text{profit (or loss)}}{\text{cost price}} \times 100\%$$

To write any quantity as a percentage of another:

1. write as a fraction — $\dfrac{\text{1st quantity}}{\text{2nd quantity}}$, (same unit)

2. multiply by 100%.

1. Change these fractions to percentages:

$\frac{1}{2}, \frac{3}{4}, \frac{7}{10}, \frac{13}{20}, \frac{1}{8}, \frac{1}{3}, \frac{3}{5}, \frac{39}{50}, 1\frac{1}{4}, 4\frac{5}{8}$

Which is her best subject?

2. Change Tina's exam results to percentages:

subject	Maths	Art	History	English	Biology	French	RE	Physics
mark	45	33	52	66	26	23	30	54
total marks	60	55	80	75	65	50	45	75

3. Calculate the percentage profit (or loss) for these:

cost price	50p	£1	$22\frac{1}{2}$p	80p	£1.80	£175	£15	£60	£260	£850
selling price	$62\frac{1}{2}$p	£1.35	$18\frac{1}{2}$p	92p	£1.65	£259	£18.75	£72	£299	£646

4. Express the first quantity as a percentage of the second:
(a) 21 cm, 1.4 m   (c) 325 ml, 5 l   (e) 460 m, 0.5 km
(b) 15 g, 2.5 kg   (d) 27 min, $2\frac{1}{2}$ h   (f) 611 mm, 1.3 m

Day trips

Sharon spends half term with her cousins in Birmingham. They like to go for day trips by train.

On Monday they plan to go to North Wales.

North Wales Seaside Day Returns

From		Outward
Birmingham New Street	d 06.25	08.55
Wolverhampton	d 06.42	09.13
Crewe	a 07.28	09.57
	change	*change*
Crewe	d 08.02	10.18
Prestatyn	a 09.24	11.23
Rhyl	a 09.33	11.31
Colwyn Bay	a 09.47	11.45
Llandudno	a 10.15	12.13

Out by the above services only. Return the same day by any train.

1. What do 'd' and 'a' stand for on the timetable?
2. When does the first train: (a) depart from Birmingham?
   (b) arrive in Llandudno?
3. Where do you have to change?
4. At which stations in Wales do the trains stop?

Sharon works out how long the first train takes from Birmingham to Llandudno.

from 1st time to next hour	06.25 to 07.00	→	35 minutes
from next hour to 2nd time	07.00 to 10.15	→	3 hours 15 minutes
add	Total time	→	3 hours 50 minutes

1. How long does the first train take from Birmingham to Prestatyn?
2. When does the second train: (a) leave Birmingham?
   (b) arrive in Colwyn Bay?
3. How long does the second train take from Birmingham to each town in Wales?

Sharon wants to see Blackpool Illuminations.
British Rail are doing two special trips.

Blackpool Day Out

From		Outward	
Birmingham New Street	d 07.38	09.10	
Wolverhampton	d 07.55	09.28	
Preston	a 09.42	10.54	
	change	*change*	
Preston	d 10.22	11.07	
Blackpool North	a 10.53	11.37	

C

1. At which stations do the trains stop?
2. How long do you have to change at Preston?

She works out how long the first train takes:

from 1st time to next hour
from next hour to 2nd time
add

07.38 to 08.00 → 22 minutes
08.00 to 10.53 → 2 hours 53 minutes   75 minutes = 1 h 15 min
Total time → 3 hours 15 minutes
1

D

1. How long does the first train take from Birmingham to Preston?
2. How long does the second train take from Birmingham to: (a) Preston?   (b) Blackpool?
3. Which train would you choose? Why?

Sharon's aunt wants to visit the colleges at Oxford and Cambridge.

Oxford Day Returns	Cambridge Day Returns
Birmingham: 07.30, 08.43, 09.58, 11.04, 12.18	Birmingham: 06.35, 07.05, 08.15, 08.36, 09.28
Journey time: 1 hour 42 minutes	Journey time: 3 hours 55 minutes

WHAT TIME DO WE ARRIVE IN OXFORD?

First train to Oxford:	hours	minutes	
Depart	07	30	
Travel time	1	42	72 minutes = 1 h 12 min
Arrive	09	12	
	1		

The first train should arrive at 09.12.
Work out when each train should arrive at its destination.

E

Sharon's family go on two 'round trips'.

Cathedral City Tour

Birmingham	d 09.15
Gloucester	a 10.10
	break of journey
Gloucester	d 13.50
Worcester	a 14.27
	break of journey
Worcester	d 16.26
Hereford	a 17.11
	break of journey
Hereford	d 19.59
Birmingham	a 21.27

Round Robin Trip

Birmingham	d 08.15
Bristol	a 10.01
	change
Bristol	d 10.14
Bath	a 10.27
	break of journey
Bath	d 12.29
Weymouth	a 14.42
	break of journey
Weymouth	d 15.33
Poole	a 16.22
	break of journey
Poole	d 17.05
Birmingham	a 20.56

1. Which cathedral cities does the first tour visit?
2. How much time do they have in each cathedral city?
3. How long is the whole tour?
4. Which places does the Round Robin Trip visit?
5. How much time do they have in each place?
6. How long do they spend on the train on the Round Robin Trip?

Here are some Saturday excursions.

Norwich
Depart: 10.15
Return: 18.32
Journey time: 3 h 52 min

Edinburgh
Depart: 07.28
Return: 18.35
Journey time: 4 h 36 min

York
Depart: 07.30
Return: 19.44
Journey time: 2 h 45 min

Cardiff
Depart: 08.55
Return: 20.45
Journey time: 2 h 10 min

Cheltenham Spa
Depart: 07.01
Return: 20.39
Journey time: 50 min

London Euston
Depart: 06.44
Return: 21.40
Journey time: 1 h 39 min

For each excursion, calculate the times the train:
(a) arrives at its destination,
(b) arrives back at Birmingham.

More directed numbers

2 means $^+2$

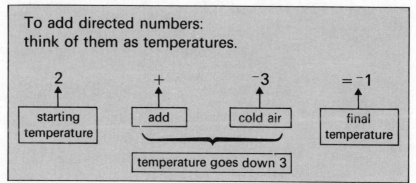

To add directed numbers:
think of them as temperatures.

2 → starting temperature
+ → add
$^-3$ → cold air
$=^-1$ → final temperature

temperature goes down 3

 Work out these:

1. $2 + ^-1$ 3. $^-3 + 4$ 5. $9 + ^-3$
2. $3 + ^-5$ 4. $^-2 + ^-1$ 6. $^-7 + 8$

5 means $^+5$
7 means $^+7$

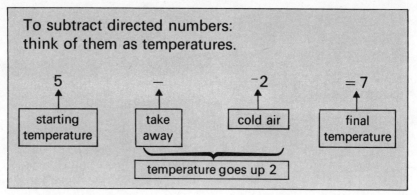

To subtract directed numbers:
think of them as temperatures.

5 → starting temperature
− → take away
$^-2$ → cold air
$= 7$ → final temperature

temperature goes up 2

 Work out these:

1. $4 - ^-1$ 3. $^-2 - 1$ 5. $^-8 - ^-2$
2. $6 - ^-3$ 4. $5 - 8$ 6. $^-9 - ^-9$

watch the signs!

Do these pairs of calculations:

1. $2 + ^-5$ 4. $^-4 + ^-5$ 7. $5 - 5$
   $2 - 5$ $^-4 - 5$ $5 + ^-5$
2. $3 + ^-6$ 5. $7 + ^-3$ 8. $9 - 6$
   $3 - 6$ $7 - 3$ $9 + ^-6$
3. $^-1 + ^-2$ 6. $^-6 + ^-8$ 9. $^-10 + ^-7$
   $^-1 - 2$ $^-6 - 8$ $^-10 - 7$

10. What do you notice about your answers?

In Exercise 1 you should have found that:

$$2 - 5 = {}^-3$$
$$2 + {}^-5 = {}^-3$$

subtracting a positive number
or adding   its negative
$\Big\}$ gave the same answer.

We use this in algebra.

For example:

subtracting y
or   adding ${}^-y$
$\Big\}$ give the same answer.

So we can rewrite $x - y$
            as $x + {}^-y$.

 Rewrite these using addition only:
1. $2x - y$
2. $m - 3n$
3. $x^2 - 2x$
4. $1 - y^2$
5. ${}^-3y - 8z$
6. $p^2 - 2q^2$
7. ${}^-2x^2 - x + 4$
8. $5x^2 - 3x - 7$
9. $x^2 + 2x - 9$

Sometimes we have to subtract negatives in algebra. We need a rule for this too.

 Do these pairs of calculations:
1. $5 - {}^-4$
   $5 + 4$
2. $3 - {}^-2$
   $3 + 2$
3. ${}^-2 + 3$
   ${}^-2 - {}^-3$
4. ${}^-1 + 5$
   ${}^-1 - {}^-5$
5. $6 - {}^-8$
   $6 + 8$
6. $9 + 2$
   $9 - {}^-2$
7. ${}^-4 + 6$
   ${}^-4 - {}^-6$
8. $10 - {}^-7$
   $10 + 7$
9. $12 - {}^-10$
   $12 + 10$
10. What do you notice about your answers?

In Exercise 2 you should have found that:

$$5 - {}^-4 = 9$$
$$5 + 4 = 9$$

subtracting a negative number
or   adding   its positive
$\Big\}$ gave the same answer.

So we can rewrite $p - {}^-q$
            as $p + q$.

 Rewrite these using addition only:
1. $a - {}^-b$
2. $4c - {}^-d$
3. $3p - {}^-4q$
4. $x^2 - {}^-x$
5. $2y^2 - {}^-y$
6. $2m - {}^-3n$
7. $5p^2 - {}^-4p$
8. $3p^2 - {}^-p - {}^-2$
9. $2x^2 - {}^-3x - {}^-1$

Summary

Subtracting a positive number
or adding   its negative } give the same answer.

Subtracting a negative number
or adding   its positive } give the same answer.

We use this in algebra to rewrite expressions using addition only.

For example: $3x^2 - 2x + 1$
                $= 3x^2 + {}^-2x + 1$

Exercise 3

Rewrite these using addition only. Find answers where you can.

1. $3 - 5$
2. $7 - 4$
3. ${}^-2 - 6$
4. $1 - {}^-2$
5. $3 - {}^-4$
6. ${}^-2 - 6$
7. $8 - 9$
8. ${}^-5 - {}^-1$
9. $7 - 12$
10. ${}^-9 - {}^-10$

11. $x - y$
12. $2x^2 - {}^-3$
13. $3p^2 - 4$
14. $c - {}^-d$
15. $4m - 3n$
16. $y^2 - 2y$
17. $2r - s$
18. $5x^2 - {}^-x$
19. $7z - w$
20. $8r - {}^-4s$

21. $x^2 - x - 2$
22. $2x^2 - 3x + 5$
23. $4p^2 - 5p + 1$
24. $6m^2 - 4m - 2$
25. $9r + 3r^2 - 1$
26. $7c^2 - 2c + 4$
27. $3e - 5e^2 + 7$
28. $8f^3 - 11f + 6$
29. $2g^4 - 7g^2 - 2$
30. $12x^2 - 8x^3 - x$

Know your Imperial units

In Britain we are now supposed to 'Think metric'.
But many people still use 'Imperial units'.

How many Imperial units do you know?
Find the ones hidden in here.

Look ⤢ for length units.
Look ⟷ for mass units.
Look ↕ for capacity units.

A	S	T	O	N	E	G	E	V	D	H	W	X	K
I	M	C	O	C	N	A	N	A	G	R	I	C	S
L	N	I	H	O	D	L	R	E	T	R	A	U	Q
T	B	C	L	A	F	L	U	O	N	W	L	Y	U
Y	M	R	H	E	I	O	Z	F	I	B	L	R	A
O	U	N	C	E	D	N	U	O	P	P	I	J	R
F	H	U	N	D	R	E	D	W	E	I	G	H	T

For charity

You need: a ruler.

Paul's class organized the school fête.
He collected the entrance money.

Paul's Ready Reckoner

Number of people

	1	2	3	4	5	6	7	8	9	10
Adult	40p			£1·60						
Child	25p						£1·75			

  Copy and complete Paul's ready reckoner.

Steve's class organized a sponsored walk.

Gary	Distance 12 km	
Name	Amount	Total
Jom Amul	10p.	1.20
Ann Jnn	15p.	1.80
Suw Cnnw	5p.	60
Lnn Ann	10p.	1.20
Tnw Lnwl	2p.	24

Everyone taking part had a sponsor form.
Steve had to check the amounts on each form.
He made a ready reckoner:

Steve's Ready Reckoner

Distance in km

Pence per km	1	2	3	4	5	8	10	12	15	18	20
1p								12p			
2p				8p							
10p					50p						£2·00

Copy and complete Steve's ready reckoner.

Tina's class did community work.
They did decorating and gardening for senior citizens.

Each job had a number of 'man hours'.

Mr. Weed's garden: 60 'man hours'.

more 'men',
less time!

1 'man' should spend 60 hours.
2 'men' should each spend $60 \div 2$ hours = 30 hours.

How long should these spend on Mr. Weed's garden?
(a) 3 'men'   (c) 5 'men'   (e) 12 'men'
(b) 4 'men'   (d) 10 'men'   (f) 15 'men'

Tina made out the work schedules.

Decorating	'Man hours'	Gardening	'Man hours'
Miss Pott	40	Mrs Rakeleaf	30
Mrs Paper	90	Mr Diggins	48
Mr Backake	100	Miss Bonfire	70

Exercise 2

How long should these spend doing each job?
(a) 1 'man'   (c) 4 'men'   (e) 15 'men'
(b) 3 'men'   (d) 10 'men'   (f) 20 'men'

Now try this mixed exercise.

Exercise 3

1. The school trip costs £2.50. Make a ready reckoner
   showing the cost for 1–20 people to travel.

2. One tractor can do a farm's ploughing in 84 hours.
   How long would it take these numbers of tractors to
   do the ploughing:
   (a) 3   (b) 4   (c) 8   (d) 12   (e) 7 ?

3. A gearwheel turns 500 times in 1 minute.
   How many times does it turn in:
   (a) 2 minutes   (b) 3 minutes   (c) 5 minutes ?

Well balanced

You need: tracing paper and a ruler.

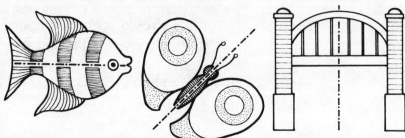

These shapes are **symmetrical**.
Each is 'balanced' about its dotted line.
This line is called the **axis of symmetry**.
It divides the shape into two matching halves. One half is the same as the other but the opposite way round.

A An axis of symmetry is a fold line.
Check by tracing each shape. Then fold each tracing along its dotted line to see if the two halves match.

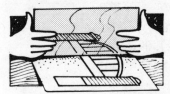

An axis of symmetry is a mirror line too.
If you hold a mirror along it, the reflection matches the other half of the shape.
You can check this at home.

B Copy and complete these shapes.
The dotted lines are axes of symmetry.

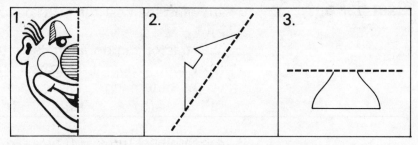

1.
2.
3.

Some shapes have more than one axis of symmetry.
This shape has four.

Copy these shapes and draw in their axes of symmetry.
Check by tracing and folding.

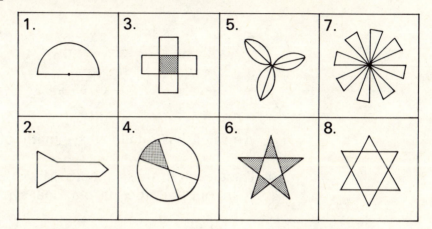

| 1. | 3. | 5. | 7. |
| 2. | 4. | 6. | 8. |

This shape is symmetrical too.
But it does not have an axis of symmetry!

 Turn this page round like this:
Look at the shape again.
What do you notice?

 top

 do⊥

We say that it has **point symmetry**.
It looks the same after it has been turned through
half a turn (180°).

 Which shapes on page 22 and on this page have point
symmetry?
Check by turning the pages round.

Point symmetry is a special kind of **rotational
symmetry**.
Rotation means 'turning round'.

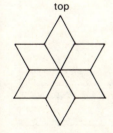 top

 Trace this star. Mark the top as shown.
Put your tracing on top of the star.
Rotate the tracing one whole turn (360°).
How many times does your tracing fit exactly on top of
the star?

Your tracing from **F** should have fitted exactly in 6 different positions:

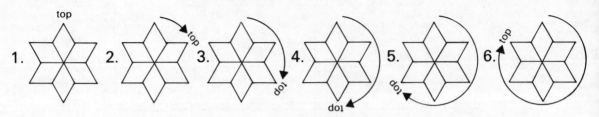

We say it has rotational symmetry of order 6.

G Trace each of these shapes. Mark the top each time. Work out the order of rotational symmetry for each one.

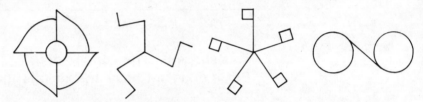

Some shapes only look the same after they have been rotated the full turn.
They do not have rotational symmetry.

H Which shapes on pages 22 and 23 do not have rotational symmetry?

Summary

An axis of symmetry divides a shape into two balanced halves. Each half is a mirror image of the other.

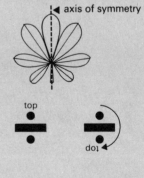
axis of symmetry

Point symmetry: the shape looks the same when rotated half a turn (180°).

Rotational symmetry: the shape looks the same in several different positions when rotated one turn (360°).
Order: the number of times it fits onto itself in one turn.

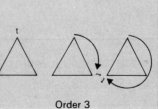
Order 3

1. Copy these shapes and draw in any axes of symmetry.

A B C D E F G H I J K L M N
O P Q R S T U V W X Y Z

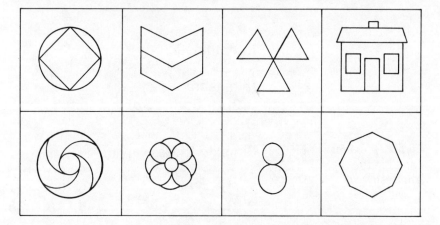

2. Draw these shapes and mark any axes of symmetry:
square, rectangle, rhombus, parallelogram, kite,
trapezium, equilateral triangle, isosceles triangle,
regular pentagon, regular hexagon, regular octagon.

3. Copy and complete these shapes.
The dotted lines are axes of symmetry.

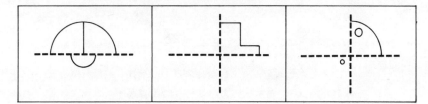

4. Which shapes in questions 1–3 have:
(a) rotational symmetry?   (b) point symmetry?
If a shape has rotational symmetry, give its order.

5. Draw some symmetrical road signs. Write about their
axes of symmetry and rotational symmetry.

6. Find some symmetrical 'company signs' (logos) in
magazines or newspapers. Write about their
symmetries.

More shorthand

You should have done: More directed numbers (pages 17–19).

In arithmetic
$$2 - 5 = {}^-3$$
In algebra
$$2p - 5p = {}^-3p$$

'simplify' means 'write in the shortest way'

 Simplify these:

1. $5a - 2a$
2. $4x - 7x$
3. $3y + y - 5y$
4. $4l - 6l + 3l$
5. $2m - 10m$
6. $^-b + 3b - 4b$

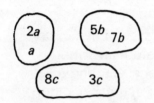

Sometimes we have different letters. But we can only put the *same* letters together.

$$2a + 5b - 8c - a + 3c - 7b$$

put the same letters together

$$= \boxed{2a - a} \; + \; \boxed{5b - 7b} \; + \; \boxed{3c - 8c}$$

work it out

$$= \quad a \quad + \quad ^-2b \quad + \quad ^-5c$$

$$= \underline{a \; - 2b \; - 5c}$$

 Write these in their simplest forms:

1. $2a - c - a + 5c$
2. $3m + n - 4m + 3n$
3. $5x - 2y - x + 5y + x$
4. $3g + 4f - 5g + 8f$
5. $5c - 4d + 6d - 2c$
6. $s - 6t + r + 5t + 3s - 2r$

Sometimes all the terms in one letter have to be subtracted.

$$5p - 2q - 3r - 2p + 8q - 5r$$

put the same letters together

$$= \boxed{5p - 2p} + \boxed{8q - 2q} - 3r - 5r$$

$- 3r = + {}^-3r$

$$= \boxed{5p - 2p} + \boxed{8q - 2q} + \boxed{^-3r - 5r}$$

work it out

$$= 3p + 6q + {}^-8r$$

$$\underline{= 3p + 6q - 8r}$$

 Simplify these:
1. $a - 2b + 3a - b$
2. $4p - 3q + r - q$
3. $x - y + 5x - 3y$

4. $3n - 4m - 2m - n$
5. $e - 2f + 5e + g - 3f$
6. $5b + 2c - 3d - c - 4d$

We can have different powers too.
Like powers of the same letter go together.

$$3x^2 - 4 + 2x - x^2 - 7x$$

put the same powers together

$$= \boxed{3x^2 - x^2} + \boxed{2x - 7x} - 4$$

work it out

$$= 2x^2 + {}^-5x - 4$$

$$\underline{= 2x^2 - 5x - 4}$$

 Simplify:
1. $2x^2 - 1 + 3x - x^2 - 2$
2. $5p + 3p^2 - 3p + 2 - 2p^2$
3. $7a^2 + 8a - a^2 - 5 - 9a$

4. $2t^2 - 3t^2 + 4t + t^2$
5. $y - 3y^2 - 2y + y^3$
6. $2n^5 + 3n^2 - 2 + 6n^2$

 Simplify these:
1. $7m - 2m$
2. $3x - 5x$
3. $4y - 2y + 3y$
4. ${}^-2a - 3a + a$
5. $10s + 6s - 5s - s$
6. $3a - b - 2a - 2b$
7. $2x^2 - x^2 + 3x^2$
8. $3q - p + 2r - 2p$
9. $m - n + n - m$
10. ${}^-2f + 6f - 4f$

11. ${}^-3a^2 + 2a^2 - a^2$
12. $7g - 12g$
13. $7 + 2y - 3y + 4y^2$
14. $4 - 11q - 6q + 3$
15. $3x^2 - 2x - 2x^2 + 4x$
16. $16r + 4s - 8r - 8s$
17. ${}^-2a - b - a - 3b$
18. $x - 2x^2 + 4x + x^3$
19. $p^2 - 3p - 2p - 4p^2$
20. ${}^-b + 3b^3 - 2b + b^3$

Ratio

Tim is Gary's little brother.

A How many 'bricks' high are they on each wall?

Ratios compare things.
Here the ratio of Gary's height to Tim's height is:

6 bricks to 3 bricks

or   6 to 3

or   6 : 3

B What is the ratio of Gary's height to Tim's height from each wall?

Gary and Tim have stayed the same height, so all these ratios must be the same. The **simplest form** is 2:1.

simplest form:
no common factors
except 1

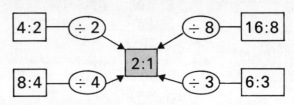

 1. Which of these are 2:1?
    (a) 12:6   (b) 7:3   (c) 9:5   (d) 10:5

2. Write these in their simplest forms:
    (a) 8:2   (b) 12:3   (c) 4:16   (d) 5:30

Sue is Steve's little sister.

1. What is the ratio of Steve's height to Sue's height from each wall?

The simplest form of this ratio is 3:2.

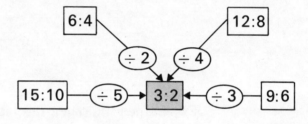

simplest form:
no common factors
except 1

1. Which of these are 3:2?
   (a) 21:14   (b) 10:6   (c) 14:8   (d) 33:22

2. Write these in their simplest forms:
   (a) 15:6   (b) 8:6   (c) 35:20   (d) 36:30

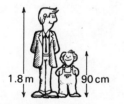

1.8 m   90 cm

Gary and Tim measured their heights.
They are 1.8 m and 90 cm tall.

To compare their heights the units must be the same.
   180 cm : 90 cm
      180 : 90
       2 : 1

Write these ratios in their simplest forms:
   (a) 1.5 m to 60 cm   (c) 2.5 m to 75 cm
   (b) 30 cm to 2.4 m   (d) 125 cm to 0.25 m

Ann is Sharon's baby sister.
The ratio of their heights is 1:3.
Ann is 4 bricks high on this wall.
We can find how many bricks high Sharon is.

4 bricks

Ann : Sharon

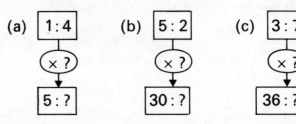

The multiplier is 4 because 1 × 4 = 4

1 : 3

× 4

4 bricks : ? bricks

1. How many bricks high is Sharon on this wall?
2. Copy and complete these:

(a) 1:4   (b) 5:2   (c) 3:7

× ?   × ?   × ?

5:?   30:?   36:?

Sometimes the given ratio is not in its simplest form.

Example

The school hall is 70 paces long and 40 paces wide.
If it is 42 m long, how wide is it?

length : width

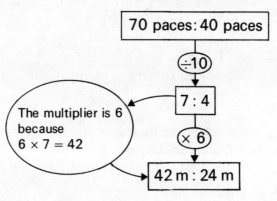

ratio you know

70 paces : 40 paces

÷10

change to
simplest form

7 : 4

The multiplier is 6 because 6 × 7 = 42

× 6

change to
ratio you want

42 m : 24 m

So the hall is <u>24 m wide.</u>

If the hall is: (a) 56 m long, how wide is it?
                 (b) 28 m wide, how long is it?

Ratios compare things.
The things must be in the same unit.
Simplest form: no common factors except 1.

Using ratios to find an unknown:

Write the ratio you know:

Change to simplest form:

Find the ratio you want:

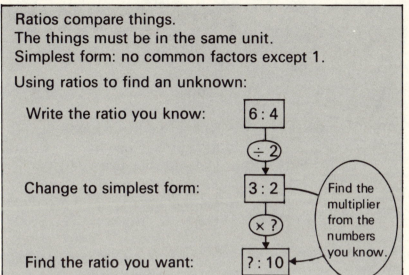

1. Simplify these ratios:
(a) 6 : 2   (c) 6 : 4   (e) 2 : 10   (g) 15 : 9
(b) 5 : 10   (d) 9 : 3   (f) 14 : 6   (h) 110 : 100

2. Write down the ratios of these lengths in simplest form:
(a)   (b)   (c)

    12 cm   10 cm   25 mm

    6 cm   15 cm   20 mm

3. Write down the ratios of these heights in simplest form:
(a)   (b)

32 cm   8 cm   15 cm   12 cm

4. Find the ratios of the marked lengths in these triangles in simplest form:
(a)   (b)

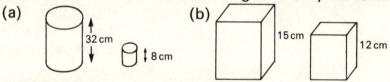

6 cm
9 cm
14 cm
10 cm

watch the units!

5. Write these ratios in simplest form:
(a) 1 m : 20 cm   (c) 1.5 kg : 750 g   (e) 1.4 km : 1 km
(b) 90 cm : 1.2 m   (d) 110 cm : 1.65 m   (f) 1.01 m : 64 cm

6. A room has a tiled floor. There are 45 tiles along a long wall and 30 along a short wall. If the room is 12 m long, how wide is it?

Foreign currency

A country's money is called its currency.

In Britain we use pounds (£). This is called sterling.
In France they use francs (fr.).
In Holland they use guilders or florins (fl.).

 Name the currency of these countries:
1. USA   2. Germany   3. Spain   4. Italy   5. Japan

Sharon went abroad last year.
She bought her foreign currency from her bank.

Banks give **exchange rates**.
These are the amounts of currency you can buy for £1.
They can change from day to day.

Exchange rates

We sell at:

Francs (fr.)	10.10
Marks (DM)	4.03
Lire (L)	2140
Yen (Y)	425
Pesetas (P)	172.5
Dollars ($)	1.825

 How much of these currencies could Sharon buy for £1?
1. fr.   2. DM   3. L   4. $ 5. yen

Sharon changed £25 into francs:

$$£1 \rightarrow 10.10 \text{ francs}$$
$$£25 \rightarrow 25 \times 10.10 \text{ francs}$$
$$= \underline{252.50 \text{ francs}}$$

 Change these into the currency shown:
1. £35 → fr.   3. £56 → L   5. £38 → yen
2. £25 → DM   4. £60 → $ 6. £40 → pesetas

Sharon went shopping in Paris.

Exchange rate: 10.10 francs cost £1

So   1   franc costs £$\dfrac{1}{10.10}$

95   francs cost £$\dfrac{95}{10.10}$

= £9.41   (to the nearest penny)

 Work out how much each item in the window costs in sterling (to the nearest penny).

After her holiday Sharon had some foreign money left.

22 DM

23·45 fl

8500 LIRE

1060 ESCUDOS

Exchange rates
We buy at:

Marks (DM)	4.27
Guilders (fl.)	4.69
Lire (L)	2240
Escudos (E)	125
Kroner (Kr.)	10.54
Dinars (D)	83

Her bank bought it back from her.
They give different exchange rates for this.

Exchange rate: 4.27 DM → £1

1 DM → £$\dfrac{1}{4.27}$

So   22 DM → £$\dfrac{22}{4.27}$

=   £5.13   (to the nearest penny)

 How much sterling did she get back for each currency?

page 33

Summary

A country's money is called its currency.
British currency is called sterling.

Exchange rates tell you how much of each currency you can buy for £1.

To change sterling to foreign currency:
    multiply by the exchange rate.
To change foreign currency to sterling:
    use the exchange rate to find how much sterling you get for 1 unit first.

Exercise

1. What are today's exchange rates for the countries listed in Sharon's bank? You can find them in a newspaper or at a bank.
   Compare them with those Sharon got.
   Have the rates increased or decreased since then?

2. Change these into the currency shown. Use the exchange rates on page 32.
   (a) £20→DM   (e) £70→fr.   (i) £95→Y
   (b) £23→L   (f) £68→L   (j) £76→P
   (c) £50→$ (g) £40→P   (k) £95→DM
   (d) £45→Y   (h) £85→fr.   (l) £120→$

3. Change these to sterling (to the nearest penny). Use the 'buying back' rates on page 33.
   (a) 625 E   (e) 17 fl.   (i) 746 D
   (b) 581 D   (f) 150 Kr.   (j) 56 DM
   (c) 38 DM   (g) 25 000 L   (k) 235 Kr.
   (d) 11 000 L   (h) 900 E   (l) 69 fl.

4. Change these into the currency shown. Use the correct 'exchange rate' tables.
   (a) £17→L   (e) 972 D→£   (i) 1250 E→£
   (b) 72 DM→£   (f) £52→DM   (j) £93→$
   (c) 15 500 L→£   (g) 87 fl.→£   (k) £132→P
   (d) £28→Y   (h) £85→fr.   (l) 426 Kr.→£

Recap 1

1. In a tennis tournament the number of 'aces' scored by each player was recorded.

No. of aces	0	1	2	3	4	5	6
No. of players	3	8	4	5	3	1	2

   (a) How many players were in the tournament?
   (b) Write down the mode of this distribution.
   (c) Calculate the mean number of aces.

2. Use sines and cosines to calculate the missing lengths in these triangles.

   (a)   (b)   (c)

3. This is a B R timetable for a day excursion from Banbury.

Banbury	d	08.16
Winchester	a	10.04
Southampton	a	10.19
Bournemouth	a	11.00
Poole	a	11.13

   (a) How long does the train take from Banbury to each station?
   (b) If the train leaves Banbury 7 minutes late and arrives at Poole at 11.46, how long does the journey take?

4. Do these:
   (a) $3 + {}^-1$ (c) $8 - {}^-2$ (e) ${}^-6 - {}^-6$
   (b) $5 - 7$ (d) ${}^-3 + 6$ (f) $17 - 7$

5. Rewrite these using addition only:
   (a) $3p - 5$ (c) $x^2 - 2x + 1$
   (b) $4m - {}^-3n$ (d) $5p^2 - 3p - 2$

6. A car takes 2 h to travel 90 km. How long should it take to travel 225 km?

7. 2 boys weed a garden in $1\frac{1}{2}$ h. How long should it take 3 boys to do the job?

8. Copy these shapes on to centimetre squared paper. Draw in any lines of symmetry.

   (a)   (b)

   (c)   (d)

   Do any of these shapes have rotational symmetry? If so, write down the order.

9. Simplify these:
   (a) $5p - 3p$ (c) $3c - 2d + c - d$
   (b) $x - 5x$ (d) $4n^2 - 5n^2 + 3n$

10. Simplify these ratios:
    (a) $2:8$ (c) $2\,\text{kg}:250\,\text{g}$
    (b) $27:12$ (d) $1.75\,\text{km}:500\,\text{m}$

11. A table has a rectangular top covered with square tiles. There are 21 tiles along a long side and 9 along a short side. If the table is 1.35 m wide, how long is it?

12. If the exchange rate is 9.8 francs to the pound, how many francs would you get for £75?

13. A bank 'buys back' Deutschmarks at 4.12 to the pound. How much would you receive for 57 D M? (Answer to nearest p.)

Conversion graphs

You need: a ruler and centimetre graph paper.
You should have done: Foreign currency (pages 32–34).

£1 → 4.5 fl.
£10 → 45 fl.

Sharon found **conversion graphs** useful abroad.
She used exchange rates to draw them.

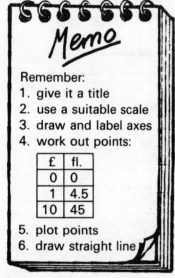

Memo

Remember:
1. give it a title
2. use a suitable scale
3. draw and label axes
4. work out points:

£	fl.
0	0
1	4.5
10	45

5. plot points
6. draw straight line

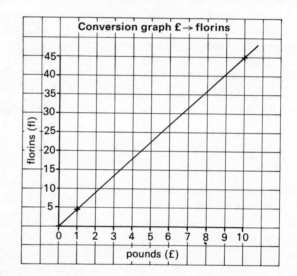

Exercise 1

Draw Sharon's graph on centimetre squared paper.
Use this scale:
  £ axis – 1 cm represents £1
  fl. axis – 1 cm represents 5 fl.

Sharon used her graph to convert sterling to florins.

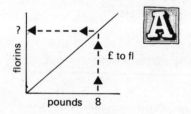

1. Find £8 on your £ axis.
   Draw a dotted line:
      up from £8 to your line,
      then across to the florin axis.
   Read off the florin value.

2. Change these to florins the same way:
   (a) £6   (b) £3.50   (c) £4.60   (d) £9.80   (e) £7.20

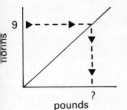

Sharon also used her graph to convert florins to sterling.

1. Find 9 fl. on your florin axis.
   Draw a dotted line across from 9 fl. to your line,
   then down to the £ axis.
   Read off the £ value.
2. Change these to sterling the same way:
   (a) 20 fl. (b) 35 fl. (c) 12 fl. (d) 3 fl. (e) 42 fl.

Sharon's conversion graph only goes from £0 to £10.
For larger or smaller amounts we can change the scales.

look at the scales
on the axes!

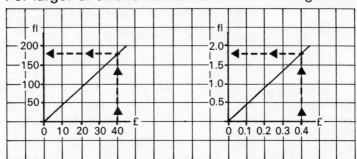

Conversion graphs can be used for other units, too.

Paul was cooking dinner. The recipe said:
   'Cook in a slow oven, Gas Mark ½/275°F.'
But the oven was marked in °C!

From science he remembered:

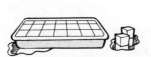

Water freezes at
32°F ≡ 0°C

Water boils at
212°F ≡ 100°C

He plotted (32, 0) and (212, 100) on a graph.
Then he drew a straight line through them.
This gave him a conversion graph.

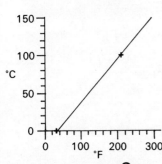

1. Draw Paul's graph on centimetre graph paper.
   Scale: °F axis – 1 cm represents 20°F
           °C axis – 1 cm represents 10°C

2. At what temperature in °C did Paul set the oven?
3. Use your graph to convert these to °C:
   130°F, 100°F, 210°F, 88°F, 30°F
4. Use your graph to convert these to °F:
   50°C, 80°C, 55°C, 32°C, 28°C

Summary

A straight line graph can be used to convert units.
It is called a conversion graph.

Use the exchange rate or conversion rate to plot points on the graph.

Exercise 3

1. (a) Draw a conversion graph for £ to yen:
      £1 → 425 yen
   (b) Use your graph to convert these to yen:
      80p, 30p, 45p, 52p, 68p.
   (c) Use your graph to convert these to £:
      400 yen, 50 yen, 170 yen, 240 yen, 315 yen

Use the scale:
£ axis – 10 cm ≡ £1
yen axis – 2 cm ≡ 10 yen

2. (a) Draw a conversion graph for kg to lb:
      1 kg → 2.2 lb
   (b) Use your graph to convert these to lb:
      6 kg, 5 kg, 8 kg, 5.5 kg, 9.6 kg
   (c) Use your graph to convert these to kg:
      10 lb, 6 lb, 14 lb, 3 lb, 20 lb

Use the scale:
kg axis – 1 cm ≡ 1 kg
lb axis – 1 cm ≡ 2 lb

3. (a) Draw a conversion graph for $ to £:
      $1 → £0.54
   (b) Use your graph to convert these to £:
      $120, $90, $65, $26, $42
   (c) Use your graph to convert these to $:
      £70, £30, £12, £26, £57

Use the scale:
$ axis – 1 cm ≡ $10
£ axis – 1 cm ≡ £5

4. (a) Draw a conversion graph for miles to km:
      1 mile → 1.61 km
   (b) Use your graph to convert these to km:
      5 miles, 13 miles, 3.5 miles, 6.8 miles, 8.2 miles
   (c) Use your graph to convert these to miles:
      12 km, 14.5 km, 18 km, 19.4 km, 4.2 km

Use the scale:
mile axis – 1 cm ≡ 1 mile
km axis – 1 cm ≡ 1 km

Fractions of a degree

You need: 3 figure tables and a ruler.
You should have done: Sines and cosines (pages 9–11).

You have measured angles with a protractor.
Its scale shows only whole degrees.

A surveyor measures angles with a theodolite.
Its scale shows fractions of degrees too.

Tables give the sines, cosines and tangents of whole degrees and fractions.
Find your tangent tables. Here is part of them:

Angle in degrees	.0	.1	.2	.3	.4	.5	.6	.7	.8	.9
45	1.00	1.00	1.01	1.01	1.01	1.02	1.02	1.02	1.03	1.03
46	1.04	1.04	1.04	1.05	1.05	1.05	1.06	1.06	1.06	1.07
47	1.07	1.08	1.08	1.08	1.09	1.09	1.10	1.10	1.10	1.11
48	1.11	1.11	1.12	1.12	1.13	1.13	1.13	1.14	1.14	1.15
49	1.15	1.15	1.16	1.16	1.17	1.17	1.17	1.18	1.18	1.19

45.6° 49.2°

tan means tangent

The table gives: tan 45.6° = 1.02
                          tan 49.2° = 1.16

We look up sines and cosines like this too.

Exercise

sin means sine

cos means cosine

Use your tables to find the values of:
1. tan 31.5°
2. tan 55.1°
3. tan 23.9°
4. sin 84.3°
5. sin 12.8°
6. sin 77.5°
7. cos 46.5°
8. cos 35.9°
9. cos 19.0°
10. tan 62.3°
11. cos 60.4°
12. sin 43.1°
13. sin 51.7°
14. tan 4.8°
15. cos 28.1°
16. tan 89.4°
17. sin 66.9°
18. sin 5.6°
19. cos 72.7°
20. cos 84.2°
21. tan 17.6°
22. tan 76.0°
23. sin 49.2°
24. cos 27.3°
25. sin 38.0°
26. tan 50.7°
27. cos 1.6°
28. sin 40.4°
29. cos 53.8°
30. tan 48.2°

Negative powers

You should have done: More directed numbers (pages 17–19).

In arithmetic
$$3 \times 3 \times 3 \times 3$$
is $\qquad 3^4$
We say '3 to the power 4'.

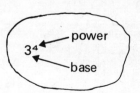

 Write these out in full:
1. 3^5 　　　　 2. 2^3 　　　　 3. 7^6 　　　　 4. 8^2 　　　　 5. 4^4

To divide numbers with the same base we subtract the powers:
$$4^5 \div 4^3 = 4^{5-3} = 4^2$$

 Use this short method to do these:
1. $2^6 \div 2^2$ 　　 2. $7^9 \div 7^6$ 　　 3. $5^3 \div 5^3$ 　　 4. $10^2 \div 10^7$

Your answer to **B** 4 should have been:

$2 - 7 = {}^-5$

$$10^2 \div 10^7 = 10^{2-7} = 10^{-5} \longleftarrow \text{negative power}$$

But what is 10^{-5}? We can work it out.

rewriting division

$$10^2 \div 10^7 = \frac{10^2}{10^7}$$

rewriting numbers and cancelling

$$= \frac{\cancel{10}^1 \times \cancel{10}^1}{\cancel{10}_1 \times \cancel{10}_1 \times 10 \times 10 \times 10 \times 10 \times 10}$$

$$= \frac{1}{10 \times 10 \times 10 \times 10 \times 10}$$

using powers

$$= \frac{1}{10^5}$$

Since both answers must be the same:
$$10^{-5} = \frac{1}{10^5}$$

1. Using both long and short methods, work out these:
   (a) $10^3 \div 10^5$ (c) $8^4 \div 8^7$
   (b) $3^2 \div 3^6$ (d) $5^6 \div 5^7$
2. Rewrite these with positive powers. Use your answers to 1 to help you.
   (a) 10^{-2} (b) 3^{-4} (c) 8^{-3} (d) 5^{-1}

We can use negative powers in multiplication:

> To multiply numbers with the same base we add the powers:
> $$10^6 \times 10^{-4} = 10^{6 + {}^-4} = 10^2$$
> $$3^{-2} \times 3^{-7} = 3^{{}^-2 + {}^-7} = 3^{-9} = \frac{1}{3^9}$$

Do these the same way:
1. $4^5 \times 4^{-3}$ 2. $6^3 \times 6^{-7}$ 3. $2^{-3} \times 2^{-2}$ 4. $5^{-4} \times 5^5$

Negative powers are used in divisions, too.

$$7^5 \div 7^{-3} = 7^{5 - {}^-3} = 7^8$$
$$6^{-8} \div 6^2 = 6^{{}^-8 - 2} = 6^{-10} = \frac{1}{6^{10}}$$

Do these the same way:
1. $3^4 \div 3^{-2}$ 2. $5^{-3} \div 5^2$ 3. $7^{-4} \div 7^3$ 4. $10^{-2} \div 10^{-3}$

There are negative powers in algebra, too.

$$a^{-7} = \frac{1}{a^7} \qquad x^{-3} = \frac{1}{x^3} \qquad y^{-1} = \frac{1}{y}$$

Rewrite these with positive powers:
1. b^{-3} 2. x^{-4} 3. p^{-5} 4. r^{-8} 5. c^{-10}

We can multiply and divide in algebra:

$$a^{-3} \times a^4 = a^{-3+4} = a^1 = a$$
$$x^{-6} \div x^{-2} = x^{{}^-6 - {}^-2} = x^{-4} = \frac{1}{x^4}$$

Do these the same way:
1. $a^2 \times a^{-1}$ 3. $p \div p^{-3}$ 5. $m^{-5} \times m^2$ 7. $c^{-2} \times c^{-5}$
2. $x^{-3} \times x^2$ 4. $r^{-2} \div r^4$ 6. $y^3 \div y^{-1}$ 8. $s^{-6} \div s^{-4}$

Summary

Numbers and letters with negative powers can be rewritten with positive powers.
For example:

$$3^{-2} = \frac{1}{3^2} \qquad a^{-5} = \frac{1}{a^5}$$

Exercise

1. Rewrite these with positive powers:
   (a) 2^{-1} (c) 4^{-7} (e) 8^{-6} (g) 12^{-2} (i) 10^{-9}
   (b) 5^{-2} (d) 10^{-3} (f) 3^{-4} (h) 6^{-10} (j) 15^{-12}

2. Rewrite these with positive powers:
   (a) a^{-2} (c) p^{-3} (e) b^{-4} (g) r^{-8} (i) n^{-10}
   (b) x^{-5} (d) c^{-6} (f) y^{-1} (h) d^{-7} (j) z^{-a}

3. Work out these numbers:
   (a) $2^3 \times 2^{-2}$ (e) $7^2 \times 7^{-5}$ (i) $12^{-2} \div 12^8$
   (b) $5^{-1} \times 5^4$ (f) $10^{-3} \div 10$ (j) $9^{-5} \times 9^6$
   (c) $8^4 \div 8^5$ (g) $6^{-4} \times 6^2$ (k) $15^8 \div 15^{10}$
   (d) $3^2 \div 3^4$ (h) $4^3 \div 4^{-7}$ (l) $20^{-6} \times 20^{-5}$

watch the signs!

4. Work out these:
   (a) $x^{-1} \times x^5$ (e) $c \div c^2$ (i) $m^7 \times m^{-10}$
   (b) $p^3 \div p$ (f) $q^5 \times q^{-8}$ (j) $d^4 \div d^{12}$
   (c) $a^2 \div a^3$ (g) $n^2 \div n^6$ (k) $g^{-1} \times g^{-1}$
   (d) $r^{-3} \times r^{-4}$ (h) $y^{-9} \times y^5$ (l) $s^3 \div s^8$

watch the signs!

☆ Want a change? Try Numbers in spaces on page 173.

Fair shares

You should have done: Ratio (pages 28–31).

Steve's and Paul's dads do the pools together.

1. What is the ratio of their stake money?
2. How much is their total stake?

They divide their winnings:

ratio   2 : 3

→ 5 'shares' get £350

So   1 'share' gets £350 ÷ 5
                        = £70

How much does
(a) Steve's dad get for his £2 'share'?
(b) Paul's dad get for his £3 'share'?

1. Two winners divide £1200 in the ratio 3 : 5.
   (a) How many 'shares' are there altogether?
   (b) How much does one 'share' get?
   (c) How much does each winner get?

2. Two pools winners divide £2200 in the ratio 7 : 4.
   (a) How many 'shares' are there altogether?
   (b) How much does one 'share' get?
   (c) How much does each winner get?

3. Now divide these the same way:
   (a) £600 in the ratio 1 : 2.
   (b) £2700 in the ratio 5 : 4.
   (c) £5500 in the ratio 3 : 7.
   (d) £450 in the ratio 7 : 8.

Tina, Gary and Jackie buy in bulk for their families.

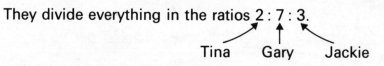

They divide everything in the ratios 2 : 7 : 3.

Tina   Gary   Jackie

Soap	£15.60
Rice	£ 4.56
Pop	£10.08
Beans	£17.28
Sugar	£23.52
Jam	£16.20
Tea	£ 9.12
Matches	£ 6.60
Total	

C

1. How many 'shares' are there altogether?
2. What was the total cost?
3. How much does one 'share' cost?
4. How much does each family pay?

Exercise 2

Divide the goods between the families.
Write down how much each gets.

Sharon wants 10 litres of Party Punch for a barbeque.
She uses

   orange juice, ginger ale, cranberry juice, lemon juice
in the ratios

3   :   10   :   6   :   1

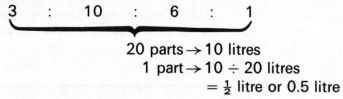

20 parts → 10 litres
1 part → 10 ÷ 20 litres
= ½ litre or 0.5 litre

D

How much of each ingredient will she need?

To divide an amount in a given ratio, work out:
(a) the total number of 'shares' (or parts) from the ratio,
(b) what one 'share' (or part) is,
(c) the amounts for the ratio.

Exercise 3

1. Divide these winnings in the given ratios:

	Winnings	Ratio
(a)	£55	2 : 3
(b)	£360	7 : 5
(c)	£59.50	4 : 3
(d)	£780	1 : 4 : 5
(e)	£367.50	2 : 58
(f)	£685	3 : 10 : 7

2. Divide these quantities in the given ratios:

	Quantity	Ratio
(a)	36 boxes of matches	2 : 1
(b)	96 beef cubes	3 : 5
(c)	5 litres cooking oil	7 : 3
(d)	1 kg drinking chocolate	3 : 2
(e)	1100 tea bags	4 : 5 : 1
(f)	1 gross pencils	7 : 1 : 4

3. Jackie is making 10 litres of Fizzy Fruit Cup for a disco party. She uses pineapple juice, grapefruit juice, passion fruit juice, lemonade in the ratios 6 : 1 : 3 : 50. How much of each liquid should she use?

4. Paul makes $4\frac{1}{2}$ litres of Hot Mulled Punch for a Christmas party. He uses apple juice, honey, orange juice, grape juice in the ratios 20 : 2 : 5 : 18. How much of each item does he use?

5. Gary makes 15 litres of Guy Fawkes Punch for Bonfire Night. He uses grenadine, egg white, orange juice, lemon juice, soda water in the ratios 2 : 3 : 50 : 5 : 15. How much of each ingredient does he use?

Standard form

You should have done: Negative powers (pages 40–42).

Steve is keen on space.
In space travel distances are very large.
They are awkward to write out in full.

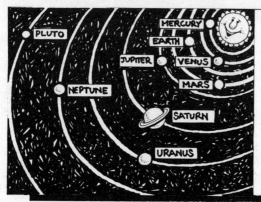

Approximate distances from Sun	
Mercury	58 000 000 km
Venus	108 000 000 km
Earth	150 000 000 km
Mars	228 000 000 km
Jupiter	778 000 000 km
Saturn	1427 000 000 km
Uranus	2870 000 000 km
Neptune	4497 000 000 km
Pluto	5950 000 000 km

Standard form

$$A \times 10^n$$

number — between 1 and 10

power of 10

Standard form is our number shorthand.

Earth's distance from sun: $150\ 000\ 000$ km
$$= 1.5 \times 100\ 000\ 000 \text{ km}$$
$$= \underline{1.5 \times 10^8 \text{ km}}$$

 Rewrite the other planet distances using standard form.

Diameters of the planets in km			
Mercury	4.84×10^3	Saturn	1.19×10^5
Venus	1.23×10^4	Uranus	4.7×10^4
Earth	1.28×10^4	Neptune	5.1×10^4
Mars	6.79×10^3	Pluto	6×10^3
Jupiter	1.43×10^5		

The diameter of the earth is 1.28×10^4 km
$$= 1.28 \times 10\ 000 \text{ km}$$
$$= \underline{12\ 800 \text{ km}}$$

 Rewrite the other planets' diameters as ordinary numbers.

Other scientists use very small numbers.

Some useful lengths in metres
Diameter of human hair: 0.000 075
Diameter of fine wire: 0.000 2
Length of human chromosome: 0.000 005
Thickness of paper: 0.000 1
Wavelength of light: 0.000 000 5
Diameter of quarz fibre: 0.000 001

Diameter of human hair $= 0.000\,075$ m

rewrite with a number between 1 and 10

$$= \frac{7.5}{100\,000}\,\text{m}$$

write using powers

$$= \frac{7.5}{10^5}\,\text{m} = 7.5 \times \frac{1}{10^5}\,\text{m}$$

$\frac{1}{10^5} = 10^{-5}$

$$= \underline{7.5 \times 10^{-5}\,\text{m}}$$

 Rewrite the other lengths in standard form.

Some useful masses in kg
House mouse: 1.5×10^{-2}
Pygmy shrew: 2.5×10^{-3}
Small bacterium: 4×10^{-15}
Grain of sand: 1×10^{-7}
Uranium atom: 4×10^{-25}
Molecule of water: 3×10^{-26}

The mass of a house mouse is 1.5×10^{-2} kg

$10^{-2} = \frac{1}{10^2}$

$$= \frac{1.5}{10^2}\,\text{kg}$$

$$= \frac{1.5}{100}\,\text{kg}$$

$$= \underline{0.015\,\text{kg}}$$

 Rewrite the other masses as ordinary numbers.

Here are some large and small numbers.

34 000 0.0015 0.000 06 0.000 79 2120 378 000
42 000 000 0.01 0.000 042 568 000 000 000

Exercise 1

1. Which of the numbers are (a) greater than 10,
   (b) less than 1?
2. Rewrite the numbers in standard form.
3. Which of the numbers written in standard form have
   (a) positive powers of 10, (b) negative powers of 10?
4. What do you notice about your answers to questions
   1 and 3?

Summary

Any number can be written in standard form like this:

$$A \times 10^n$$

Number between 1 and 10 ↲   ↳ Power of 10

Numbers greater than 10 → positive powers
For example: $31\,000 = 3.1 \times 10^4$
Numbers less than 1 → negative powers
For example: $0.000\,075\,2 = 7.52 \times 10^{-5}$

Exercise 2

1. Write these in standard form:
   (a) Height of Mount Everest: 8800 m
   (b) Width of a stamp: 0.02 m
   (c) Thickness of a penny: 0.0014 m
   (d) Radius of Moon: 1 700 000 m
   (e) Diameter of blood corpuscle: 0.000 007 5 m
   (f) Length of cricket pitch: 20 m
   (g) Distance Earth–Moon: 400 000 000 m
   (h) Period of sound: 0.0001 s
   (i) Stroboscope flash: 0.000 012 s
   (j) AC mains period: 0.02 s

2. Write these as ordinary numbers:
   (a) Maximum depth of ocean: 10^4 m
   (b) Room reverberation time: 7×10^{-1} s
   (c) Speed of a neutron: 2×10^3 m/s
   (d) Sun's diameter: 1.39×10^6 m
   (e) Thickness of oil film: 5×10^{-7} cm
   (f) Mass of Earth: 6×10^{24} kg
   (g) Wavelength of light: 5×10^{-7} m
   (h) Distance to nearest star: 4.6×10^{16} m
   (i) Period of light: 2×10^{-15} s
   (j) Mass of electron: 10^{-30} kg

Two at a time

> When multiplying directed numbers:
>   if the signs are the same, the answer is positive;
> $^+3 \times {}^+2 = {}^+6$ $^-4 \times {}^-5 = {}^+20$
>   if the signs are different, the answer is negative.
> $^-2 \times {}^+4 = {}^-8$ $^+3 \times {}^-1 = {}^-3$

Now do these:
1. $^+3 \times {}^-7 =$ 3. $^+6 \times {}^+1 =$ 5. $^-6 \times {}^-7 =$
2. $^-4 \times {}^-2 =$ 4. $^-5 \times {}^+3 =$ 6. $^+4 \times {}^-8 =$

Sometimes we have to multiply more than two numbers.
But we must do them two at a time.

put in twos

Calculate (i) $^-2 \times {}^+3 \times {}^-4$ *(ii)* $^-3 \times {}^-1 \times {}^+2 \times {}^-5$

(i) $\boxed{^-2 \times {}^+3} \times {}^-4$ (ii) $\boxed{^-3 \times {}^-1} \times \boxed{^+2 \times {}^-5}$

     $= \quad {}^-6 \quad\quad \times {}^-4$ $= \quad {}^+3 \quad\quad \times \quad {}^-10$

     $= \quad \underline{^+24}$ $= \quad \underline{^-30}$

Calculate:
1. $^-2 \times {}^+3 \times {}^-5$ 3. $^-4 \times {}^+2 \times {}^-3 \times {}^-2$
2. $^+6 \times {}^-1 \times {}^-4$ 4. $^-5 \times {}^+1 \times {}^+6 \times {}^-4$

> Always multiply directed numbers two at a time.

Calculate:
1. $^-4 \times {}^+3 \times {}^-2$ 7. $^-5 \times {}^+5 \times {}^-2 \times {}^-1$
2. $^+6 \times {}^-5 \times {}^-4$ 8. $^-10 \times {}^+2 \times {}^-4$
3. $^-3 \times {}^+2 \times {}^-1 \times {}^+9$ 9. $^+8 \times {}^+5 \times {}^-7$
4. $^+8 \times {}^+3 \times {}^-2$ 10. $^-6 \times {}^-4 \times {}^-3 \times {}^-2$
5. $^+2 \times {}^-2 \times {}^+2 \times {}^-2$ 11. $^+11 \times {}^-2 \times {}^+6 \times {}^+2$
6. $^-7 \times {}^-2 \times {}^+3$ 12. $^-1 \times {}^-2 \times {}^-3 \times {}^-4 \times {}^-5$

Significant figures

Each of Jackie's friends 'rounded off' the number.
But their answers were all the right size.

38 451

40 000

Paul looked at the
'2nd figure'.
He corrected 38 451 to
1 significant figure.

38 451

38 000

Tina looked at the
'3rd figure'.
She corrected 38 451 to
2 significant figures.

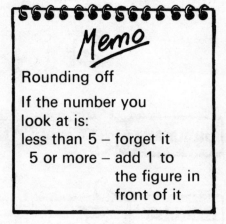

Memo

Rounding off

If the number you
look at is:
less than 5 – forget it
5 or more – add 1 to
the figure in
front of it

1. How many significant figures did Steve and Sharon
correct the number to?
Which figures did they look at?

2. Correct the other record sales figures to:
(a) 1 s.f.   (b) 2 s.f.   (c) 3 s.f.   (d) 4 s.f.

s.f. means
significant figures

Rounding off decimals is just as easy.
We look for the '1st figure' which is not zero.

0.000 492 5
↑
This is the '1st figure'.

0.000 49̌2 5	┐— Look at the '2nd figure' to correct to
0.000 5̲	1 s.f.

0.000 49̌2 5	┐— Look at the '3rd figure' to correct to
0.000 49̲	2. s.f.

1. Correct 0.000 492 5 to 3 s.f.
   Which figure did you look at?
2. Which is the '1st figure' in these numbers?
   (i)   0.003 214   (iv) 0.060 173   (vii) 0.727 23
   (ii) 0.051 672   (v)   0.814 01   (viii) 0.046 51
   (iii) 0.000 281 9   (vi) 0.001 38   (ix)   0.000 957 3
3. Correct each number in **B** 2 to: (a) 1 s.f. (b) 2 s.f.
   (c) 3 s.f.

s.f. means significant figures.

To correct a number to:
   1 s.f., look at the '2nd figure',
   2 s.f., look at the '3rd figure',
   3 s.f., look at the '4th figure', and so on...

If the number you look at is:
   less than 5 – forget it,
     5 or more – add 1 to the figure in front of it.

Correct each number to (a) 1 s.f. (b) 2 s.f. (c) 3 s.f.:
1. 14.723   6. 2385   11. 9.158 047
2. 5.8271   7. 0.006 149   12. 36.9513
3. 8.2504   8. 0.346 81   13. 0.000 852 71
4. 163.85   9. 510.962   14. 0.009 520 1
5. 0.3215   10. 0.084 71   15. 0.000 960 5

Percentages

On our calculator, to find 15% of £156.55

we press:  C 1 5 6 . 5 5 × 1 5 %

the display shows: *23.4825*

pounds pence

The answer is £23.48 (to the nearest penny).

If you have a % button

See if your % button works like ours.
If it does not, look in your instruction book or try to work it out.

No % button!

Try this:

Press: C 1 5 6 . 5 5 × 1 5 ÷ 1 0 0 =

How is it different from our way?

Now find these:
1. 15% of £234.20   3. 11% of £132
2. 23% of £31.72   4. 34% of £576.23

Gary's mum and dad went to Costa Packet in 1981.
It cost them £340.
If prices go up by 11% each year, what happens to the cost of the holiday?

Year	Cost	
1981	£340	
1982	£377.40	up by 11% of £340
1983		up by 11% of £377.40

When will the cost be more than double the 1981 price?

In 1981, Gary's dad earned £450 a month.
If wages go up by 7% each year, what happens to his monthly wages?

Year	Wage	
1981	£450	
1982	£481.50	up by 7% of £450
1983		up by 7% of £481.50

In which year does his holiday cost more than a month's wages?

What happens if prices go up by 14%,
and wages go up by 9%?

Look-alikes

 These two pictures should be exactly the same.
List the five objects missing from picture B.

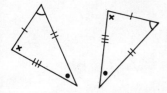 Objects which are exactly the same shape and size are congruent.
Matching angles and sides are equal.

 Which of these shapes are congruent?
You may want to trace them to check.

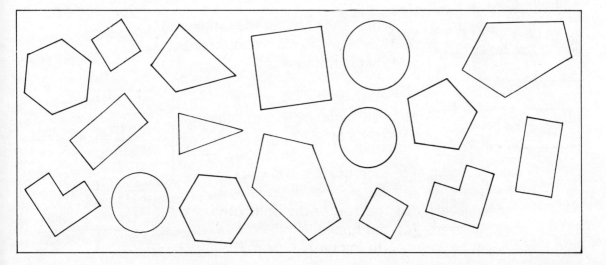

Bills! Bills! Bills!

Gary's dad gets an electricity bill every quarter.
$\frac{1}{4}$ year = 3 months

KILOWATT HOURS

METER READING		UNITS USED	UNIT PRICE (pence)	V.A.T. code	AMOUNT £
PRESENT	PREVIOUS				
28726	30051	?	5.61	0	?
STANDING CHARGE 1/11/82 TO 31/1/83				0	6.35

E = Estimated Reading Please read the advice given on the back of this bill.
C = Your own reading.

YOUR REFERENCE NUMBER	YOU CAN PHONE US ON	NORMAL READING DATE	AMOUNT TO PAY
08..0.0 /02 .001	0I-7I. 73 0	1 JAN 8.	£ ?

HOW MUCH ELECTRICITY HAVE I USED?

Their electricity meter measures the units used.
Each unit is a kilowatt hour (kWh).

A

1. What are the two meter readings on the bill?
2. How many units have been used?

Each unit costs 5.61 p.
A standing charge of £6.35 is added. This is the same for everyone.

HOW MUCH DO I PAY?

B

1. What is the cost of the units used?
2. How much is the standing charge?
3. What is the total bill?

Exercise 1

Here are some meter readings for Gary's family.

For each quarter, work out:
(a) the number of units used,
(b) the cost of the units used,
(c) the total bill
    (to the nearest penny).

	Meter Readings	
	Previous	Present
1.	19807	20821
2.	20821	22834
3.	22834	25439
4.	25439	26957
5.	26957	28726

Tina's family are on **Economy 7.**
Their electricity is cheaper for 7 hours at night.
But it is dearer during the day.

They have two electricity meters:
one measures 'day units',
the other measures 'night units'.

METER READING					
PRESENT	PREVIOUS	UNITS USED	UNIT PRICE (pence)	V.A.T. code	AMOUNT £
09160	09917	?	5.87	0	?
29944	30733	?	2.18	0	?
STANDING CHARGE 1/11/82 TO 31/1/83					9.00

1. What are the 'day meter' readings on this bill?
2. How many 'day units' have been used?
3. What are the 'night meter' readings?
4. How many 'night units' have been used?

Economy 7
tariff

A 'day unit' costs 5.87p.
A 'night unit' costs 2.18p.
The standing charge is £9.00.

1. What is the cost of:
   (a) the 'day units' used?
   (b) the 'night units' used?
2. What is the total bill?

Here are some Economy 7 meter readings:

1.

Meter Readings	
Previous	Present
day	05416	06126
night	17823	18548

3.

Meter Readings	
Previous	Present
day	07278	08327
night	23799	28719

2.

Meter Readings	
Previous	Present
day	06126	07278
night	18548	23799

4.

Meter Readings	
Previous	Present
day	08327	09160
night	28719	29944

Work out the bill (to the nearest penny) for each quarter.

Gary's house has gas as well as electricity.
The gas meter measures the volume of gas used.
This is in cubic feet.
The Gas Board changes this to the amount of heat used.
This is in therms.

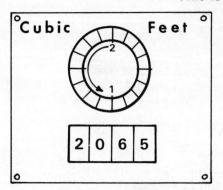

MIDLANDS GAS
P.O. Box 99, Anytown.

Meter Readings		Gas supplied		Pence per Therm	Charges £	VAT Rate	VAT Charges £	Total Amount £
Present	Previous	Cubic feet (Hundreds)	Therms					
2065	1820	245	253.57	35.4	89.76	0.00	0.00	89.76
Standing Charge					9.10			9.10

Account charged up to	Date of Account	Account Reference Number				
29.10.82	05.11.82				0.00	99.86

1. Answer these questions about Gary's gas bill:
   (a) How many therms were used?
   (b) How much does a therm cost?
   (c) How much is the standing charge?
2. There is a mistake on this bill. What is it?
3. Work out the total charge when these therms were
   used. Give your answers correct to the nearest penny.
   (a) 200   (c) 360   (e) 680   (g) 215   (i) 279
   (b) 401   (d) 511   (f) 109   (h) 321   (j) 493

Sharon's mum gets a telephone bill every quarter.

```
                    phone number              Date of bill          was prepared
                 RUSTINGTON 76_90        2 NOV 82      will be included
  Payment Is Now Due                                   in a later bill
  Rental and        from        to      £ quarterly rate    (Tax point)
  other standing                                         £
  charges        1 AUG   31 OCT         16.50           16.50

  Metered        date      meter reading    units used
  units
  (See           16 FEB    028265
  overleaf)      18 MAY    029186          921

                 UNITS AT 5.00            921           46.05

                 TOTAL (EXCLUSIVE OF VAT)        62.55
                 VALUE ADDED TAX AT 15.00%        9.38
                            TOTAL PAYABLE        71.93
```

1. What is the cost of: (a) one unit?
                          (b) the units used?
2. How much is the rental per quarter?

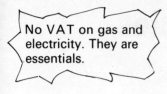
No VAT on gas and electricity. They are essentials.

She also has to pay VAT.
VAT is Value Added Tax.
It is charged on services.
A telephone is called a service.
So VAT is added to telephone bills.

1. What percentage is VAT on the telephone bill?
2. What is the total before VAT?

Sharon's mum checks the VAT like this:

$\div 10$
$\div 10$

    100% is £62.55
     10% is £ 6.255
      1% is £ 0.6255

So   15%   is   10% ⟶ £6.255
                5% → 5 × 1% → 5 × £0.6255 → £3.1275
                                            ─────────
                                            £9.3825

So VAT is £9.38 (to the nearest penny).

Work out the VAT (to the nearest penny) on these:
1. £32.50   2. £21.75   3. £45.30   4. £54.82   5. £91.21
What is the 'total payable' for each one?

Here are the meter readings from some telephone bills:

Date	Meter reading
8 Aug	023772
17 Nov	024177

Date	Meter reading
16 Feb	024983
18 May	025829

Date	Meter reading
8 Aug	026620
17 Nov	027651

Date	Meter reading
17 Nov	024177
16 Feb	024983

Date	Meter reading
18 May	025829
8 Aug	026620

Date	Meter reading
17 Nov	027651
16 Feb	028265

Exercise 4

For each quarter, work out (to the nearest penny):
(a) the cost of the units used,   (c) the VAT payable,
(b) the total bill before VAT,   (d) the total payable.

Angles from tables

You need: 3 figure tables.
You should have done: Fractions of a degree (page 39).

If we know the tangent of an angle we can find the angle.

Look for 0.063 *in* your tangent table. It comes from 3.6°.

tan a° = 0.063
a° = 3.6°

Angle in degrees	.0	.1	.2	.3	.4	.5	⑥	.7	.8	.9
0	0.000	.002	.003	.005	.007	.009	.010	.012	.014	.016
1	0.017	.019	.021	.023	.024	.026	.028	.030	.031	.033
2	0.035	.037	.038	.040	.042	.044	.045	.047	.049	.051
③	0.052	.054	.056	.058	.059	.061	.063	.065	.066	.068

 Which angles have these tangents?
1. 0.049   2. 0.477   3. 2.63   4. 0.759   5. 3.73

Find 1.01 *in* your tangent table. It appears three times.

45	1.00	1.00	1.01	1.01	1.01	1.02	1.02	1.02	1.03	1.03

The angle it comes from is 45.2° or 45.3° or 45.4°.
We choose 45.4°, the *biggest* angle.

 Which angles have these tangents?
1. 1.17   2. 1.75   3. 1.41   4. 2.01   5. 1.83

Look for 5.30 *in* your tangent table:

79	5.14	5.19	5.24	5.29	5.34	5.40	5.45	5.50	5.56	5.61

5.30 is *not in* the table.
5.29 is the one *nearest* to it. It comes from 79.3°.

 Which angles have these tangents?
1. 9.10   2. 5.97   3. 3.91   4. 4.05   5. 85.2

Look for 0.371 *in* your table. It is not there!

0.371

20	0.364	.366	.368	.370	.372	.374	.376	.378	.380	.382

↑
halfway!

We choose the *larger* angle, 20.4°.

D Which angles have these tangents?
1. 2.22   2. 2.68   3. 2.93   4. 4.42   5. 3.09

We use sine tables the same way.

Which angles have these sines?

1. 0.413	5. 0.860	9. 0.990	13. 0.512	17. 0.756
2. 0.867	6. 1.000	10. 0.946	14. 0.582	18. 0.939
3. 0.177	7. 0.962	11. 0.283	15. 0.247	19. 0.771
4. 0.939	8. 0.903	12. 0.496	16. 0.035	20. 0.717

Look at your cosine tables. They are slightly different.
As the angle increases, the cosine decreases.

Find 0.889 *in* your cosine table. It appears twice.

27	0.891	.890	.889	.889	.888	.887	.886	.885	.885	.884

We choose 27.2°, the *smaller* angle.

E Which angles have these cosines?
1. 0.869   2. 0.880   3. 0.854   4. 0.949   5. 0.978

Look for 0.256 *in* your table. It is not there!

0.256

75	0.259	.257	.255	.254	.252	.250	.249	.247	.245	.244

↑
halfway!

We choose the *smaller* angle, 75.1°.

Which angles have these cosines?

1. 0.429	5. 0.769	9. 0.997	13. 0.351	17. 0.326
2. 0.818	6. 0.959	10. 1.000	14. 0.288	18. 0.852
3. 0.174	7. 0.985	11. 0.338	15. 0.472	19. 0.908
4. 0.698	8. 0.885	12. 0.253	16. 0.349	20. 0.468

Dividing directed numbers

You should have done: Two at a time (page 49).

Division is the inverse of multiplication.
Look at this flow diagram and its inverse.

flow diagram

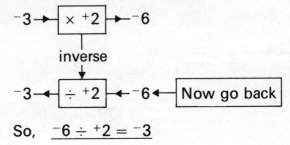

inverse diagram

So, $^-6 \div {}^+2 = {}^-3$

Copy and complete these:

1.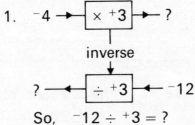

So, $^-12 \div {}^+3 = ?$

2.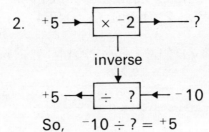

So, $^-10 \div ? = {}^+5$

3.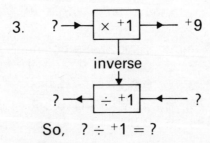

So, $? \div {}^+1 = ?$

4.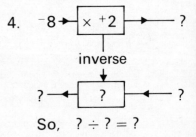

So, $? \div ? = ?$

5.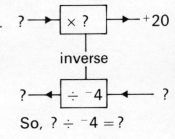

So, $? \div {}^-4 = ?$

6.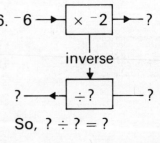

So, $? \div ? = ?$

1. Look at your answers to Exercise 1. What sort of directed numbers do you get when you divide:
   (a) a positive number by a positive number?
   (b) a negative number by a negative number?
   (c) a positive number by a negative number?
   (d) a negative number by a positive number?

2. Now do these:
   (a) $^+8 \div ^+2 =$ (d) $^+14 \div ^+7 =$
   (b) $^+12 \div ^-3 =$ (e) $^-21 \div ^-3 =$
   (c) $^-10 \div ^+5 =$ (f) $^-30 \div ^-10 =$

When dividing directed numbers:
   if the signs are the same, the answer is positive;
   if the signs are different, the answer is negative.

Do these divisions:
1. $^+4 \div ^-2 =$ 12. $^-15 \div ^+5 =$
2. $^-7 \div ^+7 =$ 13. $^-10 \div ^-2 =$
3. $^+8 \div ^+4 =$ 14. $^+20 \div ^+10 =$
4. $^+10 \div ^-5 =$ 15. $^-24 \div ^+6 =$
5. $^-12 \div ^-6 =$ 16. $^+25 \div ^-5 =$
6. $^-16 \div ^+4 =$ 17. $^-35 \div ^+7 =$
7. $^+15 \div ^+3 =$ 18. $^+42 \div ^-6 =$
8. $^-6 \div ^-6 =$ 19. $^-50 \div ^+10 =$
9. $^-18 \div ^+9 =$ 20. $^+72 \div ^-9 =$
10. $^+14 \div ^+2 =$ 21. $^-90 \div ^-45 =$
11. $^+17 \div ^-1 =$

☆ Want a change? Try Snooker squared on page 173.

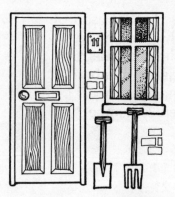

Perpendiculars

You need: ruler, compasses, protractor, pencil and plain paper.

Perpendicular lines meet at right angles.

Name ten objects with perpendicular lines in them. Use the pictures above to help you.

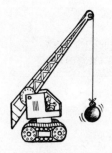

We can drop a perpendicular from a point to a line using a ruler and compasses.

Follow these steps:

1. Draw a line. Mark a point P above it. With centre P, draw an arc to cut the line twice. Call it A B.

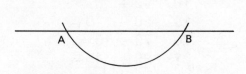

2. Open your compasses to a radius more than half A B. With centre A, draw an arc below the line.

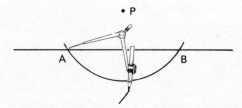

3. Keep the same radius. With centre B, draw an arc to cut your second arc.

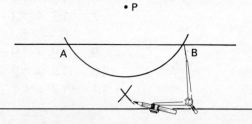

4. Draw a line through P and where the arcs cross.

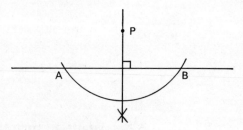

5. Use a protractor to check that your lines are perpendicular.

Exercise 1

Practise drawing some more perpendicular lines. Check them with your protractor.

We can construct a perpendicular at a given point using a ruler and compasses.

 Follow these steps:

1. Draw a line. Mark a point P on it. With centre P, draw two equal arcs to cut the line. Call them A, B.

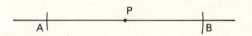

3. Keep the same radius. With centre B, draw another arc.

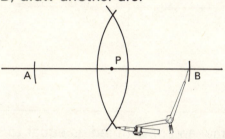

2. Open your compasses to a larger radius. With centre A, draw a big arc.

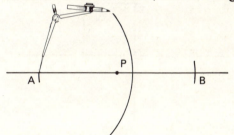

4. Draw a line through the crossing arcs.

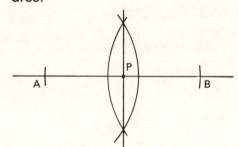

5. Measure the angles at P to check your drawing. Use a protractor.

Exercise 2

1. Practise drawing some more perpendiculars. Check them with your protractor.
2. Draw a line 6 cm long. Mark the ends A and B. Follow the steps 2, 3 and 4 in **C** to draw a perpendicular. Your perpendicular should cut AB in half. Check it with your ruler. You have drawn the **perpendicular bisector** of the line.

'bisect' means to cut in half

3. Draw the perpendicular bisectors of these lines:
   (a) AB = 7 cm (c) CD = 12 cm (e) MN = 11.8 cm
   (b) XY = 8 cm (d) PQ = 9.5 cm (f) RS = 10.6 cm
   Check them with your ruler and protractor.

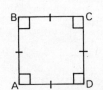

 Follow these steps to draw a square.

1. Draw a line. Mark a point P above it. Drop a perpendicular from P. Mark point A.

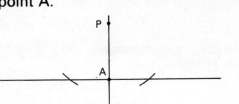

2. Draw an arc with radius equal to the square's side. Mark B and D.

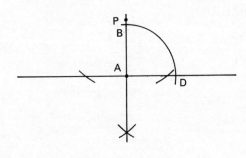

3. Keep the same radius. With B and D as centres, draw two arcs to cut at C.

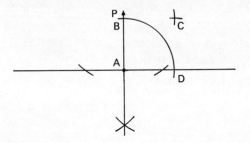

4. Complete the square ABCD.

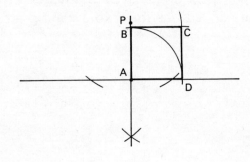

5. Check all the angles. Check all the sides.

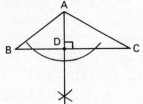

1. Draw squares with these sides:
   (a) 4 cm   (b) 5 cm   (c) 6.5 cm   (d) 8.4 cm

2. (a) Draw a large triangle ABC.
   (b) Drop a perpendicular from A to BC.
   (c) Measure AD. AD is the perpendicular height.
   (d) Measure BC.
   (e) Use a calculator to work out the area of △ABC.

3. Repeat Question 2 with 5 different triangles.

page **64**

Recap 2

1. Draw a conversion graph for £ to DM.
   £1 → 4.4 DM
   Use a scale of: 1 cm to 4.4 DM
               1 cm to £2
   (a) Use your graph to convert these to DM:
   (i) £4 (ii) £10 (iii) 80p (iv) £15.60
   (b) Use your graph to convert these to £:
   (i) 10 DM (ii) 26 DM (iii) 58 DM

2. Use tables to find the values of:
   (a) tan 24.5°   (d) sin 83.8°
   (b) sin 50.9°   (e) cos 17°
   (c) cos 4.7°   (f) tan 69.1°

3. Rewrite these with positive powers
   (a) 3^{-1} (c) 9^{-7} (e) 15^{-6}
   (b) 2^{-3} (d) 10^{-2} (f) 50^{-4}

4. Work out these:
   (a) $2^2 \times 2^{-1}$ (d) $a^3 \times a^{-2}$
   (b) $5^{-3} \times 5^4$ (e) $x^4 \times x^{-1}$
   (c) $7^{-2} \times 7$ (f) $m^{-3} \times m^{-4}$

5. Divide these quantities in the given ratios:

	quantity	ratio
(a)	£200	3 : 1
(b)	63 l	5 : 2
(c)	1 kg	3 : 2 : 5
(d)	45 m	7 : 5 : 3

6. Write these numbers in standard form:
   (a) 230   (e) 0.0087
   (b) 5630   (f) 26 500
   (c) 0.35   (g) 0.0009 .
   (d) 1 500 000 (h) 0.000 037

7. Write these as ordinary numbers:
   (a) 5×10^2 (d) 6.4×10^{-3}
   (b) 1.6×10^1 (e) 9×10^{-1}
   (c) 3.4×10^{-2} (f) 8.0×10^7

8. Calculate:
   (a) $^+2 \times ^-5$ (c) $^+8 \times ^+2 \times ^-5$
   (b) $^-3 \times ^+2 \times ^+4$ (d) $^-9 \times ^-2 \times ^-1$

9. Correct each of these numbers to:
   (a) 1 s.f., (b) 2 s.f.
   (i) 6.73   (iii) 0.006 17
   (ii) 0.265   (iv) 528.2

10. Here are the electricity meter readings for one quarter of the year:

present	previous
38425	36932

    (a) How many units were used?
    (b) What is the cost of the units used if each unit costs 5.92p?
    (c) If there is a standing charge per quarter of £7.65, what is the total bill?

11. A telephone subscriber used a total of 1156 units in one quarter. If each unit costs 5.02p, what is the cost of the units used? (Answer to nearest penny.)
    There is a rental charge of £16.50 and VAT at 15% is added to the bill.
    What is the total payable altogether?

12. (a) Which angles have these sines?
    (i) 0.584 (ii) 0.935 (iii) 0.022
    (b) Which angles have these cosines?
    (i) 0.098 (ii) 0.889 (iii) 0.704
    (c) Which angles have these tangents?
    (i) 0.458 (ii) 1.40 (iii) 7.87

13. Do these divisions:
    (a) $^+6 \div ^-2$ (d) $^-15 \div ^-3$
    (b) $^-8 \div ^+4$ (e) $^+36 \div ^-9$
    (c) $^-14 \div ^-7$ (f) $^-48 \div ^-12$

14. Using ruler, compasses and pencil only, draw a square of side 5.8 cm.

Average speed

Jackie went from Cambridge to Norwich by car.
She found the distance in the Road Atlas.

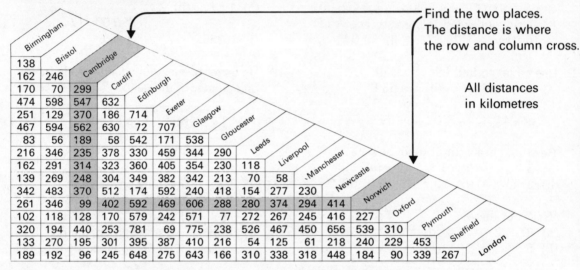

Find the two places.
The distance is where
the row and column cross.

All distances
in kilometres

Birmingham	Bristol	Cambridge	Cardiff	Edinburgh	Exeter	Glasgow	Gloucester	Leeds	Liverpool	Manchester	Newcastle	Norwich	Oxford	Plymouth	Sheffield	London
138																
162	246															
170	70	299														
474	598	547	632													
251	129	370	186	714												
467	594	562	630	72	707											
83	56	189	58	542	171	538										
216	346	235	378	330	459	344	290									
162	291	314	323	360	405	354	230	118								
139	269	248	304	349	382	342	213	70	58							
342	483	370	512	174	592	240	418	154	277	230						
261	346	99	402	592	469	606	288	280	374	294	414					
102	118	128	170	579	242	571	77	272	267	245	416	227				
320	194	440	253	781	69	775	238	526	467	450	656	539	310			
133	270	195	301	395	387	410	216	54	125	61	218	240	229	453		
189	192	96	245	648	275	643	166	310	338	318	448	184	90	339	267	

How far is it from Cambridge to Norwich?

Jackie set off at 09.45 and arrived at 10.45.

How long did the journey take?

The car went at different speeds during the journey.

But it travelled 99 kilometres in 1 hour.
So its average speed is 99 kilometres per hour
or 99 km/h.

These journeys each took one hour, too.

Find the distances in the table on page 66.

Manchester to Sheffield   Edinburgh to Glasgow
Birmingham to Gloucester   Oxford to London

 C What was the average speed for each journey?

Paul left Birmingham on a coach at 11.22.
He arrived in Liverpool at 13.22.

D
1. How far is it from Birmingham to Liverpool?
2. How long did the journey take?

use the formula

$$\text{Paul's average speed} = \frac{\text{distance travelled}}{\text{time taken}}$$

distance in km

time in h

$$= \frac{162\,\text{km}}{2\,\text{h}}$$

speed in km/h

$$= \underline{81\,\text{km/h}}$$

E Work out the average speeds for these journeys:
1. Depart Bristol 09.58. Arrive London 11.58.
2. Depart Leeds 11.45. Arrive Norwich 15.45.
3. Depart Manchester 08.30. Arrive Plymouth 17.30.
4. Depart Edinburgh 14.15. Arrive Sheffield 19.15.
5. Depart Oxford 13.05. Arrive Liverpool 16.05.

Tina left Exeter at 11.00 and arrived in Plymouth at 11.45.

use the formula

$$\text{Tina's average speed} = \frac{\text{distance travelled}}{\text{time taken}}$$

distance in km

time in h

$$= \frac{69\,\text{km}}{\frac{3}{4}\,\text{h}} \quad \longleftarrow \quad \left(45\,\text{min} = \tfrac{3}{4}\,\text{h}\right)$$

$$= \overset{23}{6\!\!\!/9} \times \frac{4}{\underset{1}{\cancel{3}}}\,\text{km/h}$$

speed in km/h

$$= \underline{92\,\text{km/h}}$$

 Memo
write the times in h

F Work out the average speeds for these journeys:
1. Depart Leeds 09.30. Arrive Sheffield 10.15.

2. Depart Bristol 11.05. Arrive Gloucester 11.35.
3. Depart Gloucester 11.40. Arrive Cardiff 12.20.
4. Depart London 15.35. Arrive Oxford 17.05.
5. Depart Cardiff 12.30. Arrive Bristol 13.45.

Steve ran for his House on Sports Day.
Here are his times:

Event	100 m	200 m	400 m	800 m	1000 m	1500 m
Time	12 s	26 s	65 s	2 min 25 s	3 min 45 s	5 min 50 s

In the 100 m race:

use the formula

distance in m
time in s

speed in m/s

$$\text{Steve's average speed} = \frac{\text{distance travelled}}{\text{time taken}}$$

$$= \frac{100 \text{ m}}{12 \text{ s}}$$

$$= 8.3 \text{ metres per second (to 1 d.p.)}$$

or 8.3 m/s

write all the
times in
seconds

 G Work out Steve's average speed in metres per second for each race. Give your answers correct to 1 decimal place.

When Steve ran his races, World Records for men were:

Event	100 m	200 m	400 m	800 m	1000 m	1500 m
Time	9.95 s	19.72 s	43.86 s	1 min 41.72 s	2 min 12.18 s	3 min 31.36 s

 H Calculate each runner's average speed in metres per second. Give your answers correct to 1 decimal place.

Gary went on a sponsored walk.
He knows that his average walking speed is 5 km/h.

This means that in 1 hour he will have walked 5 km.

Look... I'VE
SPONSORED YOU FOR
ONE WALK IN THIS
BOOK ALREADY

 I How far will he have walked in these times?
1. 2 hours   2. 3 hours   3. 4 hours   4. 5 hours

page 68

To work out your answers to you multiplied the average speed by the times.
Gary used this to make up a formula:

$$\text{distance travelled} = \text{average speed} \times \text{time taken}$$

J Use the formula to work out the distances travelled on these journeys:
1. 2 h at 7 km/h   3. 10 km/h for 5 h   5. $8\frac{1}{2}$ h at 12 km/h
2. 9 km/h for 6 h   4. $2\frac{1}{2}$ h at 6 km/h   6. $13\frac{1}{2}$ km/h for 10 h

Paul is training for the London Marathon.
His average jogging speed is 8 km/h.

K How long will it take him to jog these distances?
1. 16 km   2. 24 km   3. 32 km   4. 40 km

To work out your answers to you divided the distances by the average speed.
Paul used this to make this formula:

$$\text{time taken} = \frac{\text{distance travelled}}{\text{average speed}}$$

L Use the formula to work out the times for these journeys:
1. 16 km at 4 km/h   4. 8 km/h for 48 km
2. 20 km at 5 km/h   5. $2\frac{1}{2}$ km/h for 15 km
3. 27 km at 9 km/h   6. 6 km/h for $28\frac{1}{2}$ km

Summary

$$\text{average speed} = \frac{\text{distance travelled}}{\text{time taken}}$$

distance in km, time in h → speed in km/h
distance in m, time in s → speed in m/s

$$\text{distance travelled} = \text{average speed} \times \text{time taken}$$

$$\text{time taken} = \frac{\text{distance travelled}}{\text{average speed}}$$

1. Work out the average speeds for these journeys.
   (a) Depart Cardiff 09.15. Arrive Gloucester 10.15.
   (b) Depart Cambridge 11.17. Arrive Oxford 13.17.
   (c) Depart Newcastle 08.35. Arrive Sheffield 11.35.
   (d) Depart Sheffield 10.45. Arrive Exeter 15.15.
   (e) Depart Plymouth 05.48. Arrive Glasgow 18.18.

2. Sharon ran in the School Sports.
   Her times are given in this table:

Event	100 m	200 m	400 m	800 m	1000 m	1500 m
Time	14 s	30 s	72 s	2 min 45 s	4 min 20 s	6 min 35 s

Work out Sharon's average speed (to 1 d.p.) in metres per second for each race.

3. In August 1981 world running records for women were:

Event	100 m	200 m	400 m	800 m	1000 m	1500 m
Time	10.88 s	21.71 s	48.60 s	1 min 53.43 s	3 min 52.47 s	4 min 21.68 s

Calculate each runner's average speed in metres per second. Give your answers correct to 1 decimal place.

4. Calculate the distance travelled on these journeys:
   (a) 2 h at 15 km/h
   (b) 32 km/h for 5 h
   (c) 52.8 km/h for 10 h
   (d) $1\frac{1}{2}$ h at 60 km/h
   (e) $12\frac{1}{2}$ h at 500 km/h
   (f) $16\frac{1}{2}$ km/h for 17 h

5. Calculate the times for these journeys:
   (a) 35 km at 5 km/h
   (b) 63 km at 7 km/h
   (c) 14 km/h for 126 km
   (d) 220 km at 55 km/h
   (e) 3000 km at 600 km/h
   (f) $12\frac{1}{2}$ km/h for 125 km

6. Pironi and Jaussaud hold the record for the Le Mans 24 hour motor race. They averaged 210 km/h. How far did they travel in the 24 hours of the race?

7. The 'Indianapolis 500' motor race in the USA is run over a 4 km circuit. The average speed on the record lap was 310 km/h. What was the record lap time?

Finding lengths

You need: 3 figure tables and a ruler.
You should have done: Angles from tables (pages 58–59).

In this triangle, the hypotenuse is 1 cm.

opposite = sin 51° cm   adjacent = cos 51° cm

This triangle is an enlargement of the first one.
Its hypotenuse is 3 cm.
This is three times the length of the first one.
So the scale factor is 3.

opposite = 3 × sin 51° cm   adjacent = 3 × cos 51° cm
= 3 × 0.777 cm
= 1.554 cm

A Now calculate the length of the adjacent side.

Exercise 1 Copy these pairs of triangles. They are not drawn accurately. Work out and fill in the missing values.

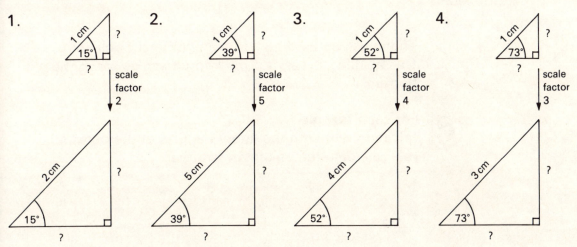

1.
2.
3.
4.

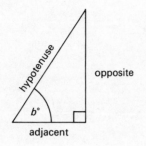

You have used the hypotenuse to find the other two sides of the triangle.

We can use:

> opposite = hypotenuse × sine of base angle
> adjacent = hypotenuse × cosine of base angle

In the given triangle, calculate the length AB.

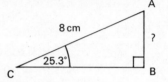

draw a diagram
put on what you know

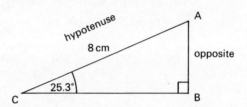

choose the formula
put in what you know
use the tables
work it out

opposite = hypotenuse × sine of base angle
      =   8   ×   sin 25.3° cm
      =   8   ×   0.427   cm
      = <u>3.416 cm</u>

Now calculate the length of BC.

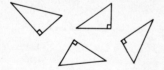

Triangles can be drawn in many different positions. Our working is easier if the known angles are at the bottom.

For each triangle:
(a) redraw it with the known angles at the bottom;
(b) calculate the unknown lengths.

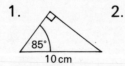

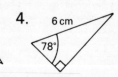

Sometimes we are given the information in words.

In △XYZ, ∠Y = 90°, ∠X = 37.9°, XZ = 5 cm.
Calculate the lengths of XY and YZ.

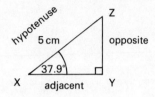

draw a diagram
put on what you know
label the sides

choose the formula
put in what you know
use the tables
work it out

adjacent = hypotenuse × cosine of base angle
$\quad\quad$ = $\quad\quad$ 5 $\quad\quad$ × $\quad\quad$ cos 37.9° $\quad\quad$ cm
$\quad\quad$ = $\quad\quad$ 5 $\quad\quad$ × $\quad\quad$ 0.789 $\quad\quad$ cm
XY = <u>3.945 cm</u>

opposite = hypotenuse × sine of base angle
$\quad\quad$ = $\quad\quad$ 5 $\quad\quad$ × $\quad\quad$ sin 37.9° $\quad\quad$ cm
$\quad\quad$ = $\quad\quad$ 5 $\quad\quad$ × $\quad\quad$ 0.614 $\quad\quad$ cm
YZ = <u>3.070 cm</u>

Calculate the lengths of the other two sides in these:
1. △ABC, ∠B = 90°, ∠A = 20°, $\quad$ AC = 4 cm.
2. △PQR, ∠Q = 90°, ∠P = 54°, $\quad$ PR = 5 cm.
3. △FGH, ∠G = 90°, ∠F = 48.5°, FH = 9 cm.

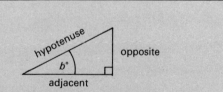

opposite = hypotenuse × sine of base angle
adjacent = hypotenuse × cosine of base angle

Calculate the marked lengths in these triangles:

1.
2.
3.
4.

5. **6.** **7.** **8.**

9. 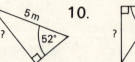 **10.** **11.** **12.**

Calculate the unknown lengths in these triangles:

13. $\triangle$XYZ, $\angle$Y = 90°, $\angle$X = 53.5°, XZ = 10 cm.
14. $\triangle$DEF, $\angle$E = 90°, $\angle$F = 79.4°, DF = 4 cm.
15. $\triangle$LMN, $\angle$M = 90°, $\angle$L = 21.9°, LN = 2.7 cm.
16. $\triangle$STU, $\angle$T = 90°, $\angle$U = 36.7°, SU = 4.9 cm.

17. Calculate CD and AC.   18. Calculate BD and BC.

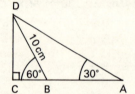 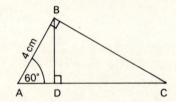

Worth repeating

'Sevenths' give recurring decimals. 'To recur' means 'to come round again'.

$$\frac{1}{7} = 0.\underbrace{142\ 857}\ 142\ 857\ 142\ldots = 0.\dot{1}42\ 85\dot{7}$$

These numbers are repeated forever.

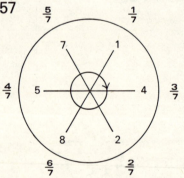

Work out $\frac{2}{7}$ and $\frac{3}{7}$ to at least 12 decimal places.
Look at your answers and the circle diagram.
Notice anything?
Can you predict what $\frac{4}{7}$, $\frac{5}{7}$ and $\frac{6}{7}$ will be?
Check by working them out.

Some other fractions give recurring decimals too. How many can you find?

Pot Black

You need: a ruler and centimetre graph paper.
You should have done: Pick your own (pages 6–8).

Paul is snooker mad.
Pot Black and Junior Pot Black are his favourites on TV.
He records all their scores.

POT BLACK

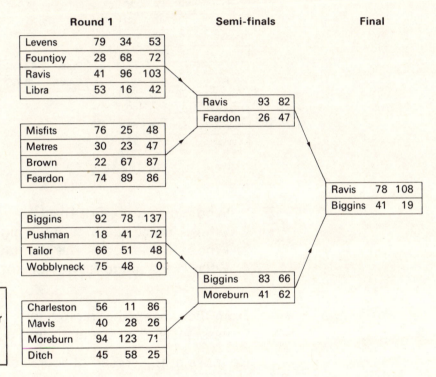

	Round 1			Semi-finals		Final	
Levens	79	34	53				
Fountjoy	28	68	72				
Ravis	41	96	103	Ravis	93 82		
Libra	53	16	42	Feardon	26 47		
Misfits	76	25	48				
Metres	30	23	47			Ravis	78 108
Brown	22	67	87			Biggins	41 19
Feardon	74	89	86				
Biggins	92	78	137				
Pushman	18	41	72				
Tailor	66	51	48	Biggins	83 66		
Wobblyneck	75	48	0	Moreburn	41 62		
Charleston	56	11	86				
Mavis	40	28	26				
Moreburn	94	123	71				
Ditch	45	58	25				

How to score:
Add the 'frame scores' for each player. The highest total wins.

1. Who won Pot Black?
2. Whose 'frame score' was the highest? What was it?
3. Whose 'frame score' was the lowest? What was it?

range =
highest − lowest

The difference between the highest and lowest scores is called the **range**.

What is the range for Pot Black?

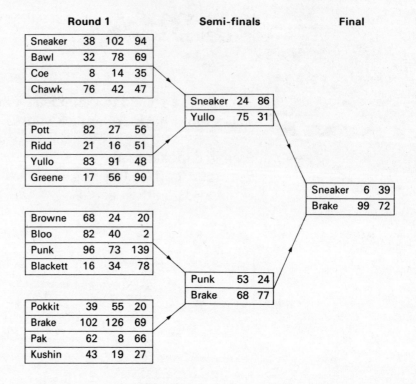

| Round 1 | Semi-finals | Final |

Sneaker	38	102	94
Bawl	32	78	69
Coe	8	14	35
Chawk	76	42	47

| Sneaker | 24 | 86 |
| Yullo | 75 | 31 |

Pott	82	27	56
Ridd	21	16	51
Yullo	83	91	48
Greene	17	56	90

| Sneaker | 6 | 39 |
| Brake | 99 | 72 |

Browne	68	24	20
Bloo	82	40	2
Punk	96	73	139
Blackett	16	34	78

| Punk | 53 | 24 |
| Brake | 68 | 77 |

Pokkit	39	55	20
Brake	102	126	69
Pak	62	8	66
Kushin	43	19	27

1. Who won Junior Pot Black?
2. Whose 'frame score' was the highest? What was it?
3. Whose 'frame score' was the lowest? What was it?
4. What is the range for Junior Pot Black?

From the ranges, the Juniors look as good as the Professionals. Paul wants to find out if they are.

He looks at the spread of scores on a **frequency table**.

POT BLACK

scores	tally	frequency
0	1	1
1		0
2		

Exercise 1

This is the mode ──▶

1. Copy and complete Paul's frequency table.
2. How many different scores are there?
3. Which score has the highest frequency?
4. What is the highest frequency?

This frequency table does not tell Paul much more.
There are too many different scores.
The frequencies are all small.

Paul thinks that scores less than 20 are pathetic.
He decides to put them into one group.
So he must group the other scores in 20s too.

POT BLACK

scores	tally	frequency
0–19	|||||	5
20–39		
40–59		
100–119		
120–139		

1. Copy and complete Paul's new frequency table.
2. Which group of scores has the highest frequency?
   This is called the **modal group**.

Paul draws a **histogram** from his new table.

This type of
bar chart
is called a
histogram.

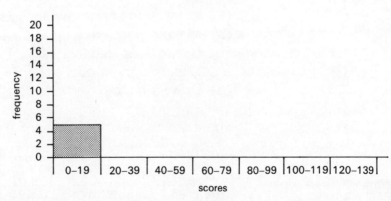

Pot Black

Copy and complete Paul's histogram.

Paul does the same for Junior Pot Black.

Exercise 3

1. Make a frequency table for Junior Pot Black. Group the scores in 20s as before.
2. Which is the modal group?
3. Draw a histogram from your table.
4. Compare your results for the Professionals and Juniors. Do the Juniors still look as good as the Professionals? Explain your answer.

Summary

Range: the difference between the largest and smallest values of the data.

Grouped data
When we have a large range of values we can group the data. Each group must have the same range of values.
A frequency table can be made using the grouped data.
Modal group: the group with the highest frequency, i.e., with the most values in it.
A histogram can be drawn from the frequency table.

Exercise 4

1. The golf scores of 30 players are given below:

92	103	85	81	96	88	108	93	73	85
70	102	95	82	103	81	96	64	91	84
103	84	102	92	76	86	85	104	86	95

   (a) What is the range for these scores?
   (b) Make a frequency table for the golf scores. Group them like this: 60–69, 70–79, ..., 100–109.
   (c) Which is the modal group?
   (d) Draw a histogram from your table.

2. The darts scores of 40 players are given below:

100	80	20	48	120	55	75	170	120	80
100	34	39	49	92	87	31	100	120	144
100	86	72	8	114	71	70	100	120	150
170	113	64	42	118	54	79	91	80	100

   (a) What is the range for these scores?
   (b) Make a frequency table for the darts scores. Group them like this: 0–19, 20–39, ..., 160–179.

(c) Which is the modal group?
(d) Draw a histogram from your table.

3. The points scored by Rugby Union clubs one Saturday are given below:

3	9	39	7	6	26	15	30	12	22
30	15	3	18	36	30	12	26	6	12
15	44	3	6	16	12	7	4	16	3
4	10	13	9	0	6	6	19	6	25

(a) What is the range for these points?
(b) Make a frequency table for the rugby points.
Group them like this: 0–4, 5–9, ..., 40–44.
(c) Which is the modal group?
(d) Draw a histogram from your table.

4. The points scored by teams in a Basketball Competition are given below:

26	12	24	42	16	18	30	24	36	8
34	24	20	16	24	16	18	26	10	32
24	12	26	12	12	20	24	18	14	22
24	14	34	24	20	12	20	24	20	26
32	12	16	42	26	22	24	20	16	18
18	30	24	36	8	26	18	24	10	16

(a) What is the range for these points?
(b) Make a frequency table for the basketball points.
Group them like this: 0–4, 5–9, ..., 40–44.
(c) Which is the modal group?
(d) Draw a histogram from your table.

5. A batsman's scores over a cricket season are given below:

61	75	9	121	182	13	133	34	0	33
110	88	169	233	6	3	169	151	40	111
30	112	24	58	112	14	66	138	84	124

(a) What is the range for these scores?
(b) Make a frequency table for the batting scores.
Group them like this: 0–24, 25–49, ..., 225–249.
(c) Which is the modal group?
(d) Draw a histogram from your table.

More substitution

You should have done: More shorthand (pages 26–27);
Dividing directed numbers (pages 60–61).

Substitution is replacing letters by numbers.

Substitute $p = {}^-3$ to find the values of:
(i) 7p, (ii) 5p − 4.

(i) $7p = 7 \times p$ (ii) $5p - 4 = \boxed{5 \times p} - 4$

$\qquad\quad = 7 \times {}^-3 \qquad\qquad\qquad = \boxed{5 \times {}^-3} - 4$

$\qquad\quad = \underline{{}^-21} \qquad\qquad\qquad\quad = \quad {}^-15 \quad - 4$

$\qquad\qquad\qquad\qquad\qquad\qquad\qquad = \underline{{}^-19}$

 Substitute $t = {}^-2$ to find the values of:

1. $2t$	3. $1 - t$	5. $4t + 2$	7. $7t + 6$
2. $5 + t$	4. $3t + 1$	6. $3 - 2t$	8. ${}^-8 + 4t$

Expressions can have more than one letter.

If $x = {}^-4$, $y = 5$ and $z = {}^-3$, find the value of
$2x + 3y - xyz$.

$2x + 3y - xyz = \boxed{2 \times x} + \boxed{3 \times y} - \boxed{x \times y \times z}$

$\qquad\qquad\quad = \boxed{2 \times {}^-4} + \boxed{3 \times 5} - \boxed{{}^-4 \times 5 \times {}^-3}$

${}^-8 + 15 = 7 \qquad\qquad = \quad {}^-8 \quad + \quad 15 \quad - \quad 60$

$\qquad\qquad\quad = \qquad\qquad\qquad 7 - 60$

$\qquad\qquad\quad = \underline{{}^-53}$

B If $p = {}^-2$, $q = {}^-1$ and $s = 4$, find the values of:
1. $2p + 3q$ 3. $3sq - 5pq$
2. $pq + s$ 4. $5p - 6q + pqs$

$b^4 = b \times b \times b \times b$

We can have powers in expressions, too.

If $a = {}^-3$, find the values of: (i) a^2, (ii) $2a^3$.

(i) $a^2 = a \times a$ (ii) $2a^3 = 2 \times a \times a \times a$

$\qquad\quad = {}^-3 \times {}^-3$ $= 2 \times {}^-3 \times {}^-3 \times {}^-3$

$\qquad\quad = \underline{9}$ $= 2 \times {}^-27$

$\qquad\qquad\qquad\qquad\qquad\qquad\quad = \underline{{}^-54}$

If $r = {}^-5$, find the values of:
1. r^2 2. r^4 3. $4r^3$ 4. $7r^5$.

Expressions can have different powers in them.

If $y = {}^-2$, find the values of:
(i) $3y^3 + 1$, (ii) $2y^2 + 5y - 1$.

$\times$ before $+$

(i) $3y^3 + 1 = \boxed{3 \times y \times y \times y} + 1$

$\qquad\qquad\quad = \boxed{3 \times {}^-2 \times {}^-2 \times {}^-2} + 1$

$\qquad\qquad\quad = \boxed{3 \times {}^-8} + 1$

$\qquad\qquad\quad = \quad {}^-24 \quad + 1$

$\qquad\qquad\quad = \underline{{}^-23}$

(ii) $2y^2 + 5y - 1 = \boxed{2 \times y \times y} + \boxed{5 \times y \times y} - 1$

$\qquad\qquad\qquad = \boxed{2 \times {}^-2 \times {}^-2} + \boxed{5 \times {}^-2} - 1$

$\qquad\qquad\qquad = \boxed{2 \times 4} + {}^-10 - 1$

$\qquad\qquad\qquad = \quad 8 \quad + \quad {}^-10 \quad - 1$

$\qquad\qquad\qquad = \underline{{}^-3}$

If $a = {}^-2$, $m = {}^-3$ and $x = {}^-5$, find the values of:
1. $2a^2 + 1$ 4. $2m^2 - 3m + 1$
2. $3m^3 - 2$ 5. $x^2 + 4a^2 - m^2$
3. $4x^2 + x$ 6. $m^3 - 3a^2 + ax$

1. If $x = {}^-3$, find the values of:
   (a) $3x$ (c) $4 - x$ (e) $8 - 2x$ (g) ${}^-x - 1$
   (b) $5x + 1$ (d) $7x - 2$ (f) ${}^-1 + 2x$ (h) ${}^-3 - 4x$

2. Substitute $m = {}^-5$ and $n = 3$ to find the values of:
   (a) $m + n$ (c) $2m + 4n$ (e) $3m + 6n - mn$
   (b) $n - m$ (d) $5n - 4m$ (f) $nm - 5m - 2n$

3. If $p = {}^-2$ and $q = {}^-5$ find the values of:
   (a) p^2 (b) q^3 (c) $4p^3$ (d) $3q^2$ (e) $5p^5$

4. Substitute $r = {}^-1$, $s = {}^-3$ and $t = 4$ to find the values of:
   (a) $3r^2 - 1$ (d) $4r^2 - 6r + 3$
   (b) $6s^2 + 5$ (e) $2s^2 + 3s - 5$
   (c) $2r^3 - s^2$ (f) $5r^3 - 2s^2 - 3rs$

Perfect routes

Jackie has a paper round.
The street map shows where she delivers papers.
She has found the 'perfect route' for her round.
It starts at the shop,
goes along each street once only
and finishes at the shop.

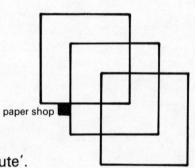

paper shop

Copy the street map and find Jackie's 'perfect route'.

Now try to find 'perfect routes' for these paper rounds.

One of these cannot be done!

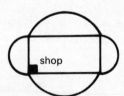

shop

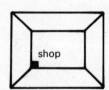

shop

shop

Get a street map for your area. Make up some 'paper rounds' from it.
Investigate the 'perfect route' for each one.

Travel graphs

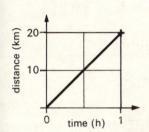

You need: a ruler and centimetre graph paper.
You should have done: Average speed (pages 66–70).

Jackie goes to visit her sister every week.
She cycles the 20 km there in 1 hour.

This graph shows her journey.

What is her average speed?

These travel graphs show journeys too.

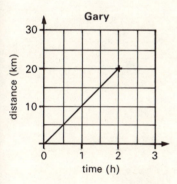
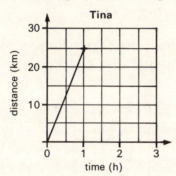
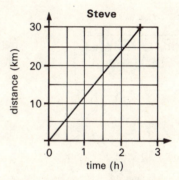

1. For each journey, what is: (a) the distance travelled?
   (b) the time taken?
   (c) the average speed?
2. Which line has: (a) the steepest slope?
   (b) the gentlest slope?
3. Which average speed is: (a) the greatest?
   (b) the least?
4. Compare your answers to 2 and 3. Write a sentence about the slopes and average speeds.

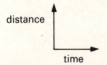

In a travel graph we plot distance against time.

Scale: time axis –
2 cm to 1 h
distance axis –
1 cm to 5 km

Draw travel graphs showing these journeys:
1. 30 km in 2 h   3. 40 km in $3\frac{1}{2}$ h
2. 70 km in 3 h   4. 25 km in $4\frac{1}{2}$ h

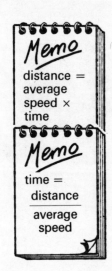

distance =
average
speed ×
time

time =

distance
─────────
average
speed

Sometimes we need to work out the distance before drawing the graph.

1. What is the distance travelled on these journeys?
   (a) 20 km/h for 3 h
   (b) 3 km/h for 4 h
   (c) 50 km/h for $\frac{1}{2}$ h
   (d) 10 km/h for $2\frac{1}{2}$ h

2. Draw travel graphs to show each journey.

Sometimes we have to find the time taken.

1. What is the time taken on these journeys:
   (a) 48 km at 8 km/h
   (b) 54 km at 27 km/h
   (c) 45 km at 36 km/h
   (d) 63 km at 42 km/h

2. Draw travel graphs to show each journey.

Paul went on a sponsored walk.
He rested at one checkpoint.

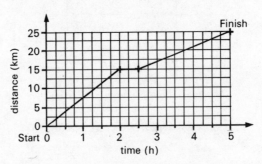

1. Copy this travel graph showing Paul's journey.
   Scale: time axis – 4 cm represents 1 h
              distance axis – 2 cm represents 5 km
2. Work out Paul's average speed (in km/h) on the 1st stage of his walk.
3. How long did he rest at the checkpoint?
4. Work out Paul's average speed (in km/h) on the 2nd stage of his walk.
5. How far did Paul walk altogether?
6. How long did he take from Start to Finish?
7. What was his average speed (in km/h) between the Start and Finish?

Steve went on the same sponsored walk.
He walked the first 15 km in 3 hours.
Then he rested for 30 minutes.
He walked the next 10 km in 1½ hours.

1. Show Steve's journey on the same graph as Paul's.
2. What was Steve's average speed (in km/h) between the Start and Finish? (Answer to 1 d.p.)

This travel graph shows Tina's sponsored walk.
She rested at two checkpoints.

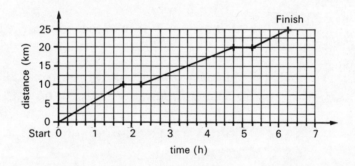

1. Copy this travel graph showing Tina's journey.
2. Work out Tina's average speed (in km/h) on each stage of her journey.
3. How long did she rest at each checkpoint?
4. What was her average speed (in km/h) between the Start and Finish? (Answer to 1 d.p.)

Sharon went on the sponsored walk too.
She walked the first 11 km in 2 hours.
Then she rested for 15 minutes.
The next 11 km took her 3 hours!
After a ¼ h rest she did the last 3 km in 45 minutes.

1. Show Sharon's journey on the same graph as Tina's.
2. What was Sharon's average speed (in km/h) between the Start and Finish?

Tina cycled from home to town.
Her mum went by bus from town to home.

These graphs
show their
journeys.

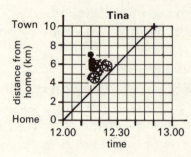

Tina

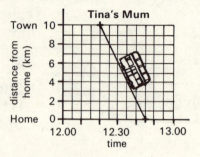

Tina's Mum

G

1. How far is it from Tina's home to town?
2. When did Tina: (a) leave home   (b) arrive in town?
3. What was Tina's average speed (in km/h)?
4. When did Tina's mum: (a) leave town,
   (b) arrive home?
5. What was her average speed (in km/h)?

Tina follows the bus route on her bike.
So Tina's mum saw her cycling into town.

H

1. Show Tina's and her mum's journeys on the same
   graph.
   Scale: time axis – 1 cm represents 5 minutes
               distance axis – 1 cm represents 1 km
2. At what time did Tina and her mum pass each other?
3. How far from home was her mum then?
4. How far from town was Tina then?

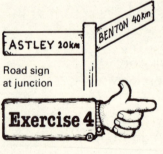

Road sign
at junction

Exercise 4

Two villages, Astley and Benton, are 60 km apart. A bus
leaves Astley at 10.00 and arrives at Benton at 11.30.
A car leaves Benton at 10.05 and follows the bus route
to Astley. It arrives at 11.05.

1. Show the bus and car journeys on the same graph.
   Scale: time axis – 1 cm represents 5 minutes
               distance axis – 1 cm represents 5 km
2. What is the average speed of each vehicle (in km/h)?
3. At what time did the bus and car pass each other?
4. How far from Benton is the bus then?
5. How far from Astley is the car then?

Steve went to visit Paul.
He walked from home. Paul's dad gave him a lift back.

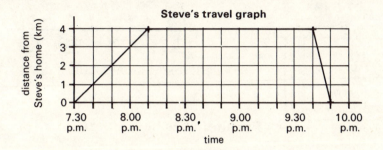

Steve's travel graph

1. Copy Steve's travel graph.
   Scale: time axis – 1 cm represents 10 minutes
               distance axis – 2 cm represents 1 km
2. How far is it from Steve's home to Paul's?
3. How long did it take Steve to walk to Paul's?
4. What was Steve's average walking speed (in km/h)?
5. How long did Steve stay at Paul's?
6. How long did the car journey home take?
7. What was the car's average speed (in km/h)?

Tina and Sharon live 6 km apart.
Sharon goes to Tina's by bus. She leaves home at
6.10 p.m. and arrives at Tina's 10 minutes later. At
7.30 p.m. she borrows Tina's bike and cycles home.
It takes her half an hour.

Exercise 5

1. Show Sharon's journey on a travel graph.
   Scale: time axis – 1 cm represents 10 minutes
               distance axis – 2 cm represent 1 km
2. How long did Sharon stay at Tina's?
3. What was Sharon's average cycling speed (in km/h)?

Summary

Travel graphs show journeys.
We plot distance against time.

distance

time

The steeper the slope,
the greater the speed.

Parallels

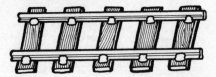

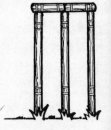

You need: a set square, ruler, pencil and plain paper.

Parallel lines never meet.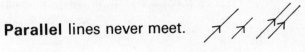

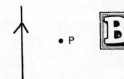 Name ten objects with parallel lines in them.
The pictures above will give you some clues.

We can draw parallel lines using a set square.

B Follow these steps:

1. Draw a straight line. Mark it with an arrow.
   Mark a point P to the right of it.

2. Place one edge of your set square along the line.

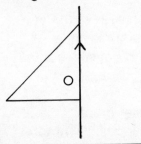

3. Place your ruler firmly against the other edge.

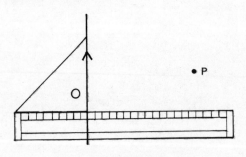

4. Hold your ruler in place.
   Slide your set square along it to P.

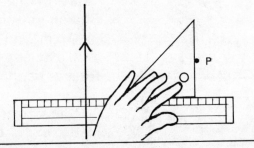

5. Draw along your set square through P.

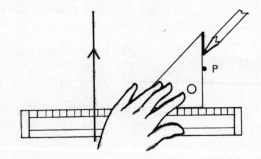

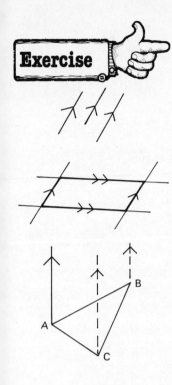

1. Practice drawing some more parallel lines.
   Mark them with matching arrows.

2. Draw two parallel lines. Now draw two more parallel lines to cut the others.
   You have made a parallelogram.

3. Draw five more parallelograms.

4. (a) Draw a large triangle A B C.
   (b) Draw a line through A.
   (c) Draw parallel lines through B and C.

5. Repeat Question 4 with two different triangles.

6. (a) Draw a large polygon.
   (b) Draw a line through a vertex (corner).
   (c) Draw parallel lines through all the other vertices.

7. Repeat Question 6 with two different polygons.

Angles of elevation and depression

Angles of **elevation** are always measured **upwards**.

angle
of
elevation

always measure from the
horizontal

angle
of
depression

Angles of **depression** are always measured **downwards**.

Squares

$17^2 = 17 \times 17$

You can do it like this:

Press: ☐C☐ ☐1☐ ☐7☐ ☐×☐ ☐1☐ ☐7☐ ☐=☐

But this is quicker

Press: ☐C☐ ☐1☐ ☐7☐ ☐×☐ ☐=☐

Try both ways for yourself.

$5^2 = ?$	$1^2 = ?$
$15^2 = ?$	$11^2 = ?$ Notice
$25^2 = ?$	$21^2 = ?$ any
.	. patterns?
$95^2 = ?$	$91^2 = ?$

What do you think 105^2 and 101^2 are?
Check your ideas.

$25^2 - 24^2 = ?$
$30^2 - 29^2 = ?$ Spot anything?
$43^2 - 42^2 = ?$ Try some more
$52^2 - 51^2 = ?$ to check.
$61^2 - 60^2 = ?$

$6^2 + 7^2 = ?$	$10^2 + 10^2 = ?$
$2^2 + 9^2 = ?$	$2^2 + 14^2 = ?$

$6^2 + 13^2 = ?$	$7^2 + 9^2 = ?$
$3^2 + 14^2 = ?$	$3^2 + 11^2 = ?$

Notice anything?
Which two pairs of squares add up to:
50, 145, 170, 185?

$13^2, 84^2, 85^2$	$12^2, 35^2, 38^2$

$36^2, 48^2, 60^2$	$15^2, 112^2, 113^2$

Which is the odd threesome? Why?

Square roots

$\sqrt{}$ means square root.

Some calculators have a ☐√☐ button.

To find $\sqrt{9}$ press: ☐C☐ ☐9☐ ☐√☐

Find: $\sqrt{196}$, $\sqrt{361}$, $\sqrt{1369}$, $\sqrt{784}$

What does your calculator show for:

$\sqrt{71}$, $\sqrt{710}$, $\sqrt{0.53}$, $\sqrt{5.3}$, $\sqrt{9876}$?

Correct each answer to:
  (a) 2 d.p.   (b) 3 s.f.

No ☐√☐ button!

You can still use
your calculator.

What is $\sqrt{7}$?
Guess 2: $2^2 = 4$ too small
Guess 3: $3^2 = 9$ too big
Try a number in between.
2   2.5   3

  $2.5^2 = 6.25$ too small
  $2.6^2 = 6.76$ still too small
  $2.7^2 = 7.29$ too big

Try a number in between.
2.6   2.65   2.7

  $2.65^2 = 7.0225$ too big
  $2.64^2 = 6.9696$ too small

Try in between
  $2.645^2 = 6.996025$ too small
  $2.644^2 = \ldots$

Find the best answer you can for $\sqrt{7}$.

Now try: $\sqrt{8}$, $\sqrt{11}$, $\sqrt{27}$, $\sqrt{23}$, $\sqrt{42}$

Flight plans

You need: a protractor, a centimetre ruler and tracing paper.
You should have done: Parallels (pages 88–89).

Gary wants to be a navigator in the RAF.
He must learn how to plot courses.

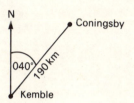

Flight plan
Kemble to Coningsby
bearing: 040°
distance: 190 km

A course in a flight plan must give:
   a **bearing** and
   a **distance**.

The bearing gives the direction to travel in.
It is an angle measured:
   in degrees,
   from North,
   turning clockwise.

bearing 212°

Bearings must have three figures.

The bearing 065° tells you to turn 65°
   This zero ↑ makes up   from N,
   the three figures   clockwise.

These diagrams show the directions of some RAF stations from Kemble (K).

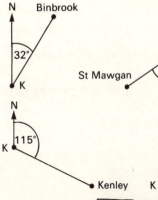
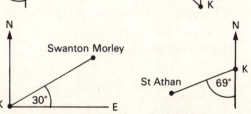
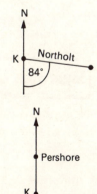

Write each direction as a bearing.

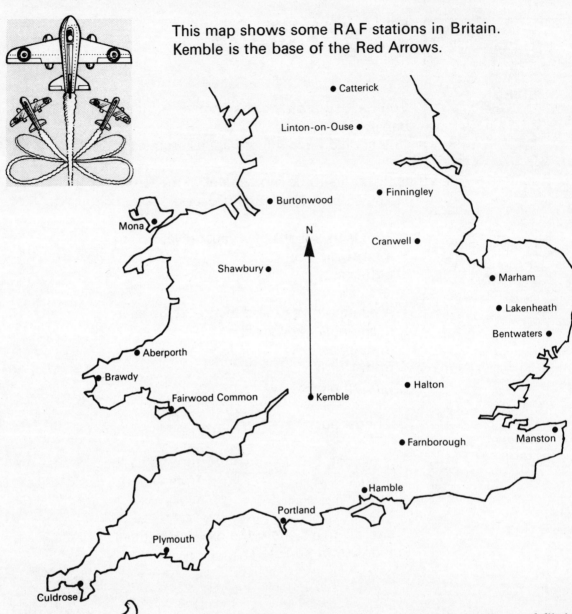

This map shows some RAF stations in Britain.
Kemble is the base of the Red Arrows.

Trace the map. On your tracing draw in the lines of flight from Kemble to each station.
Use your protractor to help you to find the bearing for each flight from Kemble.
Write your answers in a table like this:

Bearings from Kemble	
Catterick	005°
Linton-on-Ouse	

The scale on the map is:
  1 mm represents 3.5 km.

Exercise 2

Copy and complete this table. Measure the flight distances on the map in millimetres. Work out the real distances in kilometres.

Distances of airfields from Kemble		
	Map distance	Real distance
scale	mm 1 mm	km 3.5 km
Catterick Linton-on-Ouse	82 mm	$3.5 \times 82 = 287$ km

The Red Arrows give aerobatic displays around the country. Gary plots their round trip from the Farnborough Air Show.

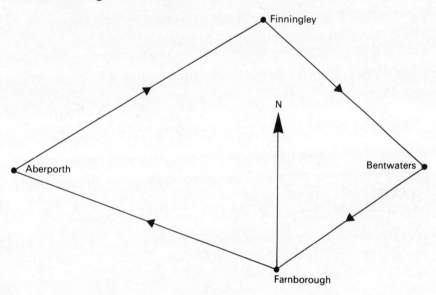

Exercise 3

1. Trace Gary's flight course.
2. Use your set square and ruler to draw North lines at each place.
   (Remember: all the North lines must be parallel.)

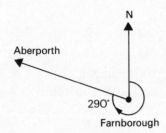

3. Copy and complete this table of bearings.
Use your protractor to find the bearing for each separate flight.

Flight From – to	Bearing
Farnborough – Aberporth Aberporth – Finningley	290°

4. Copy and complete this table of distances.

Flight From – to	Map distance scale: 1 mm	Real distance 3.5 km
Farnborough – Aberporth Aberporth – Finningley		

Summary

Navigators plot courses.

A course gives: a bearing
             and a distance.

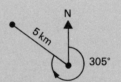

A bearing is measured: in degrees,
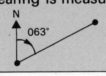
                   from North,
                   turning clockwise.
                   It must have 3 figures.

Exercise 4

1. Write each of these directions as a bearing:

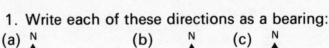

(a)   (b)   (c)   (d)

2. Compass directions can be written as bearings.
Copy and complete this table:

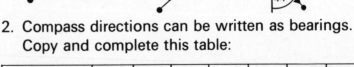

Direction	N	NE	E	SE	S	SW	W	NW
Bearing	000°							

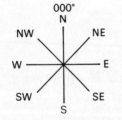

3. Trace these courses. For each flight:
  (i) find the bearing,
  (ii) work out the real distance in kilometres.
  (a) Hamble → Manston → Marham → Burtonwood → Hamble.
  (b) Portland → Brawdy → Catterick → Lakenheath → Portland.
  (c) Mona → Cranwell → Kemble → Manston → Plymouth → Mona.
  (d) Linton-on-Ouse → Shawbury → Bentwaters → Hamble → Fairwood Common → Linton-on-Ouse.
  (e) Culdrose → Brawdy → Burtonwood → Catterick → Marham → Aberporth → Culdrose.

Points of view

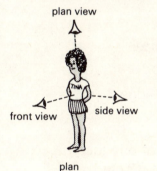

Three different views of Tina:

Which is the plan view, front view, side view?

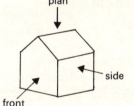

Three different views of the solid:

Which view is which?

Match each solid with its views. Mark which view is which.

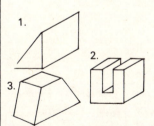

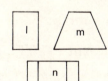

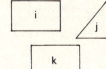

Find some pictures of solids of your own.
Try to imagine and draw the three views of each.
See if your friends can match the solids and views.

Christmas boxes

Jackie and Sharon want to make some Christmas boxes.
Sharon has a cube she got last year.
She cuts along the edges and opens it out.

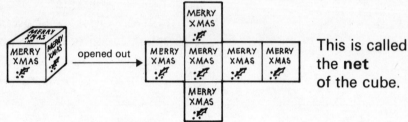

opened out

This is called
the **net**
of the cube.

A
1. How many faces has the cube?
2. What shape are the faces?
3. How many faces are the same size?

Sharon decides to make a cube of edge 3 cm.
She must find its surface area.

$$\text{surface area of cube} = 6 \times \text{area of one face}$$
$$= 6 \times 3\,\text{cm} \times 3\,\text{cm}$$
$$= 6 \times 9\,\text{cm}^2$$
$$= \underline{54\,\text{cm}^2}$$

B
Find the surface areas of cubes with these edges:
1. 5 cm   2. 10 cm   3. 12 cm   4. 25 cm

Jackie's box is a cuboid:

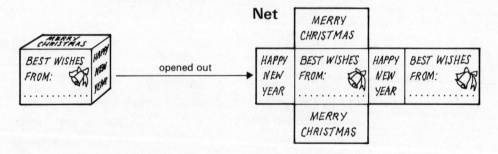

opened out

Net

1. How many faces has the cuboid?
2. What shape are the faces?
3. How many faces are the same size? Which ones?

Jackie wants to make a cuboid with edges 4 cm, 3 cm and 2 cm.

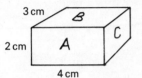

Area

2 faces like A: $2 \times (4\,cm \times 2\,cm) = 16\,cm^2$
2 faces like B: $2 \times (4\,cm \times 3\,cm) = 24\,cm^2$
2 faces like C: $2 \times (3\,cm \times 2\,cm) = \underline{12\,cm^2}$
Total surface area $\underline{52\,cm^2}$

Find the surface areas of cuboids with these edges:
1. 3 cm, 4 cm, 5 cm   3. 2.5 cm, 4 cm, 6 cm
2. 12 cm, 10 cm, 4 cm   4. 10.5 cm, 10 cm, 12.5 cm

Summary

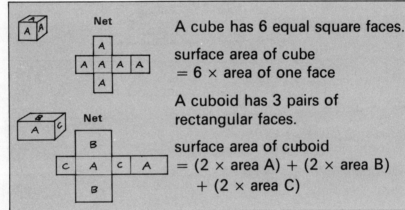

A cube has 6 equal square faces.

surface area of cube
= 6 × area of one face

A cuboid has 3 pairs of rectangular faces.

surface area of cuboid
= (2 × area A) + (2 × area B)
+ (2 × area C)

Exercise

1. Find the surface areas of cubes with these edges:
   (a) 4 cm (b) 7 cm (c) 14 m (d) 11 cm (e) 6.3 m

2. Find the surface areas of cuboids with these edges:
   (a) 2 cm, 6 cm, 8 cm   (c) 5.1 cm, 3 cm, 4 cm
   (b) 5 m, 7 m, 12 m   (d) 12 mm, 15 mm, 7 mm

watch the
units!

3. A cube has edge 75 mm.
   What is its surface area in cm^2?

4. A cuboid has edges 1.4 m, 22 cm, 80 cm.
   Calculate its surface area in (a) cm^2 (b) m^2.

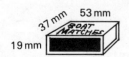

5. Calculate the surface area of this matchbox in cm^2.

page **97**

Enlargements

You need: a centimetre ruler, centimetre squared paper, scissors.
You should have done: Ratio (pages 28–31).

Gary has a 35 mm camera.
He develops, prints and enlarges his own negatives.

negative

print

Each print is an **enlargement** of the negative.

 A

1. How long is   (a) his negative?   (b) his print?
2. How many times longer is the print than the negative?

So the **scale factor** of the enlargement is 2.

B

1. On your squared paper, draw rectangles the same sizes as Gary's negative and print. Cut out your negative.
2. How many times does your 'negative' fit on to your 'print'?

So the **area factor** of the enlargement is 4.

Gary makes enlargements of these sizes:

A: 140 mm × 100 mm   C: 105 mm × 75 mm
B: 175 mm × 125 mm   D: 210 mm × 150 mm

Exercise 1

1. On your squared paper draw rectangles the same sizes as Gary's enlargements.
2. Copy and complete this table:

Print	Scale factor	Number of times your 'negative' fits	Area factor
A B			

3. If the scale factor is 10, what do you think is the area factor?

From your table, it looks as if:

area factor = (scale factor)²

Find the area factors for these scale factors:
1. 3   3. 5   5. 8   7. 13   9. 20
2. 6   4. 1   6. 10   8. 15   10. 25

When the scale factor is 2,
the original fits 4 times on to the enlargement.

So   area of enlargement = 4 × area of original

                                    area factor

or

area of enlargement = area factor × area of original

We can use scale factors and area factors to find areas of enlarged shapes.

These shapes are similar.
What is the area of
the larger shape?

find scale factor

$$\text{scale factor} = \frac{\text{length on enlargement}}{\text{matching length on original}}$$

$$= \frac{6\,\text{m}}{2\,\text{m}} = \underline{3}$$

find area factor

$$\text{area factor} = (\text{scale factor})^2$$

$$= 3^2 = 3 \times 3 = \underline{9}$$

write the formula

$$\text{area of enlargement} = \text{area factor} \times \text{area of original}$$

$$= \quad 9 \quad \times \quad 4\,\text{m}^2$$

work it out

$$= \quad \underline{36\,\text{m}^2}$$

D For each pair of similar shapes, calculate:
(a) the scale factor, (b) the area factor,
(c) the area of the larger shape.

1.

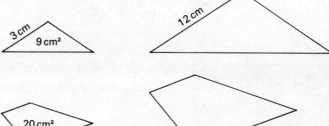

2.

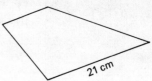

3.

Two shapes are similar if one is an enlargement (or reduction) of the other.

To enlarge (or reduce) a shape, multiply all its lengths by the scale factor.

$$\text{scale factor} = \frac{\text{length on enlargement}}{\text{matching length on original}}$$

$$\text{area factor} = (\text{scale factor})^2$$

$$\text{area of enlargement} = \text{area factor} \times \text{area of original}$$
$$\text{(or reduction)}$$

 **Exercise 2**

1. For each pair of similar shapes, calculate:
   (a) the scale factor, (b) the area factor,
   (c) the area of the larger shape.

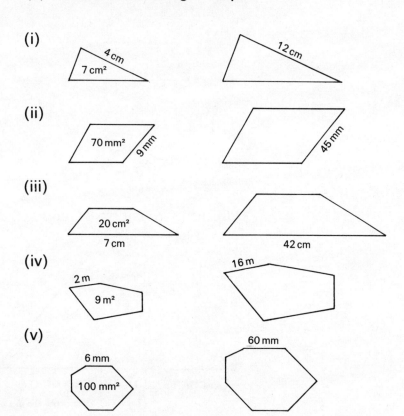

(i)

4 cm
7 cm²

12 cm

(ii)

70 mm²
9 mm

45 mm

(iii)

20 cm²
7 cm

42 cm

(iv)

2 m
9 m²

16 m

(v)

6 mm
100 mm²

60 mm

2. For each pair of similar shapes, calculate:
   (a) the area of the smaller shape,
   (b) the scale factor,
   (c) the area factor.
   Use your answers to work out the areas of the larger shapes.

(i)

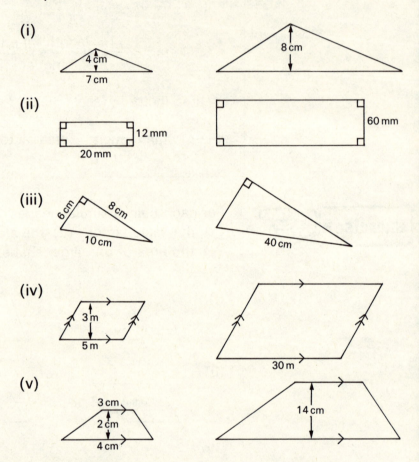

(ii)

(iii)

(iv)

(v)

3. In the diagram △ABE and △CDE are similar.

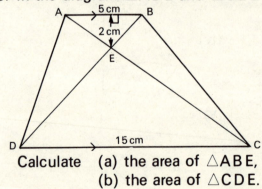

Calculate   (a) the area of △ABE,
            (b) the area of △CDE.

Recap 3

1. Work out the average speeds for these journeys:

	distance	depart	arrive
(a)	234 km	09.18	11.18
(b)	180 km	08.35	10.05
(c)	225 km	09.10	11.40
(d)	288 km	10.27	13.27

2. Calculate the distance travelled for these:
   - (a) 2 h at 27 km/h
   - (b) 650 km/h for 4 h
   - (c) 15 s at 12 m/s
   - (d) 53 m/s for 8 s
   - (e) $3\frac{1}{2}$ h at 87 km/h
   - (f) $7\frac{1}{2}$ s at 365 m/s

3. Calculate the missing lengths in these triangles:

   (a)

   (b)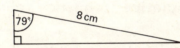

4. A class of 32 pupils scored these marks in a maths test:

   15 59 62 81 67 80 64 27
   28 58 31 75 59 36 59 58
   47 91 59 41 45 60 50 51
   69 47 58 47 30 39 27 19

   - (a) What is the range for these marks?
   - (b) Make a frequency table for the marks. Group them: 10–19, 20–29, ..., 90–99.
   - (c) What is the modal group?
   - (d) Draw a histogram from your table.

5. If $p = {}^-2$, $q = 3$ and $r = {}^-7$ work out:
   - (a) $3p$
   - (b) q^2
   - (c) $2pr$
   - (d) qr
   - (e) $p + q + r$
   - (f) $4p - 2q + r$
   - (g) $2p^2 - q$
   - (h) $5q^2 - 3pr$

6. Draw a travel graph for this journey. Mr Reed leaves home at 8.00 a.m. and arrives at work at 8.55 a.m. He walks 1 km to the station and waits 5 minutes for the 8.15 train. It reaches the town centre, 15 km away, at 8.35 a.m. He walks 2 km from the station to work.

7. Write each of these directions as a bearing:

   (a)   (b)   (c)

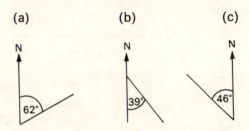

8. A cube has a total surface area of 150 cm². What is the length of one edge?

9. Calculate the surface area of a cuboid measuring 8 cm by 5 cm by 7 cm.

10. For this pair of similar shapes, calculate:
    - (a) the scale factor,
    - (b) the area factor,
    - (c) the area of the larger shape.

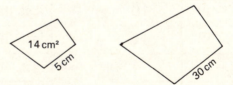

11. The triangles A B C and X Y Z are similar. Calculate the area of triangle XYZ.

Running totals

You need: a ruler and centimetre graph paper.
You should have done: Pot Black (pages 75–79).

Here is Paul's frequency table for Pot Black:

scores less than 60

score	0–19	20–39	40–59	60–79	80–99	100–119	120–139
frequency	5	10	17	14	10	2	2

32 players

  How many players in Pot Black scored:
1. less than 20?   4. less than 100?
2. less than 40?   5. less than 120?
3. less than 80?   6. less than 140?

Paul makes a **cumulative frequency table** from these results:

Frequency table   **Cumulative frequency table**

score	frequency		score	cumulative frequency (CF)
0–19	5	→	less than 20	5
20–39	10	→	less than 40	10 + 5 = 15
40–59	17	→	less than 60	17 + 15 = 32
60–79	14	→	less than 80	14 + 32 =
80–99	10	→	less than 100	10 + =
100–119	2	→	less than 120	2 + =
120–139	2	→	less than 140	2 + 58 = 60

This gives a 'running total'.

B Copy and complete Paul's cumulative frequency table for Pot Black.

Paul draws a graph from his cumulative frequency table:

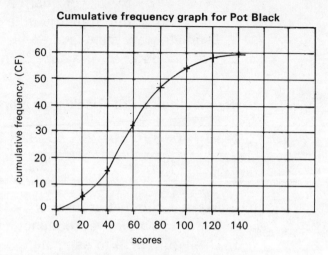

This curve is called an **ogive**.
It is a curve used in architecture.

1. Which points did Paul plot?
2. Copy Paul's graph. Use the scale:
     scores axis – 2 cm to 20 units
     CF axis – 2 cm to 10 units.
3. Divide your 'cumulative frequency axis' into four equal parts like this:

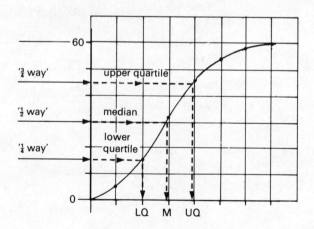

'$\frac{1}{4}$ way' gives the **lower quartile** score, LQ.
'$\frac{1}{2}$ way' gives the **median** score, M.
'$\frac{3}{4}$ way' gives the **upper quartile** score, UQ.

4. What is (a) the median score?
   (b) the lower quartile score?
   (c) the upper quartile score?
5. Estimate how many scored less than 65.
   Use dotted lines on your graph as shown.

Here is Junior Pot Black's frequency table:

score	0–19	20–39	40–59	60–79	80–99	100–119	120–139
frequency	9	15	11	12	9	2	2

1. Make a cumulative frequency table for Junior Pot Black.
2. Draw a cumulative frequency curve.
3. Use your curve to estimate:
   (a) the median score,
   (b) the lower quartile score,
   (c) the upper quartile score,
   (d) how many scored less than 65.

Summary

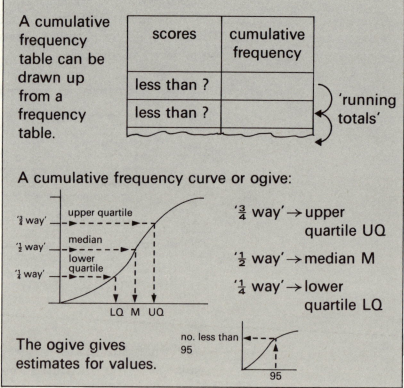

A cumulative frequency table can be drawn up from a frequency table.

scores	cumulative frequency
less than ?	
less than ?	

'running totals'

A cumulative frequency curve or ogive:

'¾ way' → upper quartile UQ

'½ way' → median M

'¼ way' → lower quartile LQ

The ogive gives estimates for values.

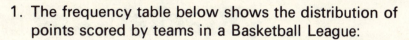

1. The frequency table below shows the distribution of points scored by teams in a Basketball League:

points	0–4	5–9	10–14	15–19	20–24	25–29
frequency	4	6	6	14	12	8

(a) Draw up the cumulative frequency table.
(b) How many teams scored less than 20 points?
(c) How many teams scored 10 or more points?
(d) Draw a cumulative frequency curve.
(e) Use your curve to estimate:
   (i) the median number of points,
   (ii) the lower quartile,
   (iii) the upper quartile,
   (iv) the number of teams scoring less than 13 points.

Scale:
points axis–
   2 cm to 5 units
CF axis–
   2 cm to 10 units

2. This frequency table shows the distribution of scores in a golf competition:

score	65–69	70–74	75–79	80–84	85–89	90–94
frequency	5	9	19	31	20	6

(a) Construct a cumulative frequency table.
(b) Use it to draw an ogive (cumulative frequency curve).
(c) Use your curve to estimate:
   (i) the median,
   (ii) the lower quartile,
   (iii) the upper quartile,
   (iv) the number of golfers scoring less than par (72).

Scale:
score axis–
   2 cm to 5 units
CF axis–
   2 cm to 10 units

3. This frequency table shows the distribution of batsmen's scores in a cricket league:

no. of runs	0–9	10–19	20–29	30–39	40–49	50–59	60–69	70–79	80–89	90–99	100–109	110–119
frequency	3	5	9	15	18	22	26	24	18	12	6	2

Scale:
2 cm to 20 units
on each axis

(a) Draw up the cumulative frequency table.
(b) Plot a cumulative frequency curve.
(c) Use your graph to find:
   (i) the median number of runs,
   (ii) the upper and lower quartiles,
   (iii) the number of batsmen scoring less than 35.

Brackets and equations

You should have done: More shorthand (pages 26–7); Two at a time (page 49).

$$^-2(y + 3) \quad \text{means} \quad ^-2 \times (y + 3)$$

We can remove the brackets like this:

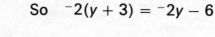

$$= \quad ^-2y \quad + \quad ^-6$$

So $\quad ^-2(y + 3) = ^-2y - 6$

 Remove these brackets:

1. $^-3(a + 2)$ 4. $^-1(q + 4)$ 7. $^-p(p + 1)$
2. $^-2(m + 1)$ 5. $^-7(3b + 4)$ 8. $^-x(3 + x)$
3. $^-5(3 + p)$ 6. $^-4(2c + 5)$ 9. $^-a(b + c)$

It is just as easy with a minus sign:

$$^-5(a - 2) = \boxed{^-5 \times a} \quad - \quad \boxed{^-5 \times 2}$$

$$= \quad ^-5a \quad - \quad ^-10$$

So $\quad ^-5(a - 2) = \underline{^-5a + 10}$

 Remove these brackets:

1. $^-3(x - 4)$ 4. $^-5(3 - p)$ 7. $^-c(c - 1)$
2. $^-4(a - 7)$ 5. $^-7(2x - 1)$ 8. $^-y(6 - 2y)$
3. $^-2(5 - m)$ 6. $^-4(2 - 3x)$ 9. $^-p(q - 3r)$

Some equations have brackets.
To solve them we remove the brackets first.

rewrite equation
$- 2$ means $+ ^-2$

Solve $\quad 7 - 2(3x - 4) = 3$

$$7 - 2(3x - 4) = 3$$

$$7 + {}^-2(3x - 4) = 3$$

$$7 + {}^-2(3x - 4) = 3$$

remove brackets	$7 + \boxed{^-2 \times 3x} - \boxed{^-2 \times 4} = 3$		

$$7 + \quad ^-6x \quad - \quad ^-8 \quad = 3$$

$$7 - \quad 6x \quad + \quad 8 \quad = 3$$

collect like terms

$$15 - \quad 6x \quad = 3$$

use a □

$$15 - \boxed{6x} = 3$$

find □

$$15 - \boxed{12} = 3$$

$$\text{So,} \quad 6x = 12$$

find x

$$\underline{x = 2}$$

Check: $7 - 2(6 - 4) = 7 - \boxed{2 \times 2} = 7 - 4 = 3 \checkmark$

 Solve these equations:
1. $7 - 2(x + 1) = 1$ 3. $5 - (2x - 3) = 10$
2. $8 - 3(2 - x) = 14$ 4. $32 - 5(3 - x) = 2$

Sometimes equations have more than one bracket.
We must remember to collect like terms.

Solve $3(x + 4) - 2(x - 1) = 11$

$$3(x + 4) + {}^-2(x - 1) = 11$$

rewrite equation

remove brackets

$$\boxed{3 \times x} + \boxed{3 \times 4} \quad + \boxed{^-2 \times x} - \boxed{^-2 \times 1} = 11$$

$$3x \quad + \quad 12 \quad + \quad ^-2x \quad - \quad ^-2 \quad = 11$$

collect like terms

$$\boxed{3x + {}^-2x} + \boxed{12 - {}^-2} = 11$$

$$x \quad + \quad 14 \quad = 11$$

use a □

$$\boxed{^-3} \quad + \quad 14 \quad = 11$$

$$\text{So} \quad \underline{x = {}^-3}$$

Check: $3(^-3 + 4) - 2(^-3 - 1) = \boxed{3 \times 1} - \boxed{2 \times {}^-4}$

$$= 3 - {}^-8 = 11 \checkmark$$

Solve these equations:
1. $3(x + 1) - 2(x - 4) = 12$
2. $(a - 7) - 3(4 - a) = 1$
3. $3(3 + y) - 7(y - 1) = 20$
4. $2(3 - p) - 5(p + 1) = 8$

1. Remove these brackets:
   (a) $^-2(x + 3)$ (e) $^-1(4 - b)$ (i) $m(^-3 + n)$
   (b) $^-3(5 + r)$ (f) $e(1 + c)$ (j) $^-6(1 - x)$
   (c) $^-5(t - 2)$ (g) $^-4(2x + 1)$ (k) $^-r(s + p)$
   (d) $a(x + y)$ (h) $^-y(3 - 2x)$ (l) $^-x(y - z)$

2. Solve these equations:
   (a) $7 - 2(x + 1) = 1$ (d) $6 - 5(2m + 3) = {}^-4$
   (b) $13 - 4(5 - 2y) = 5$ (e) $9 + 2(4 - p) = 3$
   (c) $5 - 3(2 + p) = {}^-1$ (f) $7 - (2 - 2x) = {}^-1$

3. Solve these equations:
   (a) $6(x + 2) - (x - 1) = 3$
   (b) $2(2m + 2) - 3(m + 1) = {}^-4$
   (c) $6(1 + p) - 2(2p - 3) = 20$
   (d) $2(2x - 5) - 3(x - 6) = 10$
   (e) $5(4y + 3) - 3(6y + 10) = 1$
   (f) $6(2r - 5) - 3(3x - 7) = 0$

Common codes

What do these codes mean?
Where can you see them?
Why do you think we
use codes like these?

EGGS SIZE 3

8 PAIRS OF SOCKS

SHORT STORIES — JOHN SHORT

Look for some more 'common codes'.
Find out what they mean.

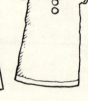

How many other people know what they mean?
You could do a survey to find out.

Areas of circles

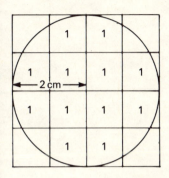

You need: centimetre squared paper, a ruler, a pair of compasses, plain paper, scissors and glue.

Here is a circle of radius 2 cm.
We can estimate its area by counting squares.

Each full square counts as 1.
If a 'bit' looks bigger than a $\frac{1}{2}$ square it counts as 1 too.

  Estimate the area of the circle.

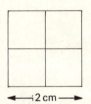

Here is a square of side 2 cm.

B
1. What is the area of the square?
2. Compare the areas of the circle and square.
   What do you notice?

Exercise 1

1. Draw circles with these radii on cm squared paper:
   (a) 3 cm   (b) 4 cm   (c) 5 cm   (d) 10 cm

2. Estimate the area of each circle by counting squares.

3. Copy and complete this table using your results:

radius of circle r or side of square (cm)	Area of circle A (cm²)	Area of square $r \times r = r^2$ (cm²)	$A \div r^2$
2	12	$2 \times 2 = 4$	$12 \div 4 = 3$
3		$3 \times 3 =$	

Your answers to $A \div r^2$ should all be about 3.

This value looks very like π.
If it is, then:
$$A \div r^2 = \pi$$

We can rearrange the formula like this:

flow diagram

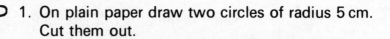

inverse   equals

inverse diagram

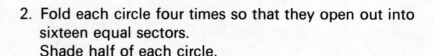

The new formula is:

$$A = \pi r^2$$

Here is another way to find this formula.

Exercise 2

1. On plain paper draw two circles of radius 5 cm.
   Cut them out.

2. Fold each circle four times so that they open out into sixteen equal sectors.
   Shade half of each circle.

3. Stick one circle into your book.

4. Cut out the 16 sectors of the other circle.
   Cut one unshaded sector in half.
   Stick them into your book like this:

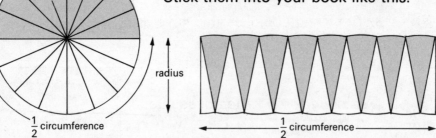

$\frac{1}{2}$ circumference

radius

$\frac{1}{2}$ circumference

This is almost a rectangle.
More sectors make it even more like a rectangle!

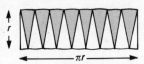

From the diagrams we can see that:

length of rectangle = ½ circumference = ½ × 2πr = πr
breadth of rectangle = radius = r

> area of rectangle = length × breadth
> $= \pi r \times r$
> $= \pi r^2$

So   area of circle = πr^2

If you know the radius of a circle, you can find its area.

Calculate the areas of circles with:

(a) r = 14 cm
     (use π = 22/7)

(b) r = 5 m
     (use π = 3.14)

write the formula

(a) $A = \pi r^2$

(b) $A = \pi r^2$

put in what you know

$= \dfrac{22}{7} \times 14 \text{ cm} \times 14 \text{ cm}$

$= 3.14 \times 5\,\text{m} \times 5\,\text{m}$

work it out

$= \underline{616\,\text{cm}^2}$

$= \underline{78.50\,\text{m}^2}$

Use π = 22/7. Calculate the areas of circles with:
1. r = 7 cm   2. d = 21 cm   3. r = 63 mm   4. r = 3½ m

Use π = 3.14. Calculate the areas of circles with:
5. r = 4 m   6. r = 10 cm   7. r = 2 km   8. d = 12 m

$r = \frac{1}{2}d$

We can rearrange the formula like this:

flow diagram

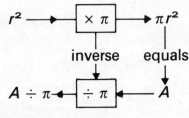

inverse diagram

So $r^2 = A \div \pi$

and $r = \sqrt{A \div \pi}$

If we know the area of a circle, we can find its radius.

Find the radius of a circle of area 33 cm². Use $\pi = \frac{22}{7}$

write the formula

$$A = \pi r^2$$

rearrange it

$$r^2 = A \div \pi$$

put in what you know

$$= 33 \text{ cm}^2 \div \frac{22}{7}$$

work it out

$$= \overset{3}{\cancel{33}} \times \frac{7}{\underset{2}{\cancel{22}}} \text{ cm}^2$$

$$= \frac{21}{2} \text{ cm}^2$$

$$r^2 = 10.5 \text{ cm}^2$$

square root

So $\qquad r = \sqrt{10.5} \text{ cm}$

use tables

$$= \underline{3.24 \text{ cm}}$$

 Use $\pi = \frac{22}{7}$. Find the radii of circles with these areas:

1. 22 cm² 2. 55 cm² 3. 242 mm² 4. 704 mm² .

Area of circle: $A = \pi r^2$

Rearranging this gives:
$r^2 = A \div \pi$

Use $\pi = \frac{22}{7}$. Calculate the areas of circles with:
1. $r = 35$ cm 2. $d = 42$ m 3. $r = 56$ mm 4. $r = 1\frac{3}{4}$ km

Use $\pi = 3.14$. Calculate the areas of circles with:
5. $d = 6$ cm 6. $r = 11$ cm 7. $d = 26$ m 8. $r = 11$ mm

| answers to 1 decimal place |

Take $\pi = \frac{22}{7}$. Calculate the radii of circles with these areas:
9. 36 cm² 10. 84 m² 11. 506 mm² 12. 198 m²

Take $\pi = 3.14$. Calculate the radii of circles with these areas:
13. 10 m² 14. 21 mm² 15. 78 m² 16. 5 km²

Simple interest

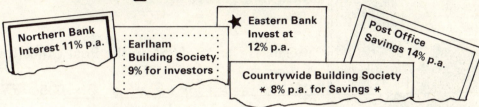

Northern Bank Interest 11% p.a.

Earlham Building Society 9% for investors

★ Eastern Bank Invest at 12% p.a.

Post Office Savings 14% p.a.

Countrywide Building Society ＊ 8% p.a. for Savings ＊

per annum (p.a.) means 'each year'

Gary has been given £250. If he invests it in a Bank or Building Society they will pay him some interest. Their rate of interest tells him what percentage he will be paid each year.

Gary works out how much the Post Office Investment Account will pay him.

Gary's working:
   100% is £250
÷ 10   10% is £25
÷ 10   1% is   £2.50

14%   10% ⟶ £25
         4% → 4 × 1% → 4 × £2.50 = £10
                              £35

The Post Office will pay £35 interest each year.

How much interest would these pay him each year?
1. Countrywide BS   3. Northern Bank
2. Eastern Bank   4. Earlham BS

Exercise 1

Work out the interest per annum on these investments:

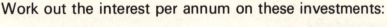

	money invested	rate of interest		money invested	rate of interest
1.	£200	8%	6.	£750	9%
2.	£150	11%	7.	£880	10%
3.	£500	12%	8.	£2000	12½%
4.	£375	5%	9.	£3500	13%
5.	£1000	15%	10.	£4750	15½%

If you withdraw your interest each year it is called **Simple Interest.**

If Gary leaves his £250 in the Post Office for more than 1 year:

Simple Interest for 2 years is $2 \times £35 = £70$
3 years is $3 \times £35 = £105$
4 years is $4 \times £35 = £140$
and so on.

Work out Gary's Simple Interest if he leaves his £250 in the Northern Bank for:
1. 2 years   2. 3 years   3. 5 years   4. 8 years   5. 20 years

Work out the Simple Interest on these investments:

	money invested	rate of interest	time
1.	£200	7%	2 years
2.	£450	9%	5 years
3.	£600	11%	3 years
4.	£850	10%	10 years
5.	£2000	$10\frac{1}{2}$%	3 years

If you borrow money you have to pay interest. It is worked out in the same way.

Work out the Simple Interest owed on these loans:

	money borrowed	rate of interest	time
1.	£500	12%	1 year
2.	£350	14%	2 years
3.	£650	15%	5 years
4.	£700	13%	3 years
5.	£1000	$11\frac{1}{2}$%	20 years

Summary

Interest is paid to you when you invest money in a Bank or Building Society.
If you borrow money, you have to pay interest to the lender.

The rate of interest is a percentage per annum.

Simple Interest is withdrawn (or paid) each year.

Exercise 4

1. Work out the Simple Interest on these investments:

	money invested	rate of interest	time
(a)	£50	7%	1 year
(b)	£100	8%	3 years
(c)	£375	9%	2 years
(d)	£700	12%	5 years
(e)	£3500	$11\frac{1}{2}$%	4 years

2. Work out the Simple Interest on these loans:

	money borrowed	rate of interest	time
(a)	£500	11%	5 years
(b)	£650	17%	2 years
(c)	£1050	10%	4 years
(d)	£3000	9%	10 years
(e)	£15 000	$12\frac{1}{4}$%	20 years

 Want a change? Try Music by chance on page 172.

Crossed lines

You need: a ruler and centimetre graph paper.

The graph of $x - y = 1$ is a straight line.
We can draw it if we know at least two points (x, y).
It is easy to find them when $x = 0$ and $y = 0$.

(i) Put $x = 0$ in the equation

$$x - y = 1$$
$$0 - y = 1$$
$$^-y = 1$$
$$y = {}^-1$$

(ii) Put $y = 0$ in the equation

$$x - y = 1$$
$$x - 0 = 1$$
$$x = 1$$

So $(0, {}^-1)$ is on the line.   So $(1, 0)$ is on the line.

Our graph needs positive and negative axes.

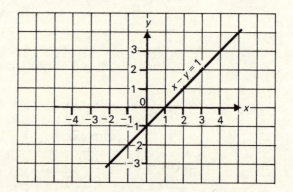

1. Draw two axes on centimetre graph paper.
2. Plot the two points $(0, {}^-1)$ and $(1, 0)$.
3. Draw and label the straight line $x - y = 1$.

The graph of $x + 2y = 4$ is a straight line too.

1. Substitute $x = 0$ in the equation.
2. Substitute $y = 0$ in the equation.
3. Write down 2 points on the line.
4. On the same axes as draw and label $x + 2y = 4$.

Your two lines should cross.
So one point lies on both lines.

 Write down the coordinates of this point.

 Draw these pairs of lines. For each pair, write down the coordinates of the point where they cross.

1. $y = x - 1$
   $y = 3 - x$

2. $y = 2x + 1$
   $y = x + 2$

3. $y = 7x$
   $y = x + 3$

4. $x + y = 7$
   $y = x - 5$

5. $y - x = 4$
   $4 - y = x$

6. $x + y = 1$
   $3y = 2x - 12$

7. $2y = 2 - x$
   $2y = 3x + 3$

8. $y = x$
   $x + y = {}^-4$

9. $x + y = 0$
   $x - y = 0$

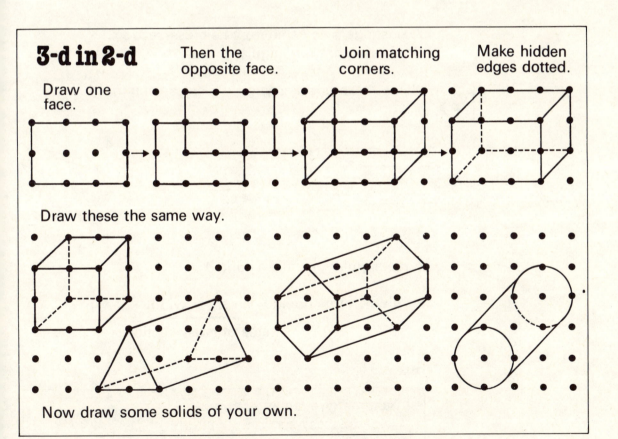

3-d in 2-d

Draw one face.

Then the opposite face.

Join matching corners.

Make hidden edges dotted.

Draw these the same way.

Now draw some solids of your own.

Prisms

You should have done: Areas of circles (pages 111–114).

Sharon used a **prism** in physics to make the colours of the rainbow.

Prism comes from a Greek word meaning 'sawn off'.

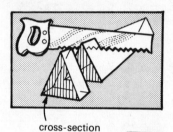

cross-section

If you 'saw through' a prism like this, then all the 'ends' are the same shape and size.
We call the end the **cross-section.**

 What shape is the cross-section of Sharon's prism?

A prism gets its name from its cross-section.
So Sharon has a triangular prism.

 Name these prisms using their cross-sections.

1.
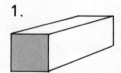

2.
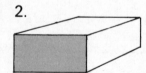

3.
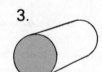

4.
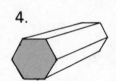

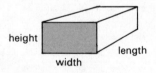

height
width
length

A rectangular prism is a cuboid.

volume of a cuboid = height × width × length

area of cross-section

So,

volume of a rectangular prism
= area of cross-section × length

 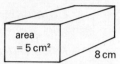

Calculate the volume of this rectangular prism:

area = 5 cm² 8 cm

check the units
make sure they match!

area of cross-section: 5 cm²
length: 8 cm

write the formula

volume of a rectangular prism
= area of cross-section × length

use the numbers

=   5 cm²   × 8 cm

work it out

=   40 cm³

C Find the volumes of these rectangular prisms:

1.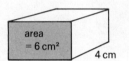

area = 6 cm² 4 cm

2.

area = 10 m² 7 m

3.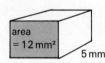

area = 12 mm² 5 mm

4.

area = $9\frac{1}{2}$ m² 3 m

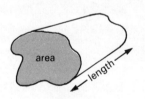

area length

We can find the volume of any prism this way.

> **volume of a prism = area of cross-section × length**

D Find the volumes of these prisms:

make sure the
units match!
m² and m
cm² and cm
and so on

1.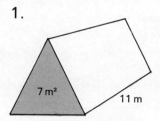

7 m² 11 m

2.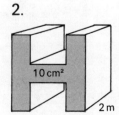

10 cm² 2 m

3.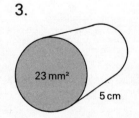

23 mm² 5 cm

Sometimes we have to find the area of the cross-section.

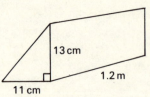

Calculate the volume of this prism in cubic centimetres (cm³).

change the units

length: 1.2 m = 120 cm

find cross-section
use the numbers

area of triangle = $\frac{1}{2}$ × base × height
= $\frac{1}{2}$ × 11 cm × 13 cm

= $\frac{143}{2}$ cm²

write the formula
use the numbers

volume of prism = area of cross-section × length

= $\frac{143}{2}$ cm² × 120 cm

work it out

$= \frac{143}{\underset{1}{2}} \times \overset{60}{120}$ cm³

$= \underline{8580 \text{ cm}^3}$

 Calculate the volumes of these prisms:
(a) in cm³   (b) in m³

1.
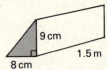
9 cm
1.5 m
8 cm

2.
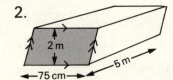
2 m
75 cm
5 m

 Summary

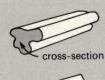
cross-section

A prism is a solid.
It has the same cross-section throughout.

triangular prism

A prism is named using the shape of its cross-section.

area
length

Volume of a prism
= area of cross-section × length

Make sure the units match!

Exercise

1. Calculate the volumes of these prisms.
   Watch the units!

(a)
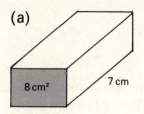
8 cm²   7 cm

(c)
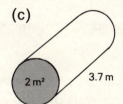
2 m²   3.7 m

(e)
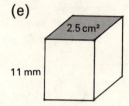
2.5 cm²   11 mm

(b)
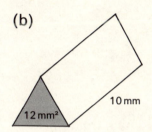
12 mm²   10 mm

(d)
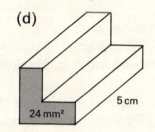
24 mm²   5 cm

(f)
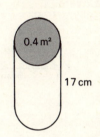
0.4 m²   17 cm

2. Calculate the volumes of these prisms.
   Take $\pi = \frac{22}{7}$ when needed. Watch the units!

(a)
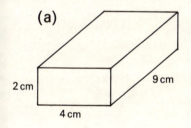
2 cm   9 cm   4 cm

(d)
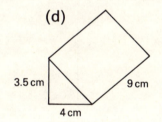
3.5 cm   9 cm   4 cm

(g)
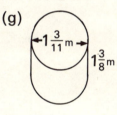
$1\frac{3}{11}$ m $1\frac{3}{8}$ m

(b)
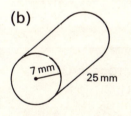
7 mm   25 mm

(e)
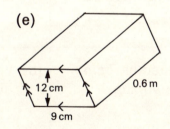
12 cm   0.6 m   9 cm

(h)
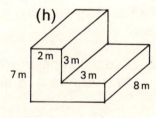
2 m   3 m   7 m   3 m   8 m

(c)
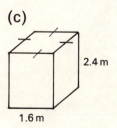
2.4 m   1.6 m

(f)
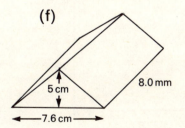
5 cm   8.0 mm   7.6 cm

(i)
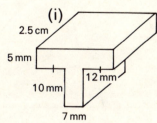
2.5 cm   5 mm   10 mm   12 mm   7 mm

Drawing triangles

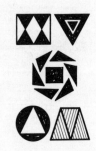

You need: a centimetre ruler, a protractor and a pair of compasses.

Tina, Jackie and Steve have to do an Art Project.
They have to design a logo for the Triangle Company.

Tina must use triangle ABC in her logo.
Its sides are:
  AB = 8 cm, AC = 7 cm, and BC = 4 cm.
She draws a rough sketch first.

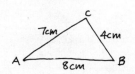

1. Copy Tina's rough sketch.
2. Follow these steps to construct Tina's triangle:

(a) Draw a line. Mark a point A.
Open compasses to radius 8 cm.
Use them to mark AB = 8 cm.

(c) Open compasses to radius 4 cm.
With centre B, draw an arc to cut
the first arc.

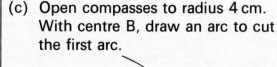

(b) Open compasses to radius 7 cm.
With centre A, draw an arc.

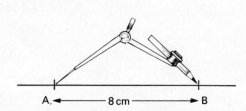

(d) Where the arcs cross is C.
Join AC and BC.

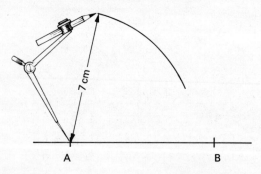

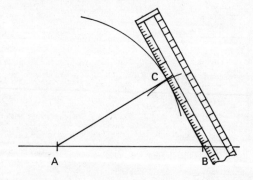

Construct these triangles:
1. △ABC,   AB = 7 cm,   AC = 5 cm,   BC = 3 cm.
2. △PQR,   PQ = 4 cm,   PR = 6.5 cm,   QR = 2.5 cm.
3. △KLM,   LM = 8 cm,   KL = 5.6 cm,   KM = 6 cm.
4. △RST,   TR = 9.3 cm,   RS = 4.7 cm,   ST = 7.2 cm.

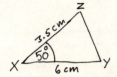

Jackie is given △XYZ for her logo.
She is told that:
   XY = 6 cm,   XZ = 3.5 cm   and   ∠X = 50°.
She draws a rough sketch of it.

B 1. Copy Jackie's rough sketch.
     2. Follow these steps to construct Jackie's triangle:

(a) Draw a line. Mark a point X.
     Use your compasses to mark
     XY = 6 cm.

(c) Use your compasses to mark
     XZ = 3.5 cm.

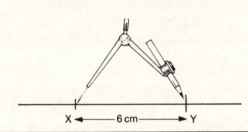

(b) Use your protractor to draw
     ∠X = 50°.

(d) Join YZ.

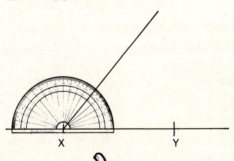

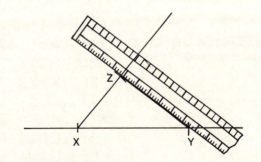

Construct these triangles:
1. △TUV,   TU = 9 cm,   TV = 7.5 cm,   ∠T = 30°.
2. △CDE,   CD = 8.6 cm,   DE = 5.9 cm,   ∠D = 45°.
3. △LMN,   LM = 6.2 cm,   MN = 3.7 cm,   ∠M = 70°.
4. △EFG,   EF = 10 cm,   FG = 9.4 cm,   ∠F = 55°.

Steve's triangle is P Q R.
It has:
$\quad$ PQ = 9 cm, $\quad \angle$ P = 30° $\quad$ and $\quad \angle$ R = 45°.

He draws a rough sketch, too.

C
1. Copy Steve's rough sketch.
2. Follow these steps to construct △ P Q R.

(a) Work out ∠Q.
Mark it on your sketch.

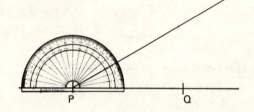

add the $\qquad$ 30° $\qquad$ angle sum
2 angles $\qquad$ +45° $\qquad$ of a △
we know $\qquad$ 75° $\qquad$ 180°
$\qquad\qquad\qquad\qquad$ → −75°
$\qquad\qquad\qquad\qquad$ 105°

(c) Use your protractor to draw
∠ P = 30°.

(b) Draw a line. Mark a point P.
Use your compasses to mark
PQ = 9 cm.

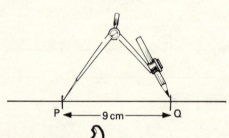

(d) Use your protractor to draw
∠ Q = 105°.
R is where the two lines cross.

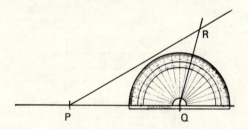

Exercise 3 👉 Construct these triangles:
1. △ A B C, $\quad$ AB = 7.2 cm, $\quad \angle$ A = 40°, $\quad \angle$ B = 35°.
2. △ R S T, $\quad$ RS = 8.3 cm, $\quad \angle$ R = 60°, $\quad \angle$ T = 75°.
3. △ X Y Z, $\quad$ YZ = 9.8 cm, $\quad \angle$ X = 50°, $\quad \angle$ Z = 45°.
4. △ J K L, $\quad$ JL = 6.7 cm, $\quad \angle$ K = 65°, $\quad \angle$ J = 58°.

Now draw these triangles:
5. △ C D E, $\quad$ CD = 9.5 cm, $\quad$ D E = 7.6 cm, $\quad$ C E = 6 cm.
6. △ U V W, $\quad$ UV = 10.4 cm, $\angle$ U = 50°, $\quad \angle$ V = 70°.
7. △ E F G, $\quad$ EF = 8.2 cm, $\quad$ FG = 7.6 cm, $\quad \angle$ F = 40°.
8. △ P Q R, $\quad$ QR = 9 cm, $\quad \angle$ R = 53°, $\quad \angle$ P = 38°.
9. △ L M N, $\quad$ LM = 11.3 cm, $\quad$ LN = 6.6 cm, MN = 8.1 cm.
10. △ F G H, $\quad \angle$ G = 64°, $\qquad$ GF = 8.8 cm, $\quad$ GH = 9.5 cm.

Design your own logo using some of your triangles.

Multiplying and dividing in algebra

You should have done: Dividing directed numbers (pages 60–61).

2 means $^+2$

In arithmetic,
$$2 \times {}^-3 = {}^-6$$
In algebra,

put numbers together

$$2 \times {}^-3p = \boxed{2 \times {}^-3} \times p$$

$$= {}^-6 \times p$$
$$= \underline{{}^-6p}$$

 Multiply these:
1. $3 \times {}^-2z$ 3. $^-3 \times a$ 5. $^-b \times 7$
2. $^-4 \times 5a$ 4. $^-6 \times {}^-m$ 6. $^-8 \times {}^-4q$

We can multiply with more letters, too.
Put the numbers together and the letters together first.

$$^-4ab \times {}^-5bc = {}^-4 \times a \times b \times {}^-5 \times b \times c$$

$$= \boxed{{}^-4 \times {}^-5} \times \boxed{a \times b \times b \times c}$$

$$= 20 \times ab^2c$$

$b \times b = b^2$

$$= \underline{20ab^2c}$$

 Multiply these:
1. $2a \times {}^-3b$ 4. $6r^2s \times {}^-2rs^2t$
2. $^-pq \times 8pr$ 5. $^-4p^2q^3 \times {}^-pq$
3. $^-5xy^2 \times {}^-2yz$ 6. $^-2cd \times {}^-3c^2 \times {}^-4cd^2$

Exercise 1

simplify means 'write in the shortest way'

Simplify these:
1. $2 \times {}^-4n$ 6. $^-3x^2y \times {}^-4y^2z$
2. $^-3 \times {}^-6e$ 7. $2pr \times {}^-8$
3. $^-7pq \times 2pq$ 8. $4a^2 \times 5abc$
4. $5rt \times {}^-4s^2$ 9. $^-8ef \times gf \times {}^-5efg$
5. $4 \times {}^-3d^3$ 10. $^-7a^2b \times {}^-4cd \times {}^-2d$

12 means $^+12$

You know that
$$12 \div {}^-4 = {}^-3$$
In algebra,
$$12d \div {}^-4 = {}^-3d$$

Do these divisions:
1. $8p \div {}^-2$ 3. $12a^2 \div {}^-2$ 5. ${}^-15ab \div {}^-5$
2. ${}^-10x \div 5$ 4. ${}^-16p^2 \div 4$ 6. $24x^2y^2 \div {}^-6$

Sometimes we have to divide by letters, too.

Memo

When dividing terms with the same letters, subtract the powers:
$$m^6 \div m^2 = m^{6-2} = m^4$$

$^-15 \div {}^-3 = {}^+5$

So
$$\begin{aligned} {}^-15\,m^6 \div {}^-3\,m^2 &= 5\,m^{6-2} \\ &= \underline{5\,m^4} \end{aligned}$$

Do these divisions:
1. $6p^2 \div {}^-3p$ 3. ${}^-9a^4 \div {}^-3a$ 5. ${}^-18r^6 \div 3r^3$
2. $5z^3 \div {}^-z$ 4. ${}^-12x^3 \div 2x^2$ 6. ${}^-25n^7 \div {}^-n^2$

Exercise 2

Simplify these:
1. $6r \div {}^-3$ 6. $25x^4 \div {}^-5x^3$
2. ${}^-12m \div {}^-4$ 7. ${}^-100p \div {}^-10$
3. ${}^-15a^2 \div 5$ 8. $36r^8 \div {}^-9r^5$
4. $14p^2 \div {}^-2p$ 9. ${}^-42y^5 \div {}^-7y^5$
5. ${}^-10a^7 \div {}^-5a^6$ 10. ${}^-50a^8 \div 100a^3$

Exercise 3

Simplify these:
 1. $3 \times {}^-4p$ 11. $7r^2st \times {}^-3t^3$
 2. ${}^-5 \times 6a$ 12. ${}^-18xy^2 \div 9xy$
 3. ${}^-2 \times {}^-b$ 13. $2cd \times {}^-4a \times {}^-5bd^2$
 4. ${}^-4xy \times 3yz$ 14. ${}^-3 \times {}^-14z^3$
 5. $7pq \times {}^-4q^2p$ 15. ${}^-90m \div 45$
 6. ${}^-21c \div 7$ 16. ${}^-7e^2f \times {}^-5fg^2 \times {}^-fg$
 7. $24a^2 \div {}^-2$ 17. $27r^2s \div {}^-3r$
 8. ${}^-8b^2ac \times {}^-abc$ 18. ${}^-8kl \times {}^-5k^2l^2m$
 9. ${}^-3p^3 \div p$ 19. ${}^-35m^4 \div 7m^3$
10. $15m^2l \div {}^-5m$ 20. ${}^-48y^5z \div {}^-6y^2z$

watch the signs!

page 128

π (or Pi)

circumference
$= \pi \times$ diameter

For thousands of years mathematicians have searched for π.
Its exact value is not known.
Here are some of the values they have used.

Egyptians *c.* 1650 B C	$\frac{256}{81}$
Greeks *c.* 240 B C *c.* 150 A D	between $\frac{223}{71}$ and $\frac{22}{7}$ $\frac{377}{120}$
Chinese *c.* 480	$\frac{355}{113}$ $\frac{454}{147}$
Hindu *c.* 530 *c.* 1150	$\frac{62\,832}{20\,000}$ $\frac{3927}{1250}$ $\sqrt{10}$
European *c.* 1585 *c.* 1671	between $\frac{377}{120}$ and $\frac{333}{106}$ $4(1 - \frac{1}{3} + \frac{1}{5} - \frac{1}{7} + \ldots)$

Change all these values to decimals.
Now you can compare them.
Which is the largest?
        the smallest?

Which is closest to the value we use?

Fibonacci numbers

Here is a famous number pattern:
    1, 1, 2, 3, 5, 8, 13, …
and how it is made:

$$1$$
$$1 + 1 = 2$$
$$1 + 2 = 3$$
$$2 + 3 = 5$$
$$3 + 5 = 8$$
$$5 + 8 = 13$$

Carry on as far as the 20th number.

An adding pattern

Add together:
  (a) the first five whole numbers,
  (b) the first twelve whole numbers,
  (c) the first fifteen whole numbers.

What do you notice?
Try five more examples of your own.

A dividing pattern

1
1
  $1 \div 1 = ?$
2
  $2 \div 1 = ?$
3
  $3 \div 2 = ?$
5
  $5 \div 3 = ?$

Give your answers correct to 3 decimal places.

and so on to the 20th number.
Spot anything?

This is called the Golden Ratio.
Find out about it.

Cyclic quadrilaterals

You need: a centimetre ruler, a pair of compasses and a protractor.

A quadrilateral has four vertices.
A **cyclic quadrilateral** has all its vertices on one circle.

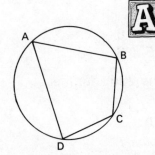

A

1. (a) Draw a circle with radius 6 cm.
    (b) Mark four points A, B, C, D on it.
    (c) Join them to make a cyclic quadrilateral A B C D.

2. (a) Measure two opposite angles (e.g. ∠A and ∠C).
        Work out their sum (∠A + ∠C).
    (b) Measure the other two opposite angles.
        Work out their sum.
    (c) What is special about your two sums?

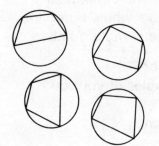

3. Draw four more different large cyclic quadrilaterals.
    Repeat Question 2 for each one.

Your friends may have different cyclic quadrilaterals.
What did they find about their opposite angles?

You should have found that:

> Opposite angles of a cyclic quadrilateral add up
> to 180°.

B Copy these diagrams.
Work out the missing angles marked with letters.

1.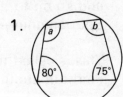

2.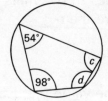

3.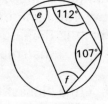

A cyclic quadrilateral has its four vertices on the same circle.

Opposite angles of a cyclic quadrilateral add up to 180°.

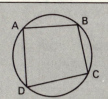

$\angle A + \angle C = 180°$
$\angle B + \angle D = 180°$

Exercise

Work out the size of the angles marked with letters.

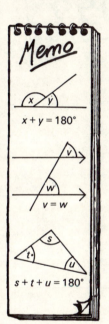
Memo

$x + y = 180°$

$v = w$

$s + t + u = 180°$

1.
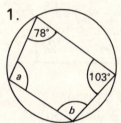

4.
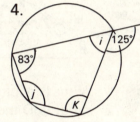

7.
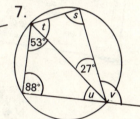

2.
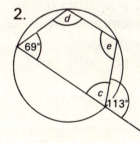

5.
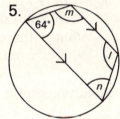

8.
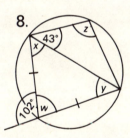

3.
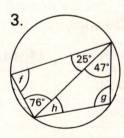

6.
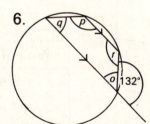

9.
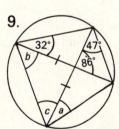

Cash or credit

Paul wants to buy a Tony Music Centre.
He has found three places selling it.

DANDY
TONY MUSIC CENTRE
£232
15% SALE

PACKHAMS
TONY MUSIC
CENTRE £223
5% DISCOUNT FOR CASH
* CREDIT TERMS AVAILABLE

METEOR
TONY MUSIC CENTRE
OUR PRICE £199

1. What is Meteor's price?
2. What is Dandy's usual price?
   What is the 'percentage off' in the Sale?
   So what is the Sale Price?
3. What is Packhams usual price?
   How much discount is given for cash?
   What is the cash price?
4. Which is the best 'cash' buy?

Packhams offer Credit terms.

amount you pay
at start

amount left
to pay

Credit Terms
→ 20% deposit
→ Balance paid monthly

No. of months	Monthly payments
9 months	£24.75
12 months	£19.66
18 months	£14.35
24 months	£11.90

B

1. What deposit do Packhams want?
2. What is the total of the monthly payments if he pays over:
   (a) 9 mths? (b) 12 mths? (c) 18 mths? (d) 24 mths?
3. What is the total credit price if he pays over:
   (a) 9 mths? (b) 12 mths? (c) 18 mths? (d) 24 mths?
4. How much more than the cash price is each credit price?
5. Which way would you buy the Music Centre if you were Paul? Why?

Sharon wants to buy a Hiscrachi radio cassette player. Here are two shops selling it:

Nixons

Cash price
£49.60

Credit terms: 15% deposit
Monthly payments:
9 mths – £5.72   18 mths – £3.39
12 mths – £4.56   24 mths – £2.81

Hurrys
£58.50

12% off in the sale!

Exercise 1

1. How much is the cash price at each shop? Which is the best buy?
2. Find the price if she pays by credit over:
   (a) 9 mths (b) 12 mths (c) 18 mths (d) 24 mths
3. How much more money is Nixons getting if she pays by credit?

Gary would like a Yobboha motor bike.
He has seen it in two garages

Cash discount 4%
Hire Purchase (HP) terms:
10% deposit
Monthly payments:
12 mths – £42.75
24 mths – £24.05

£475

£490

Cash discount 7½%
HP terms:
15% deposit
Monthly payments:
12 mths – £41.65
24 mths – £23.35

Exercise 2

1. Which is the best 'cash' buy?
2. Who offers the lower HP terms over:
   (a) 12 months, (b) 24 months?
   What is the difference?
3. How much more is each garage getting if he pays by HP?

Finding angles

You need: 3 figure tables and a ruler.
You should have done: Finding lengths (pages 71–74).

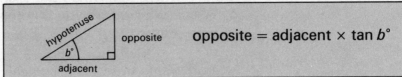

$$\text{opposite} = \text{adjacent} \times \tan b°$$

We can rearrange the formula like this:

flow diagram

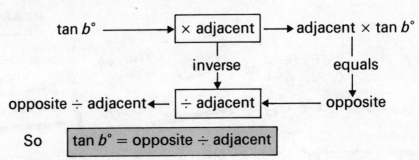

inverse flow diagram

So $\boxed{\tan b° = \text{opposite} \div \text{adjacent}}$

You know that:
$$\text{opposite} = \text{hypotenuse} \times \sin b°$$
$$\text{adjacent} = \text{hypotenuse} \times \cos b°$$

A Rearrange these formulae to find $\sin b°$ and $\cos b°$.

We can use these new formulae to calculate angles.
The sides you are given tell you which formula to use.

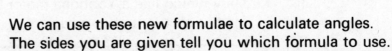

B 1. Copy these triangles:

(a)   (b)   (c)   (d)

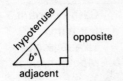

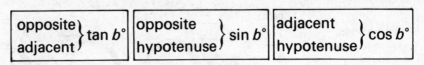

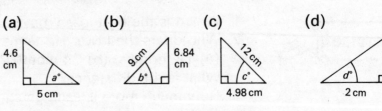

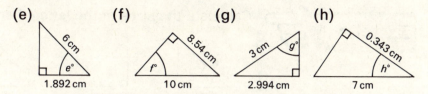

(e)   (f)   (g)   (h)

2. Label the sides 'opposite', 'adjacent', 'hypotenuse'.
3. For each triangle, say:
   (i) which sides you are given;
   (ii) whether you would use tan, sin or cos to find the
        lettered angle.

*Calculate the size of
the lettered angle in
this triangle.*

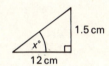

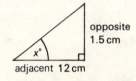

draw a diagram
label the sides

choose the formula   opposite = adjacent × tan $x°$
rearrange it   tan $x°$ = opposite ÷ adjacent
put in what you know   = 1.5 cm ÷ 12 cm
work it out   = 0.125
use the tables $x° = 82.8°$

 Calculate the sizes of the lettered angles in **B**.

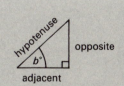

opposite = adjacent × tan $b°$
opposite = hypotenuse × sin $b°$
adjacent = hypotenuse × cos $b°$

These formulae can be rearranged to find angles:
tan $b°$ = opposite ÷ adjacent
sin $b°$ = opposite ÷ hypotenuse
cos $b°$ = adjacent ÷ hypotenuse

Exercise

Calculate the sizes of the lettered angles:

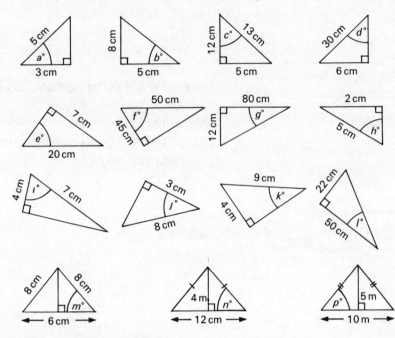

About the right size

Which answer is about the right size? Choose the 'right sized answers' for these too:

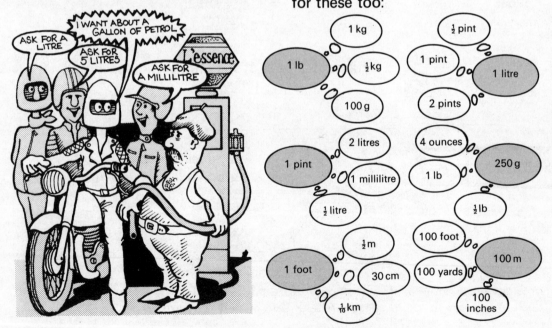

Recap 4

1. The times taken by 100 pupils to travel to school are given in the table below.

time (min)	0–10	10–20	20–30	30–40	40–50
frequency	20	40	20	10	10

   (a) Draw up the cumulative frequency table.
   (b) Plot a cumulative frequency curve.
   (c) On your graph mark the median time taken. State this time to the nearest minute.

2. Solve these equations:
   (a) $9 - 2(x - 1) = 5$
   (b) $10 - 3(2 - 5x) = 1$
   (c) $2(x + 1) - (x + 3) = 1$
   (d) $5(x - 4) - 3(1 - x) = 17$

3. Calculate the area of a circle of radius 49 mm. Give your answer in:
   (a) mm², (b) cm². (Take $\pi = 3\frac{1}{7}$.)

4. Calculate the radius of a circle whose area is 314 cm². (Take $\pi = 3.14$.)

5. Work out the simple interest on these investments:

	money	rate of interest	time
(a)	£30	12%	1 year
(b)	£150	9%	3 years
(c)	£900	$11\frac{1}{2}$%	2 years
(d)	£2500	$14\frac{1}{4}$%	7 years

6. Draw these pairs of lines. For each pair, write down the coordinates of the point where they cross.
   (a) $y = 2x + 3$ (b) $2x + y = 1$
   $ x + y = 6$ $ 2y = x - 8$

7. Calculate the volumes of these prisms:
   (a) $\qquad$ (b)

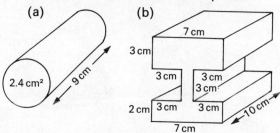

8. Construct these triangles.
   (a) $\triangle$ABC: $\quad$ AB = 9 cm $\quad$ AC = 5.9 cm, CB = 6.2 cm.
   (b) $\triangle$PQR: $\quad$ PQ = 8.7 cm, PR = 13 cm, $\angle$P = 35°.

9. Simplify:
   (a) $2 \times {}^-3a$ $\qquad$ (d) $16m^2 \div {}^-2m$
   (b) ${}^-4 \times 3p$ $\qquad$ (e) ${}^-9rs^2 \times {}^-3r^2s$
   (c) ${}^-2ab \times {}^-4bc$ $\quad$ (f) ${}^-15x^2y \div 5xy$

10. Calculate the size of the lettered angles:

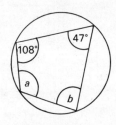
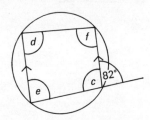

11. A shop offers a 20% cash discount.
   (a) How much will you pay for an article priced at £280?
   (b) If you pay £35.60 for a radio, what was the original price?

12. Calculate the size of the lettered angles:

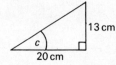

Similar solids

You should have done: Enlargements (pages 98–102);
Prisms (pages 120–123).

 A Which doll is a different shape?

All the others look alike.
They are **similar**.
Each is an enlargement (or reduction) of the others.

 Which objects are similar in these sets?

1.

(a)   (b)   (c)   (d)

2.

(a)   (b)   (c)   (d)

3.

(a)   (b)   (c)   (d)

4.

(a)   (b)   (c)   (d)

Here are some cubes.
Each is an enlargement (or reduction) of the others.

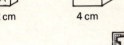 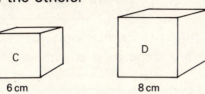 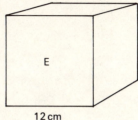

2 cm   4 cm   6 cm   8 cm   12 cm

 How long are the edges of A and B?

Scale factor of enlargement $A \rightarrow B = \dfrac{\text{length on B}}{\text{matching length on A}}$

$$= \frac{4\text{ cm}}{2\text{ cm}}$$

$$= \underline{2}$$

What are the volumes of A and B?

Volume factor of enlargement $A \rightarrow B = \dfrac{\text{B's volume}}{\text{A's volume}}$

$$= \frac{64\text{ cm}^3}{8\text{ cm}^3}$$

$$= \underline{8}$$

But $8 = 2 \times 2 \times 2 = 2^3$

So for this enlargement: volume factor = (scale factor)^3

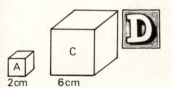

2cm   6cm

1. What is the scale factor of the enlargement $A \rightarrow C$?
2. What are the volumes of A and C?
3. What is the volume factor of enlargement $A \rightarrow C$?
4. Any connection between scale factor and volume factor?

Exercise 2

For each of these enlargements, calculate:
(a) the scale factor,   (b) the volume factor.
1. $A \rightarrow D$ 2. $A \rightarrow E$ 3. $B \rightarrow D$ 4. $B \rightarrow E$ 5. $C \rightarrow E$

Any connection between scale factor and volume factor?

From your answers to Exercise 2, it looks as if:

$$\text{volume factor} = (\text{scale factor})^3$$

But this may be true only for cubes.
Here are some pairs of similar prisms:

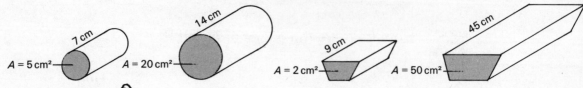

Exercise 3

1. Calculate the volume of each solid.
2. For each enlargement, calculate:
   (a) the scale factor,   (b) the volume factor.
3. Is   volume factor = (scale factor)³
   true for these solids?

We can use scale factors and volume factors to find volumes of enlarged solids.

Example

*These cylinders are similar.
What is the volume of
the larger one?*

$V = 200$ cm³ 7 cm	$V = ?$ 21 cm

find the
scale factor

$$\text{scale factor} = \frac{\text{length on enlargement}}{\text{matching length on original}} = \frac{21 \text{ cm}}{7 \text{ cm}} = \underline{3}$$

find the
volume factor

$$\text{volume factor} = (\text{scale factor})^3$$

$$= 3^3 = 3 \times 3 \times 3 = \underline{27}$$

use the formula for
volume factor

$$\text{volume factor} = \frac{\text{volume of enlargement}}{\text{volume of original}}$$

rearrange it

volume of enlargement

$$= \text{volume factor} \times \text{volume of original}$$

$$= \quad 27 \quad \times 200 \text{ cm}^3$$

work it out

$$= \underline{5200 \text{ cm}^3}$$

page **140**

For each enlargement, calculate:
(a) the scale factor, (b) the volume factor,
(c) the volume of the enlargement.

1.
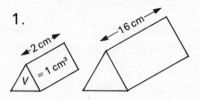

2.
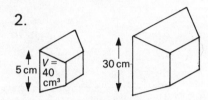

Summary

Two solids are similar if one is
an enlargement (or reduction)
of the other.

$$\text{scale factor} = \frac{\text{length on enlargement}}{\text{matching length on original}}$$

$$\text{volume factor} = (\text{scale factor})^3$$

$$\text{volume factor} = \frac{\text{volume of enlargement}}{\text{volume of original}}$$

Rearranging this gives:
volume of enlargement (or reduction)
    = volume factor × volume of original

Exercise 4

For each enlargement, calculate:
(a) the scale factor, (b) the volume factor,
(c) the volume of the enlargement.

1.

2.
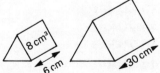

3.

4.
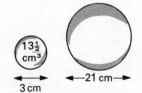

5.

6.
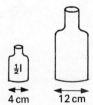

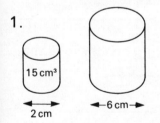

page 141

Drawing flight plans

You need: a protractor, a centimetre ruler and a set square.
You should have done: Flight plans (pages 91–95).

Gary is making a scale drawing of this flight plan.

> **Flight plan: Dishforth to Wittering**
>
> Bearing: 155°   Distance: 65 km
>
> Scale: 1 cm represents 10 km

He makes a rough sketch first.

A

1. Copy Gary's rough sketch.
2. Follow these steps to do the scale drawing:

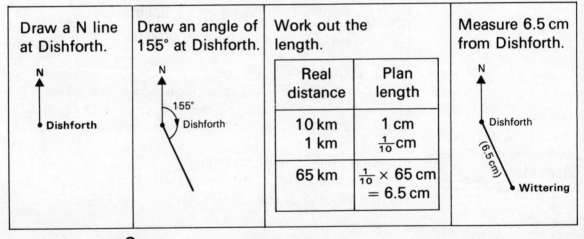

Draw a N line at Dishforth.	Draw an angle of 155° at Dishforth.	Work out the length.		Measure 6.5 cm from Dishforth.
		Real distance	**Plan length**	
		10 km	1 cm	
		1 km	$\frac{1}{10}$ cm	
		65 km	$\frac{1}{10} \times 65$ cm = 6.5 cm	

Exercise 1

Draw rough sketches and scale drawings of these flights:

	Bearing	Distance	Scale
1.	140°	75 km	1 cm to 10 km
2.	065°	120 km	1 cm to 20 km
3.	215°	190 km	1 cm to 20 km
4.	308°	74 km	1 cm to 10 km
5.	173°	226 km	1 cm to 20 km

This flight plan has two stages:

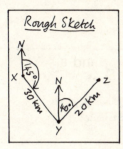

Rough Sketch

Flight plan: X to Y to Z

X to Y: 145°, 30 km
Y to Z: 040°, 20 km

Scale: 1 cm represents 5 km

1. Copy Gary's rough sketch.
2. Follow these steps to do the scale drawing:

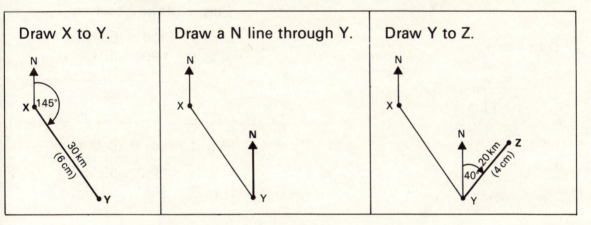

| Draw X to Y. | Draw a N line through Y. | Draw Y to Z. |

Gary works out the direct course X to Z from his drawing.

1. Follow these steps to find Gary's direct course.

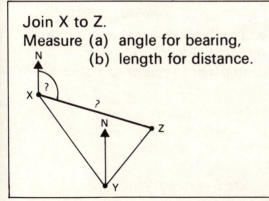

Join X to Z.
Measure (a) angle for bearing,
        (b) length for distance.

Work out the real distance.

Plan length	Real distance
1 cm	5 km
? cm	? km

2. Write down the direct course X to Z.
3. Find the direct course to fly from Z back to X.

Exercise 2 Draw rough sketches and scale drawings of these flights (Scale: 1 cm to 5 km).
Work out the direct course for each one.

1. A to B to C.

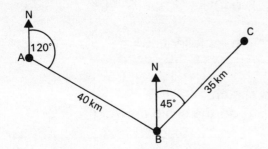

3.

Flight plan: G to H to I

G to H: 030°, 30 km
H to I: 165°, 55 km

2. D to E to F.

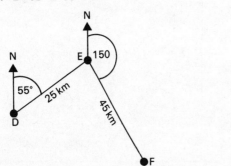

4.

Flight plan: J to K to L

J to K: 305°, 50 km
K to L: 190°, 60 km

5.

Flight plan: P to Q to R

P to Q: 215°, 65 km
Q to R: 345°, 95 km

Ships' navigators plot courses, too.

Example *A ship sails from Lowestoft for 8 km on a bearing of 060°. It then turns and sails for 7 km on a bearing of 120°. Finally it turns again and sails for 4 km on a bearing of 215°. How far is the ship from Lowestoft now? What bearing must the ship sail to return to Lowestoft?*

draw rough sketch

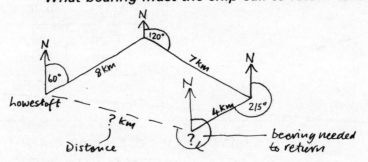

Scale: let 1 cm represent 1 km.

Do an accurate scale drawing for the example.
Use it to answer the questions.

To do a scale drawing of a course:

1. Do a rough sketch first.
2. Choose a suitable scale if not given.
3. For each stage of the course:
   (a) draw a N line,
   (b) draw the bearing angle with a protractor,
   (c) work out the 'plan length' using the scale,
   (d) measure the length along the drawn direction.

Do these by scale drawing:

1. A ship sails 7 km on a bearing of 050°, then 3 km at 100°, then 2 km at 210°. What is the distance and bearing of the ship from its starting place? (Use a scale 1 cm to 1 km.)

2. A man walks 350 m at 090°, then 210 m at 200°, then 150 m at 050°. How far is the man from his starting point? What bearing must he walk to return to his starting point? (Use a scale 1 cm to 50 m.)

3. A plane flies 350 km at 100°, then 200 km at 075°, then 150 km at 300°. What is the final distance and bearing from its starting point? (Use a scale 1 cm to 50 km.)

4. Two ships leave port. Ship 1 sails 9 km at 050°, then 5 km at 115°. Ship 2 sails 6 km at 110°, then 4 km at 060°. How far apart are the ships? What is the bearing of ship 2 from ship 1? (Use a scale 1 cm to 1 km.)

Rates

Gary's mum and dad get a rates bill every April.
It is sent by their local council.

Rates are a tax on property such as houses, shops, ...
The money is used to help to pay for local services.

A List some local services councils provide.

Rateable Value £	Rate in £
174	142p

Every property is given a rateable value.
Each council fixes its local rate or rate in the £.

B
1. What is the rateable value of Gary's house?
2. What is the local rate for Gary's council?

To check their bill Gary works out:

rates due = rateable value × rate in the £

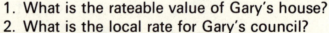

$$= \quad 174 \quad \times \quad 142\text{p}$$

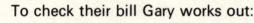

C How much is their rates bill for the year?

Gary's parents can pay their rates in instalments.

D How much is each instalment if they pay:
(a) half yearly? (b) monthly (to the nearest penny)?

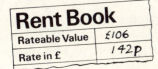

Rent Book

Rateable Value	£106
Rate in £	142p

Jackie's family rent a council house near Gary's home. They pay their rates each week with their rent.

1. What is the rateable value of Jackie's house?
2. What rates are due for a year?
3. How much do they pay each week (to the nearest p)?

Rateable values are fixed by a Valuation Officer.
He has set rules to use.

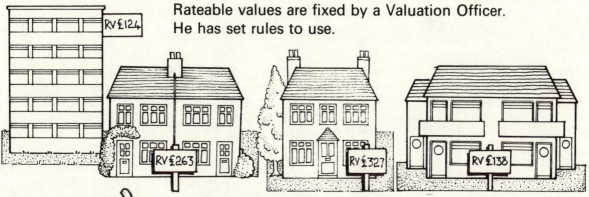

RV £124
RV £263
RV £327
RV £138

answers to the nearest penny

1. What do you think rateable value depends on?
2. The properties shown all pay rates to Gary's council. What rates are due on each one?
3. How much is each instalment if they pay:
   (a) half yearly? (b) monthly? (c) weekly?

Gary's Water Authority charges 35p in the £ water rate.
This helps to pay for the water and sewerage services.

water rates = rateable value × water rate in the £

Work out the annual water rates for Gary's house, Jackie's house and the properties in Exercise 1.

These properties are in different areas.

Type of property	flat	semi-detached	maisonette	detached	bungalow
Rateable value	£108	£223	£174	£368	£163
Rate in the £	103p	112p	126p	168p	119p
Water rate in the £	32p	25p	41p	37p	28p

Work out the rates and water rates for each property.

A council's Treasurer is responsible for the rates.
He knows the total rateable value for his area.

The total rates due are:

total rateable value × rate in the £
= 19 500 000 × 137p

G How much is due in rates altogether?

Work out the total rates due in these areas:

area	total rateable value	rate in the £
Liverpool	£31 m	148p
Exeter	£6.2 m	103p
Luton	£13.5 m	121p
Manchester	£28 m	186p
Norwich	£8.2 m	138p
Birmingham	£75 m	123p

The Treasurer's council needs £29 640 000 for next year.

He calculates the new local rate:

= amount needed ÷ total rateable value
= £29 640 000 ÷ 19 500 000

H Work out the new local rate.

Calculate the new rate in the £ for these councils.

council	amount needed	total rateable value
Chesterfield	£7.48m	£5.5m
Blackpool	£11.59m	£9.5m
Newcastle	£38.25m	£17m
Bristol	£36.5m	£25m
Colchester	£11.73m	£10.2m
Westminster	£60.39m	£49.5m

Summary

Rates are a tax on property.
They are paid to local councils.

rates due = rateable value × rate in the £

Water rates are worked out the same way.
They are paid to water authorities.

A council's total rates
= total rateable value × rate in the £

rate in the £ = amount needed ÷ total rateable value.

Exercise 5

1. This table lists properties in different areas:

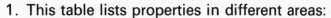

type of property	rateable value	rate in the £	water rate in the £
semi-detached	£224	138p	26p
detached	£358	173p	34p
bungalow	£179	119p	28p
maisonette	£136	208p	25p
flat	£107	184p	37p

Work out the rates and water rates for each property.

2. Work out the totals due in these areas for:
   (a) rates,   (b) water rates.

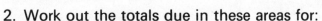

area	total rateable value	rate in the £	water rate in the £
Barnsley	£9.6m	168p	43p
Cambridge	£8.6m	112p	29p
Walsall	£19.5m	140p	27p
Leeds	£39m	112p	42p
Bristol	£25m	123p	36p

3. For these councils calculate:
   (a) the rate in the £,   (b) the water rate in the £.

council	amount needed for rates	amount needed for water rates	total rateable value
Blackburn	£7.502m	£1.55m	£6.2m
Milton Keynes	£10.168m	£2.952m	£8.2m
Darlington	£7.452m	£1.836m	£5.4m
Liverpool	£48.36m	£8.99m	£31m
Luton	£18.495m	£2.565m	£13.5m

Solving problems

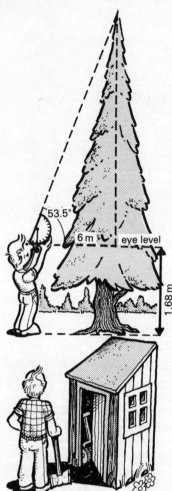

You need: 3 figure tables and a ruler.
You should have done: Angles of elevation and depression (page 89), Finding angles (pages 134–136).

Tangents, sines and cosines are used to solve practical problems.

Gary has to find the height of the tree.

He stands 6 m from its base.
With a clinometer he measures the angle of elevation to its top. It is 53.5°.
He works out the tree's height.

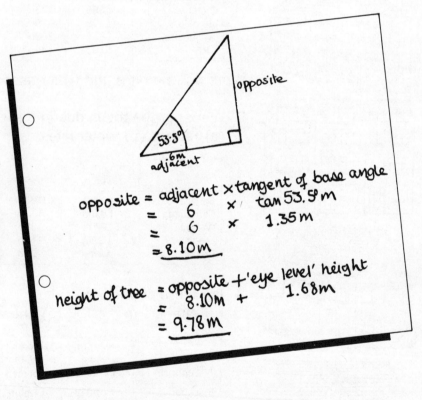

opposite = adjacent × tangent of base angle
= 6 × tan 53.5° m
= 6 × 1.35 m
= 8.10 m

height of tree = opposite + 'eye level' height
= 8.10 m + 1.68 m
= 9.78 m

A Work out the height of the tree if the angle of elevation is:
1. 46.7°   2. 58.4°   3. 32.9°   4. 61.3°.

WHY CAN'T WE JUST USE A CLINOMETER?

DON'T BE SILLY— YOU COULD BLIND YOURSELF.

Tina and Jackie work together on a project.

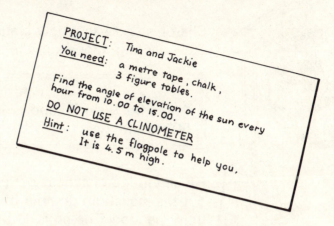

PROJECT: Tina and Jackie
You need: a metre tape, chalk, 3 figure tables.
Find the angle of elevation of the sun every hour from 10.00 to 15.00.
DO NOT USE A CLINOMETER
Hint: use the flagpole to help you, It is 4.5 m high.

 B Why are they told not to use a clinometer?

Tina and Jackie measure the flagpole's shadow every hour.

time	10.00	11.00	12.00	13.00	14.00	15.00
shadow's length	9.8 m	7.5 m	6.0 m	7.3 m	9.6 m	13.4 m

They work out the angle of elevation at 10.00 like this:

draw a diagram
put on what you know
label the sides

opposite 4.5 m

adjacent

$b°$

Call the angle of elevation $b°$.

write the formula

$$\text{opposite} = \text{adjacent} \times \tan b°$$

rearrange it
put in what you know
work it out
use the tables

$$\tan b° = \text{opposite} \div \text{adjacent}$$
$$= 4.5\,\text{m} \div 9.8\,\text{m}$$
$$= 0.459$$
$$b° = 24.7° \quad \text{The angle of elevation}$$

 C Work out the angles of elevation for the other times.

Sines and cosines are useful, too.

Sharon's dad has a new crane.
This warning appears in the cab.

WARNING!
Angle between jib and ground must be greater than 50° at all times.

He can judge distances better than angles. So he works out the maximum number of metres the crane can be from the load. The jib is 11 m long.

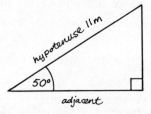

draw a diagram
put in what you know
label the sides

write the formula
put in what you know
use the tables
work it out

$adjacent = hypotenuse \times cosine$
$= 11 \times \cos 50° \, m$
$= 11 \times 0.643 \, m$
$= \underline{7.073 \, m}$

So the maximum distance the crane can be from the load is 7m.

 Work out the maximum distance if the angle must always be bigger than 55°.

To solve problems:
1. Draw a clear diagram.
2. Pick out the right-angled triangle you are going to use. Label the sides 'hypotenuse', 'opposite', 'adjacent'.
3. Decide if you are going to use tan, sin or cos.
4. Write the chosen equation.
5. Work it out.

1. The angle of elevation of the top of a tower from a point 30 m away is 41°. Calculate the height of the tower.

2. A ladder, 10 m long, rests against a wall. The angle between the ladder and the ground is 65°. How far up the wall does the ladder reach? Give your answer to the nearest metre.

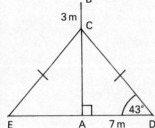

3. AB is a radio mast. Two ropes CD and CE, of equal length, hold it upright. If CB = 3 m, AD = 7 m and ∠CDA = 43°, calculate:
   (a) the height of the mast,
   (b) the length of each rope.

4. A dustbin is made from a cylinder 70 cm high with diameter 50 cm.
   A stick is placed in the bin as shown, 24 cm of it sticking out.
   Calculate:
   (a) the length of the stick,
   (b) the angle between the stick and the bottom of the bin.

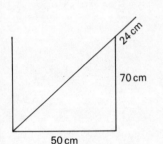

5. A man stands at the top of a cliff 55 m high. He finds the angle of depression to a ship is 24°.
   How far is the ship from: (a) the man,
                             (b) the base of the cliff?
   The ship sails to a point 150 m from the base of the cliff. What is the angle of depression now?

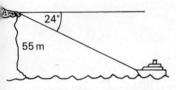

6. ABCDE represents the side of a lean-to shed. ACDE is a square of side 4 m and ∠BAC = 37°.
   Calculate:
   (a) the length AB,
   (b) the height of B above the ground.

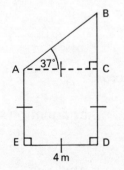

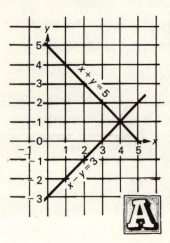

Simultaneous equations

You should have done: More substitution (pages 80–82); Crossed lines (pages 118–119).

One way to find where two lines cross is to draw them.

A Where do the lines $x + y = 5$ and $x - y = 3$ cross?

There is a better way to find where two lines cross. The equations are solved by getting rid of x or y. First we write the equations like this:

x's in line
y's in line
$x - y = x + {}^-y$

$$\begin{bmatrix} x \\ x \end{bmatrix} + \begin{bmatrix} y \\ {}^-y \end{bmatrix} = \begin{bmatrix} 5 \\ 3 \end{bmatrix}$$

Adding the equations gets rid of y.

$$\boxed{x + x} + \boxed{y + {}^-y} = \boxed{5 + 3}$$

adding
$$2x \quad + \quad 0 \quad = \quad 8$$
$$2x = 8$$

find x
$$\underline{x = 4}$$

We can now find y from either equation.
Choose the easier.

easy equation $\quad x + y = 5$
use $x = 4$ $\qquad 4 + y = 5$
find y $\qquad \underline{y = 1}$

So $(4, 1)$ is the point where the lines cross.

B Substitute $x = 4$ and $y = 1$ in the other equation. We do this to check.

C Solve these pairs of equations. Check your answers.

1. $x + y = 3$ 2. $x - y = 7$ 3. $x + y = 11$
   $x - y = 1$ $x + y = 3$ $y - x = 2$

Sometimes we have to multiply one equation by a number.

Solve $2m + n = 5$ *and* $6m - 2n + 15 = 0$

$$2m + n = 5 \quad and \quad 6m + {}^-2n = {}^-15$$

rewrite the equations

It is easier to get rid of the n's.
So we want $2n$ in each equation.

$2 \times n = 2n$

$$2m + n = 5 \qquad \xrightarrow{\times 2} \qquad \boxed{4m} + \boxed{2n} = \boxed{10}$$
$$6m + {}^-2n = {}^-15 \qquad \xrightarrow{\times 1} \qquad \boxed{6m} + \boxed{{}^-2n} = \boxed{{}^-15}$$

Add the new equations:

$$\boxed{4m + 6m} \;+\; \boxed{2n + {}^-2n} \;=\; \boxed{10 + {}^-15}$$

adding

$$10m \quad + \quad 0 \quad = \quad {}^-5$$

$$10m = {}^-5$$

find m

$$m = {}^-\tfrac{5}{10} \text{ or } \underline{{}^-\tfrac{1}{2}}$$

To find n, substitute $m = {}^-\tfrac{1}{2}$ in $2m + n = 5$.

easy equation
use $m = {}^-\tfrac{1}{2}$

$$2m + n = 5$$
$$2 \times {}^-\tfrac{1}{2} + n = 5$$
$${}^-1 + n = 5$$

find n

$$\underline{n = 6}$$

So the solution is $m = {}^-\tfrac{1}{2}, \quad n = 6$.

Substitute these values into the other equation to check.

Solve these pairs of equations:

1. $5m + n = 3$ 3. $4r - 5s = 1$ 5. $2x - y = {}^-12$
    $m - 2n = 5$ $r + s = {}^-2$ $3x + 2y = 3$

2. $3x + y = 2$ 4. $p + 3q = 6$ 6. $4a + 3b = 9$
    $x - 2y = 10$ $2p - q = 5$ $5a - 6b = 8$

page 155

Example

Some equations need a negative multiplier.

Solve $2x + 3y = 5$
$\quad\quad\quad x + 4y = 10$

It is easier to get rid of the x's.

$^-2 \times x = ^-2x$

$$
\begin{array}{ll}
2x + 3y = 5 & \quad \times 1 \\
x + 4y = 10 & \quad \times ^-2
\end{array}
\longrightarrow
\begin{array}{l}
\boxed{2x} + \boxed{3y} = \boxed{5} \\
\boxed{^-2x} + \boxed{^-8y} = \boxed{^-20}
\end{array}
$$

Add the new equations:

$$\boxed{2x + {}^-2x} + \boxed{3y + {}^-8y} = 5 + {}^-20$$

adding
$$0 \quad + \quad ^-5y \quad = {}^-15$$
$$^-5y = {}^-15$$

find y
$$\underline{y = 3}$$

Substitute $y = 3$ in $x + 4y = 10$.

use $y = 3$
$$
\begin{aligned}
x + 4y \quad\;\; &= 10 \\
x + 4 \times 3 &= 10 \\
x + 12 \quad\;\; &= 10
\end{aligned}
$$

find x
$$\underline{x = {}^-2}$$

So the solution is $x = {}^-2, \quad y = 3$.

F
G

Check this answer using the other equation.

Solve these equations:

1. $x + 2y = 6$ 2. $2r + 3s = {}^-4$ 3. $x + y = 17$
   $3x + y = 8$ $3r + s = 1$ $3x + y = 31$

Exercise

Solve these equations:

1. $x + y = 7$ 4. $4m - n = 1$ 7. $^-2x + y = {}^-14$
   $x - y = 5$ $m + 3n = 10$ $2x - 3y = 34$

2. $3p - q = 4$ 5. $5r + 4s\;\; = 2$ 8. $2p - 3q = 1\frac{1}{2}$
   $2p + q = 11$ $5r + 12s = 4$ $p + q = 4\frac{1}{2}$

3. $c - 2d = {}^-3$ 6. $4a - b = 11$ 9. $3m + 2m = 4$
   $3c + 2d = 31$ $a + 2b = {}^-13$ $m + n = 1$

Angles in circles

You need: a centimetre ruler, a pair of compasses, a piece of card (approx. 12 cm long), scissors and a protractor.
You should have done: Cyclic quadrilaterals (pages 130–131).

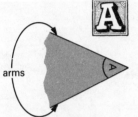

1. (a) Draw a circle with radius 6 cm.

   (b) On card draw an acute angle A with 'arms' about 12 cm long.
       Cut along the 'arms'.

   (c) Place your cardboard angle on your circle like this.
       The vertex must touch the circle.

   (d) Draw along each 'arm'.
       Mark the angle A.

   (e) Draw in the chord.
       Shade in the segment with the angle.

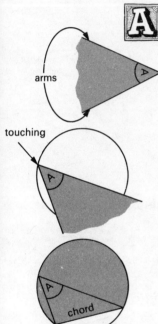

   (f) Place your cardboard angle on your circle again like this.
       Draw along each arm again.
       Mark the angle A.

   (g) Repeat (f) three times.

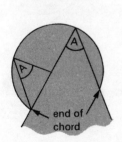

2. What can you say about:
   (a) the sizes of the angles marked A?
   (b) where they are in the circle?

page 157

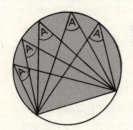

You have found that:
    all the angles A are equal;
    they are in the same segment.

Your friends may have different angles for A.
Did they find the same result?

We say that:

> Angles in the same segment are equal.

 Which angles are in the same segment?

1. 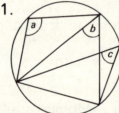   2. 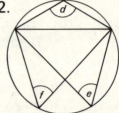   3.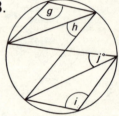

 Calculate the size of the lettered angles.

1. 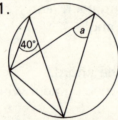   2. 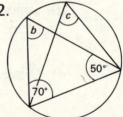   3.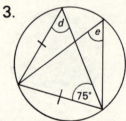

Angle at the centre

1. Draw the angle at the centre of your circle from **A**
   Mark the angle O.

2. (a) Measure ∠A and ∠O with your protractor.
   (b) Compare their sizes. What do you notice?

Your angles A and O may be special.
Have your friends found the same result for their angles?

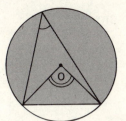

You should have found that:

> The angle at the centre is twice
> the angle at the circumference.

 Which is the 'angle at the circumference' for ∠O?

C is the centre
of the circle

1. 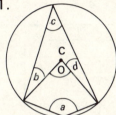   2.   3.

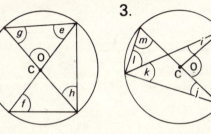

 Calculate the size of the lettered angles.

C is the centre
of the circle

1. 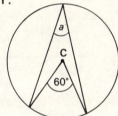   2. 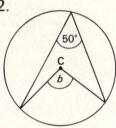   3.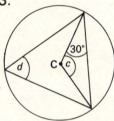

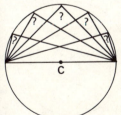

Angle in a semicircle

 Draw a circle, radius 6 cm, and a diameter.
The diameter divides the circle into two semicircles.

Draw five angles in one of the semicircles as shown.
Measure each angle.

What do you notice about the size of your angles?
Did your friends find the same result?

We say that:

> An angle in a semicircle is a right angle.

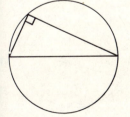

Which angles are right angles in these circles?

1.
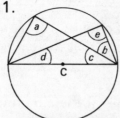

2.
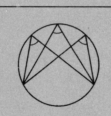

3.
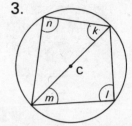

C is the centre
of the circle

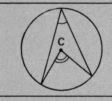

Summary

Angles in the same segment are equal.

An angle in a semicircle is a right angle.

The angle at the centre is twice the angle at the circumference.

Exercise 3

Calculate the size of the lettered angles.

C is the centre
of the circle

1.
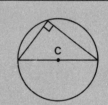
48°

a

b

c

3.
i

34°

53°

g

h

5.
l

m

2.
26°

e

f

d

4.
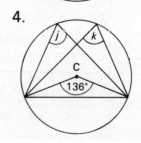
j

k

136°

6.
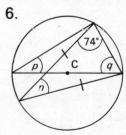
74°

p

q

n

Drawing curves

You need: a ruler and centimetre graph paper.
You should have done: More substitution (pages 80–82);
Crossed lines (pages 118–119).

$y = x^2$ can be drawn as a graph.
It is not a straight line.

Straight lines		
$y = 2x - 1$	$y = 3x$	$\dfrac{x}{2} + \dfrac{y}{3} = 1$
$4y = 5x - 3$	$7 - 2x = 3 - y$	$x + y = 6$

Not straight lines
$$x^2 + y^2 = 4 \qquad y = 5x^2$$
$$y = 2x^2 - x - 1 \qquad \dfrac{1}{x} - \dfrac{1}{y} = 3$$
$$y = x^3$$

To draw the curve we must find some points on it.
We choose positive and negative values of x. Then we
work out the y values.

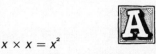

1. Copy and complete this table.

$x \times x = x^2$
$^-4 \times {}^-4 = {}^+16 = 16$

x	$^-4$	$^-3$	$^-2$	$^-1$	0	1	2	3	4
$y = x^2$	16				0			9	

2. Write these values as ordered pairs (x, y).
   Start with $(^-4, 16)$.

We can see from the table that:
   the x values go from $^-4$ to 4,
   the y values go from 0 to 16.

Exercise 1

1. On squared paper, draw x and y axes.
   Number them using this scale:
     x axis — 2 cm represents 1 unit
     y axis — 1 cm represents 1 unit

2. Plot the ordered pairs you have worked out.

3. Try to draw a smooth curve through all the points.
   Label your curve $y = x^2$.

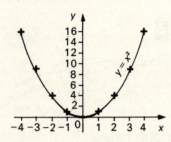

Your graph of $y = x^2$ should look like this.
It is a **parabola.**

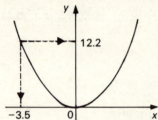

From your graph you can see that:
when $x = {}^-3.5$, $y \approx 12.2$.

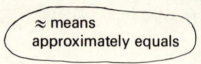

$\approx$ means approximately equals

B From your graph, find y when:
1. $x = 3.5$ 2. $x = {}^-1.5$ 3. $x = 0.5$ 4. $x = {}^-2.5$

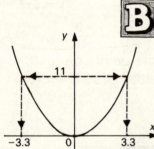

When $y = 11$ we can find two rough answers for x:
$x \approx {}^-3.3$ and $x \approx 3.3$.

C From your graph, find x when:
1. $y = 2$ 2. $y = 14$ 3. $y = 5$ 4. $y = 7.5$

$y = 2x^2 - 3x - 1$ is a curve too.
We draw its graph in the same way.
Its table of values needs more rows, like this:

Add these to get y

x	$^-4$	$^-3$	$^-2$	$^-1$	0	1	2	3	4
$2x^2$	32				0				
^-3x	12		6					$^-9$	
$^-1$	$^-1$	$^-1$			$^-1$		$^-1$		
$y = 2x^2 - 3x - 1$	43				$^-1$				

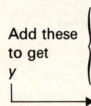

Exercise 2

1. Copy and complete this table.

2. Write the values as ordered pairs (x, y).
   Start with $({}^-4, 43)$.

3. In your ordered pairs, what is:
    (a) the smallest x value?
    (b) the largest x value?

4. In your ordered pairs, what is:
    (a) the smallest y value?
    (b) the largest y value?

5. On squared paper draw x and y axes.
    Number them using this scale:
        x axis – 2 cm represents 1 unit
        y axis – 1 cm represents 2 units

6. Plot the ordered pairs you have worked out.

7. Draw a smooth curve through all the points.
    Label your curve $y = 2x^2 - 3x - 1$.

8. What are the coordinates of the turning point?

9. From your graph, find y when:
    (a) $x = {}^{-}1.5$ (b) $x = 3.4$ (c) $x = 1.5$ (d) $x = {}^{-}3.7$?

10. From your graph, find x when:
    (a) $y = 4$ (b) $y = 18$ (c) $y = {}^{-}1$ (d) $y = 0$?
    (Your answers to (d) are the solutions of
    $2x^2 - 3x - 1 = 0$.)

Summary 👉

To draw a curve from an equation:
1. Make a table for the given values of x.
2. Work out the y values using the equation.
3. Write down the ordered pairs.
4. Draw and label the axes. Use the given scale.
5. Plot the ordered pairs.
6. Draw and label the smooth curve.

1. (a) Copy and complete this table for the curve
   $y = x^2 + 1$.

x	$^-4$	$^-3$	$^-2$	$^-1$	0	1	2	3	4
x^2	16						4		
1				1					1
$y = x^2 + 1$					2	1			

Scale:
1 cm to 1 unit
on each axis

(b) On squared paper draw x and y axes using the given scale. Draw the curve.

(c) Use your curve to find:
   (i) y when $x = 3.5$ (ii) x when $y = 9$

2. (a) Copy and complete this table for the curve
   $y = x^2 + x - 2$.

x	$^-5$	$^-4$	$^-3$	$^-2$	$^-1$	0	1	2	3	4	5
x^2					1						
x				$^-3$							
$^-2$						$^-2$				$^-2$	
$y = x^2 + x - 2$	18							4			

Scale:
x axis – 1 cm to 1 unit
y axis – 1 cm to 2 units

(b) On squared paper draw x and y axes using the given scale. Draw the curve.

(c) Use your graph to find:
   (i) the values of x when $y = 0$,
       (these are the solutions of $x^2 + x - 2 = 0$)
   (ii) the coordinates of the turning point.

3. (a) Copy and complete this table for the curve
   $y = 2x^2 - 5x - 3$.

x	$^-2$	$^-1$	0	1	2	3	4	5
$2x^2$		2					32	
^-5x					$^-10$			
$^-3$				$^-3$				
$y = 2x^2 - 5x - 3$			$^-3$			0		

(b) On squared paper draw x and y axes using the given scale. Draw the curve.

(c) Use your graph to find:
   (i) the solutions of $2x^2 - 5x - 3 = 0$, (find the values of x when y = 0)
   (ii) the coordinates of the turning point,
   (iii) the values of x when y = 10.

4. (a) Copy and complete this table for the curve $y = 3 + 2x - x^2$.

x	-3	-2	-1	0	1	2	3	4
3				3				3
2x				0			6	
$-x^2$	-9					-4		
$y = 3 + 2x - x^2$		-5			4			

(b) On squared paper draw x and y axes using the given scale. Draw the curve.

(c) From your graph, find:
   (i) the solutions of $3 + 2x - x^2 = 0$,
   (ii) the coordinates of the turning point,
   (iii) the values of x when y = -4.5.

5. (a) Copy and complete this table for the curve $y = (x + 1)(x - 2)$.

multiply these to get y →

x	-4	-3	-2	-1	0	1	2	3	4
(x + 1)	-3							4	
(x - 2)				-3					
$y = (x + 1)(x - 2)$		10		-2					

(b) On squared paper draw x and y axes using the given scale. Draw the curve.

(c) Use your graph:
   (i) to solve the equation $(x + 1)(x - 2) = 0$,
   (ii) to find the coordinates of the turning point,
   (iii) to find the values of x when y = 4.5.

Packages

You should have done: Prisms (pages 120–123).

Paul has to design a label for a can of beans.

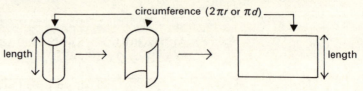

area of label = length × circumference of can

$$= 11 \text{ cm} \times (\pi \times 7 \text{ cm})$$

$$= 11 \times \frac{22}{7} \times 11 \text{ cm}^2$$

$$= \underline{242 \text{ cm}^2}$$

A Work out the areas of these labels:

use $\pi = \frac{22}{7}$

1. $10\frac{1}{2}$ cm / 15 cm
2. 7 cm / 90 mm
3. $3\frac{1}{2}$ cm / 12 cm
4. 5 cm / 70 mm
5. 7 cm / 11 cm

Sharon has to design a biscuit packet.

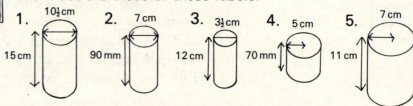

circular 'end' — 7 cm   'label' — 14 cm   circular 'end'

B Work out the area of:
(a) each end (b) the label (c) the total surface.

Exercise

use $\pi = \frac{22}{7}$

Find the total surface area of these 'packets'.

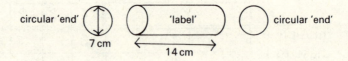

1. 7 cm / 11 cm
2. $3\frac{1}{2}$ cm / 7 cm
3. 105 mm / 85 mm
4. 7 cm / 21 cm

Diagonals

You need: a centimetre ruler, protractor and centimetre dotty paper.

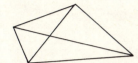

This shape has its diagonals drawn in.
Diagonals join opposite corners (vertices).

Exercise 1

On your dotty paper make large drawings of a square, rectangle, rhombus, parallelogram, kite and trapezium. Draw in their diagonals.

Some of your shapes have special diagonals.

Exercise 2

Which of your shapes have:
1. diagonals equal in length?
2. both diagonals bisected (halved)?
3. only one diagonal bisected?
4. diagonals crossing at right angles?
5. all the corner angles bisected?
6. only two corner angles bisected?

Your squares, rectangles, ... may be very special ones.
Have your friends got the same results as you?

Exercise 3

This table is a summary of your work

Copy and complete this table.
Only mark the property if all your class agree.

quadrilateral	equal diagonals	diagonals bisected	cross at right angles	bisect corner angles
square				yes
rectangle			no	
rhombus		yes		
parallelogram	no			
kite		1 only		
trapezium	no			

Banger Bean Bake (serves 10)

600 g	cocktail sausages
1.2 kg	potatoes
65 g	butter
80 g	grated cheese
550 g	baked beans

Party planners

You should have done: For charity (pages 20–21).

Tina is making the food for the end-of-term party.
16 people are coming.
She uses this recipe for Banger Bean Bake.
But it is for 10 people, not 16!
She works out the amounts for 16 people.

amounts

Ingredient	for 10 people	÷ 10 →	for 1 person	× 16 →	for 16 people
sausages	600 g		600 ÷ 10 = 60 g		60 g × 16 = 960 g
potatoes	1.2 kg		1.2 kg ÷ 10 = 0.12 kg		0.12 kg × 16 = kg
butter					
cheese					
baked beans					

 Copy and complete Tina's table for Banger Bean Bake.

The party starts with tomato soup and a soft bap.

Soft Crust Baps – makes 10

150 ml hand hot milk
150 ml hand hot water
5 ml spoon of sugar
25 g fresh yeast *or*
10 g dried yeast
450 g strong plain flour
5 ml spoon of salt
50 g lard, cubed

Tomato soup – for 6

450 g tomatoes
30 g butter
75 g long grain rice
1.5 l stock

 **Exercise 1**

Work out the amounts Tina needs for each recipe for 1 person and for 16 people. Put your working in a table as before.

Tina makes 2 chocolate squares and 3 glasses of mulled cider for each person.

1. How many chocolate squares does she make?
2. How many glasses of mulled cider does she make?

Chocolate squares – makes 9	Mulled cider – serves 5
180 g plain chocolate	15 ml spoon of soft
45 g margarine	brown sugar
225 g digestive biscuits	pinch of salt
135 g sultanas	1.2 l cider
45 g glacé cherries	2.5 ml spoon of whole
9 halves of glacé cherries	allspice berries
to decorate	pinch of grated nutmeg
orange rind	$2\frac{1}{2}$ cm cinnamon stick
	orange for decoration

Exercise 2

Work out the amounts Tina needs for each recipe.
Put your working in a table as before.

Summary

To alter a recipe or mixture:
   work out the amounts for one,
   then multiply by the number needed.

Exercise 3

Work out the amounts needed to make each recipe for
(a) 6 people,   (b) 10 people,   (c) 21 people.

Steak and Kidney Casserole (serves 5)

900 g	stewing steak	50 g	beef dripping
450 g	ox kidney	825 ml	stock
50 g	plain flour	15 ml	Worcestershire sauce
125 g	onions		salt
100 g	mushrooms		pepper

Tipsy oranges (for 4)

100 g	sugar
160 ml	water
4	large oranges
20 ml	orange liqueur

Rice salad (serves 15)

750 g	long-grain rice
900 g	frozen mixed vegetables
60 g	chopped walnuts
105 g	sultanas
180 ml	French dressing

Two solutions

To solve $x^2 + x - 2 = 0$ using your calculator, copy and complete this table:

x	$^-4$	$^-3$	$^-2$	$^-1$	0	1	2	3	4
$x^2 + x - 2$	10	4	0						

Look for 0 in this line. This gives the solutions.

$x^2 + x - 2 = 0$ when $x = {}^-2$ and $x = 1$.
So $x = {}^-2$ and $x = 1$ are the solutions of the equation.

Solve these the same way:
1. $x^2 - 2x - 3 = 0$ 2. $x^2 - 6x + 8 = 0$ 3. $x^2 + 4x + 3 = 0$

Copy and complete this table for $x^2 - 2x - 7 = 0$:

x	$^-4$	$^-3$	$^-2$	$^-1$	0	1	2	3	4
$x^2 - 2x - 7$	17	8	1	$^-4$					

Look for 0 in this line. It doesn't appear! So we look for where the sign changes.

The sign changes between $x = {}^-2$ and $^-1$, and $x = 3$ and 4.
So the solutions are between these values.

You can find the solution between $x = {}^-2$ and $^-1$ like this:

1 is nearer to 0 than − 4. So the solution is near to − 2. Try − 1.9.

x	$x^2 - 2x - 7$
Try $^-1.9$	0.41
$^-1.8$	$^-0.16$

Sign changes, so try in between
Try $x = {}^-1.85$.

Try $^-1.85$	0.1225
$^-1.84$	0.0656
$^-1.83$	0.0089
$^-1.82$	$^-0.0476$

Sign changes, so try in between.
Try $x = {}^-1.825$.

and so on ... until you find the best answer you can.

Find the other solution the same way. Try $x = 3.5$ to start.

Solve these the same way:
1. $x^2 - 2x - 2 = 0$ 2. $x^2 + 7x - 2 = 0$ 3. $x^2 - 8x + 3 = 0$

Recap 5

1. For this pair of similar solids, calculate:
   (a) scale factor,   (b) volume factor,
   (c) the volume of the larger solid.

 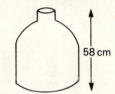

2. A ship sails 8 km on a bearing 050°, then turns and sails 12 km at 150°, then turns again and sails 10 km at 300°.
   Draw an accurate scale drawing for this course. Use your drawing to find:
   (a) the distance and bearing of the ship from its starting point,
   (b) the bearing on which the ship must be steered to get back to its starting point.

3. What are the rates payable on a house with a rateable value £275 if the rate in the pound is 132p? The householder pays the rates each month. How much is each monthly payment? (Answer to nearest p.)

4. A town has a total rateable value of £3.3m. If £3 861 000 is needed to finance its services one year, how much should the rate in the pound be?

5. This diagram shows the cross-section of a roof.

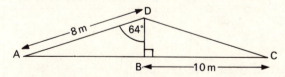

   Calculate:
   (a) the height B D,
   (b) the angles D A B and D C B,
   (c) the total width of the roof A C.

6. Solve these pairs of equations:
   (a) $x + y = 9$ (c) $x + 2y = 2$
       $x - y = 7$ $2x + y = 4$
   (b) $2x - y = 12$ (d) $3x + 5y = {}^-4$
       $x + y = 3$ $4x + y = 6$

7. Calculate the size of the lettered angles. O is the centre of the circle.

8. Copy and complete this table of values for $y = x^2 + 5x + 2$.

x	-5	-4	-3	-2	-1	0
x^2						
$5x$						
2						
y						

   Use your table to plot the graph of $y = x^2 + 5x + 2$.
   (a) What are the coordinates of the turning point?
   (b) What are the solutions of $x^2 + 5x + 2 = 0$?

9.

Bolton Hot Pot – Serves 4			
900 g	lamb	900 g	potato
120 g	onion	30 g	lard
4	kidneys	2 tbs	flour
120 g	mushrooms	420 ml	stock

   Work out the amount of each ingredient for: (a) 3 people,   (b) 7 people.

Music by chance

Have you ever composed a tune?
Here is one way.

It uses only the white notes
on a piano.

middle
C D E F G A B

C D E F G A B

Choose three of them,
for example CGB.

Write out all the different
ways you can arrange them:

1. CGB   2. CBG   3. BCG   4. BGC   5. GCB   6. GBC

Now throw a die to choose which ones to play:

and so on . . .

CBG   GBC   BGC   GBC   CBG   CGB

This gives your tune:

C B G G B C B G C G B C C B G C G B

When it is finished, try it on a piano and choose the tempo.

Compose some different tunes this way. Perhaps you could write a song.
You could try choosing four notes, or using the black notes.

Numbers in spaces

Use the given numbers. Obey the given rules.

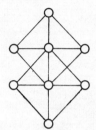

Digits 1–8.

No line must join 2 consecutive numbers.

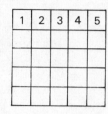

Digits 1–5.

No digit must be repeated in any row, column or diagonal.

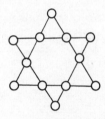

Integers 1–12.

The sum of numbers in each of the six rows must be 26.

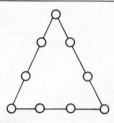

Digits 1–9.

Each side of the triangle must add up to the same total.

How many different solutions can you find?

Snooker squared

This snooker table is rather odd.
It's covered in squares!

The cue ball is odd too.
It always travels along the squares' diagonals.

Will this cue ball hit ball A?
Draw its path on squared paper to find out.

Which ball will the cue ball hit here?
Which others can it hit starting from here?
Draw the cue ball's paths on squared paper.

Make up some snooker problems of your own.
Challenge your friends to solve them.

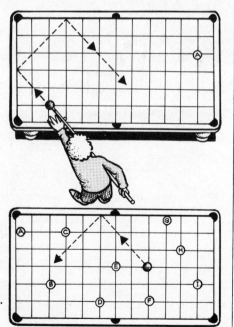

Why

To remind you
of the work done.

To practise answering
questions.

To help you to
pass your exam.

The plan

Start revising early
– in the year and in
the day.

Make a timetable of
2 hour sessions.

Plan breaks: 5 minutes
every $\frac{1}{2}$ hour, longer
after 2 hours.

Where

In a quiet room,
not too warm, with
plenty of light and air.

Work at a table or desk,
with a good light.

Make it 'your
study place'.

Your revision

How

For each topic:
Read the revision page and
the work in your books.
Make notes about it.
Try to understand it.
Do questions.
Test yourself.

How often

Revise and practise
each topic more than once.

To improve your memory,
revise each topic again:
– after 10 minutes,
– after a day,
– after a week.

Exam practice

Practise exam questions
and whole exam papers.

Do them like 'mock exams'.
Allow yourself only:
– the normal exam time,
– the things you can
take into the exam.

Before the day

Make sure you know:
- the name of your exam,
- the number of papers,
- the days, dates and times,
- where they are,
- how to get to them,
- your exam number and centre number.

On the day

Arrive early.
Bring all 'you need'.
Listen carefully to the invigilator – there may be changes.
Read the paper carefully.
Follow the instructions.
Don't forget to fill in your exam number!

You need

pens and ink,
pencils and sharpener,
rubber, ruler, compasses,
protractor, set squares,
a watch, calculator
(if allowed) and
spare batteries.

Your exam

The questions

Find out:
What type of questions are on each paper – multiple choice, short, long, ...?
Do you have a choice?
How many must you do?
How much time is there for each one?

Your answers

Do what the question asks. Work neatly and clearly.
Show your working.
If you get 'stuck', leave a space, try another question, go back later.
Check: are your answers sensible?

Which questions?

If you have a choice:
Read all the questions.
Cross the ones you can't do.
Tick those you can definitely do. Do your best questions first. Do the required number of questions.

0. Copy and complete the following table values of $y = x^2 + x - 1$ from $x = -3$ to $x = 2$.

(b) Write down the coordinates of the point B.

(c) Calculate angle BAO.

8. (a) Share £350 in the ratio 3:4.

takes 15 minutes. Using the axe below draw a graph to illustrate

7. A sum of money was divid Julie and Joanne. Julie re and Joanne received £4. |

(a) Find the coordinates in the simplest possible fo

(c) the minimum value of $x^2 + x - 1 = 0,$

4. The diagram shows a sketch o of $y = 5x - 7$.
Calculate the coordinates of

6. (a) Divide £10 between two me ratio 1:3.

(b) If five pencils cost $22\frac{1}{2}$p, wor cost of (i) one pencil (ii) twel pencils.

Exam words: what do they mean?

Exam questions often use complicated words. But many have simple meanings.

Here are some common 'exam words'
... and what they mean.

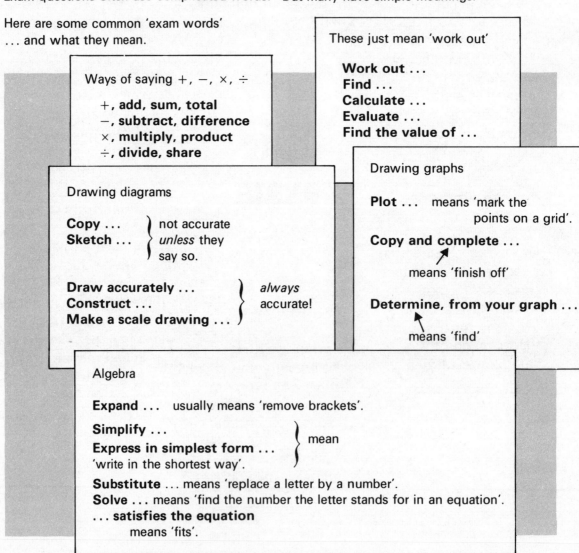

Ways of saying $+$, $-$, $\times$, $\div$

- **$+$, add, sum, total**
- **$-$, subtract, difference**
- **$\times$, multiply, product**
- **$\div$, divide, share**

These just mean 'work out'

- **Work out ...**
- **Find ...**
- **Calculate ...**
- **Evaluate ...**
- **Find the value of ...**

Drawing diagrams

Copy ... } not accurate
Sketch ... } *unless* they say so.

Draw accurately ... } *always*
Construct ... } accurate!
Make a scale drawing ... }

Drawing graphs

Plot ... means 'mark the points on a grid'.

Copy and complete ...
↗
means 'finish off'

Determine, from your graph ...
↖
means 'find'

Algebra

Expand ... usually means 'remove brackets'.

Simplify ...
Express in simplest form ... } mean
'write in the shortest way'.

Substitute ... means 'replace a letter by a number'.
Solve ... means 'find the number the letter stands for in an equation'.
... satisfies the equation
means 'fits'.

Your exam board may have its own favourite 'exam words'. Ask your teacher about them.

Arithmetic

1. (a) $1567 + 45 + 2983$ (c) 768×9
   (b) $567 - 289$ (d) $1819 \div 17$

2. (a) Use the numbers 38 and 106 to find:
       (i) their sum   (ii) their product
   (b) Express $81 \div 108$ as:
       (i) a fraction in its lowest terms,
       (ii) a decimal,
       (iii) a percentage.

3. Calculate the exact value of 363×4.

4. Write in figures: nineteen million, seventy thousand, one hundred and four.

5. (a) Which is bigger, 32 or 8.9?
   (b) Find the difference between 16.2 and 25.
   (c)   1061   (d)   15.86
          $-$ 783 $-$ 9.07

6. Two men load a lorry with sand. The sand is in 50 kg bags. It takes each man $2\frac{1}{2}$ minutes to carry and load each bag onto the lorry. How long does it take to load the lorry with 3 tonnes of sand?

7. (a) What is $\frac{1}{3}$ of 57?
   (b) What is 70% of 30?
   (c) Express $\frac{1}{4}$ of a kilometre in metres.

8. Find the exact values of:

   (a) $8\overline{)368}$ (c) $7\overline{)18.55}$

   (b) $12\overline{)5052}$ (d) $4\overline{)£2.92}$

9. Work out:
   (a) $£5 - (£1.43 + £2.76)$
   (b) $1\,l - 384\,ml$

10. A car does 8 km per litre of petrol. How far will it travel on $3\frac{1}{2}$ litres of petrol?

11. Instead of multiplying a number by 26 a boy multiplied it by 62. His answer was 4526.
    (a) Find the number.
    (b) Find the answer he should have got.

12. Work out $3^4 - 4^3$.

13. In the number 23.026:
    (a) write down the value of the digit 6,
    (b) calculate the *difference* between the two digits 2.

14. Calculate the exact values of:
    (a) $9.8 + 3.05 - 8.206$
    (b) $5\frac{2}{3} - 2\frac{3}{4}$
    (c) $4\frac{3}{4} \times 8$
    (d) $(0.65)^2 - (0.35)^2$

15. What is the remainder when 3206 is divided by 9?

16. In a sponsored swim, a girl does 34 lengths.
    If each length is 25 m, how far has she swum altogether?

17. Gary travelled from Manchester to Liverpool 15 times in May. The distance from Manchester to Liverpool is 58 km. Work out the total distance Gary travelled.

18. A boy moves 35 packages. The most he can carry at once is 4. How many journeys must he make?

19. How many pieces of string each 40 cm long can be cut from a piece 4.8 m long?

20. Each compartment in a railway carriage seats six people. There are eight compartments in a carriage. How many carriages are needed to carry 670 football supporters?

Factors and primes

To find factors of a number n:
1. try dividing by 1, 2, 3, 4, ..., n,
2. factors are those that divide exactly.

To find common factors:
1. write down factors of each number,
2. pick out the factors common to all.

Prime number: has only two factors, 1 and itself. 1 is not a prime number.

Prime factor: a factor which is a prime.

To write a number as a product of primes: find the primes by repeatedly dividing by primes in turn.

Squares
Perfect squares: 1, 4, 9, 16, 25, ...

To square a number, multiply it by itself.
e.g. $5.9^2 = 5.9 \times 5.9 = 34.81$
To get an exact answer, work it out.

Squares tables give approximate answers for numbers 1–10. e.g. $5.9^2 \approx 34.8$

For other numbers, use standard form then tables. e.g. $5900^2 = (5.9 \times 10^3)^2$
$$= 5.9^2 \times 10^6$$
$$34.8 \times 10^6 = \underline{34\,800\,000}$$

Square roots $\sqrt{}$
For perfect squares, rewrite as multiplication:
e.g. $\sqrt{25} = \sqrt{5 \times 5} = 5$

Square root tables give approximate answers for numbers 1–10 and 10–99.

For other numbers:
1. rewrite as:
$B \times 10^m$
number between 1 and 99 } { even powers of 10
2. then use the correct table.

Directed numbers

Positive$^+$ and negative$^-$ numbers.

On a number line:

negative   positive
$-5\ -4\ -3\ -2\ -1\ 0\ +1\ +2\ +3\ +4\ +5$

← Move to left, numbers get smaller.
→ Move to right, numbers get bigger.
< means 'is smaller than'.
> means 'is bigger than'.

Addition and subtraction
1. Think of them as temperatures: hot air ($^+$), cold air ($^-$).
2. Use a number line to help you.
3. Ask yourself:
   (a) What is the starting temperature?
   (b) Does it go up or down?
      + hot air : it goes up
      + cold air: it goes down
      − hot air : it goes down
      − cold air: it goes up
   (c) By how many degrees?
   (d) What is the final temperature?

or Subtracting a positive adding its negative } give the same answer.

e.g. $^+5 - {}^+3 = {}^+2$
$^+5 + {}^-3 = {}^+2$

or Subtracting a negative adding its positive } give the same answer.

e.g. $^-7 - {}^-4 = {}^-3$
$^-7 + {}^+4 = {}^-3$

Multiplication and division
Signs the same → $^+$ answer.
e.g. $^+4 \times {}^+2 = {}^+8$ $^+9 \div {}^+3 = {}^+3$
$^-3 \times {}^-5 = {}^+15$ $^-6 \div {}^-3 = {}^+2$

Signs different → $^-$ answer.
e.g. $^+6 \times {}^-3 = {}^-18$ $^-15 \div {}^+5 = {}^-3$

1. Write down the factors of 210.

2. Find the common factors of 70 and 330.

3. How many factors does the number 64 have?

4. From this set of numbers $\{1, 3, 4, 6, 10, 12\}$ write down:
   (a) a prime number,
   (b) a square number,
   (c) the square root of 144.

5. Express 12 as a product of prime numbers.

6. Here is list of numbers: 2, 3, 4, 5, 6, 7, 8, 9.
   (a) From the list, write down the prime numbers.
   (b) From the list, write down the factors of 72.

7. Which two prime numbers lie between 30 and 40?

8. List all the prime numbers between 26 and 40.

9. Write down the exact values of:
   (a) 4^2 (b) 13^2 (c) 1.3^2

10. Use tables or a calculator to find the values of these to 3 significant figures:
    (a) 2.31^2 (b) 17.5^2

11. What is $\sqrt{121}$?

12. Give the values of these to three significant figures:
    (a) $\sqrt{2.4}$ (b) $\sqrt{8.7}$ (c) $\sqrt{46.4}$

13. Work out the sum of the four prime numbers between 20 and 40.

14. Insert $>$ or $<$ in the following to make each one true:
    (a) 3 7   (b) $^-2$ $^-4$

15. Find the value of: $2 - (1 - 5)$.

16. Work out: $10 - (4 - 7)$.

17. What is $7 - (6 - 4)$?

18. Find the values of:
    (a) $^-5 \times {}^-7$ (c) $^-5 - {}^-7$
    (b) $^-5 + {}^-7$ (d) $40 \div {}^-10$

19. The answers to each part of this question are in this list of numbers: 3 6 10 15 21
    (a) Write down the prime number.
    (b) Write down the number which is a multiple of 7.
    (c) Three of the numbers add up to 24. Write them down.

20. (a) Write down the whole number which is nearest to $\sqrt{23}$.
    (b) Write down the whole number which is nearest to $\sqrt{230}$.
    (c) Write down the next prime number after 13.
    (d) Write down the whole number which is nearest to the value of $\dfrac{0.2 \times 9.86}{0.01}$

21. Write down the value of n in each of the following.
    (a) $n = (^-6) \times (^-3)$
    (b) $8n = {}^-32$
    (c) $\dfrac{^-6}{n} = {}^+2$

22. From the following numbers:
    9 14 25 29 33 42
    write down:
    (a) a factor of 72,
    (b) a prime number,
    (c) two numbers which give 1050 when multiplied together.

23. Find the values of:
    (a) $^-2 + {}^-9$ (c) $4 - {}^-8$
    (b) $^-3 \times 7$ (d) $^-26 \div 13$

24. In each of the following, write down the sign $+$ or $-$ to make each one correct:
    (a) $28 + 4 - 12 = 28 + (4 \ldots 12)$
    (b) $15 - 4 + 7 = 15 \ldots (4 - 7)$

25. What is $\sqrt{169}$?

Fractions

$3 \leftarrow$ numerator (number of equal parts taken)

$\overline{5} \leftarrow$ denominator (total number of equal parts)

$1 = \frac{2}{2} = \frac{3}{3} = \frac{4}{4} = \ldots$

Improper fraction: numerator bigger than denominator, e.g. $\frac{21}{5}$.

Mixed number: whole number and fraction, e.g. $4\frac{1}{5}$.

Equivalent fractions have the same value, e.g. $\frac{3}{5} = \frac{6}{10} = \frac{9}{15} = \frac{12}{20} = \ldots$

Multiplying top and bottom by the same number gives an equivalent fraction, e.g. $\frac{3}{5} \overset{\times 3}{\underset{\times 3}{\longrightarrow}} \frac{9}{15}$.

Cancelling: dividing top and bottom by the same number, e.g. $\frac{12}{20} \overset{\div 4}{\underset{\div 4}{\longrightarrow}} \frac{3}{5}$

Simplest form of a fraction: you cannot cancel it.

Comparing fractions: 1. write equivalent fractions of each,

2. then compare ones with the same denominator.

Addition and subtraction

1. Work out any whole numbers.
2. Use equivalent fractions to make denominators the same.
3. Work out fractions – think of them 'in words'.
4. Change to mixed numbers if you can.

e.g. $2\frac{3}{4} + 1\frac{2}{3}$

$= 3\frac{3}{4} + \frac{2}{3}$

$= 3\frac{9}{12} + \frac{8}{12}$

$= 3\frac{17}{12}$

$= 3 + 1\frac{5}{12} = \underline{4\frac{5}{12}}$

Working

$\frac{3}{4} = \frac{6}{8} = \boxed{\frac{9}{12}} = \ldots$

$\frac{2}{3} = \frac{4}{6} = \frac{6}{9} = \boxed{\frac{8}{12}} = \ldots$

$\frac{17}{12} = 1\frac{5}{12}$

Multiplication

1. Change any mixed numbers to improper fractions.
2. Cancel if you can.
3. Multiply top, then multiply bottom.
4. Change to a mixed number if you can.

e.g. $3\frac{3}{4} \times 4\frac{2}{5}$

$= \frac{\overset{3}{\cancel{15}}}{\underset{2}{\cancel{4}}} \times \frac{\overset{11}{\cancel{22}}}{\underset{1}{\cancel{5}}}$

$= \frac{33}{2}$

$= \underline{16\frac{1}{2}}$

A fraction multiplied by its reciprocal is 1.   e.g. $\frac{3}{7} \times \frac{7}{3} = 1$

Reciprocal of $\dfrac{a}{b}$ is $\dfrac{b}{a}$.

Division

1. Change any mixed numbers to improper fractions.
2. Find reciprocal of 'divider'.
3. Change '÷' to '× by reciprocal'.
4. Work it out.

e.g. $\frac{7}{8} \div 4\frac{2}{3}$

$4\frac{2}{3} = \frac{14}{3}$

Reciprocal of $\frac{14}{3}$ is $\frac{3}{14}$

$\frac{7}{8} \div \frac{14}{3} = \frac{7}{8} \times \frac{3}{14}$

$= \frac{\overset{1}{\cancel{7}}}{8} \times \frac{3}{\underset{2}{\cancel{14}}} = \frac{3}{16}$

---

1. (a) Arrange the fractions $\frac{5}{22}, \frac{5}{21}, \frac{5}{23}$ in order with the smallest first.
   (b) Write down a fraction between $\frac{1}{2}$ and $\frac{3}{4}$.

2. Calculate $\frac{1}{2} + \frac{2}{3}$.

3. Simplify $\frac{5}{8} + \frac{3}{16}$.

4. Find the value of $2\frac{1}{2} \div \frac{1}{2}$.

5. Calculate
   (a) $6 - 1\frac{7}{8}$, (b) $3\frac{1}{5} \times 1\frac{7}{8}$.

6. Work out $\frac{1}{5} + \frac{2}{3}$.

7. Calculate $1\frac{1}{2} + 2\frac{3}{4}$.

8. Work out $\frac{7}{8} - \frac{3}{4}$.

9. Find, in its simplest form, the value of $\frac{1}{4} + (\frac{1}{4} \times \frac{1}{4})$.

10. Find the value of $\frac{1}{4} + 1\frac{1}{2} - \frac{1}{16}$.

11. Calculate
    (a) $\frac{1}{3} + \frac{1}{6}$ (b) $\frac{1}{3} - \frac{1}{6}$ (c) $\frac{1}{3} \times \frac{1}{6}$ (d) $\frac{1}{3} \div \frac{1}{6}$

12. Simplify, giving your answer in its lowest terms:
    (i) $\frac{1}{2} + \frac{1}{4}$ (ii) $\frac{1}{4} \div \frac{1}{2}$

13. Simplify $\frac{3}{7} \times \frac{4}{5}$.

14. Work out $(\frac{3}{5} \times \frac{5}{6}) - (\frac{2}{3} \times \frac{1}{4})$. Give your answer in its simplest form.

15. Simplify
    (a) $\frac{1}{12} + \frac{5}{6}$ (b) $\frac{3}{4} \div \frac{7}{12}$

16. Give the answers to the following in their lowest terms:
    (a) $\frac{3}{5} \times \frac{10}{21}$ (c) $\frac{7}{8} - \frac{2}{3}$
    (b) $\frac{5}{8} \div 2\frac{3}{4}$ (d) $1\frac{1}{3} + 2\frac{3}{4}$

17. Calculate $2\frac{3}{8} \div \frac{7}{8}$.

18. Multiply $1\frac{1}{2}$ by (a) 2, (b) 10, (c) 7.

19. Calculate:
    (a) $\frac{2}{3} + \frac{3}{5}$ (b) $1\frac{3}{4} \times \frac{2}{7}$ (c) $7\frac{1}{2} \div \frac{3}{4}$

20. (a) $\frac{1}{3} + \frac{2}{5}$ (c) $\frac{2}{3} \times \frac{3}{5}$
    (b) $2\frac{1}{4} - 1\frac{1}{2}$ (d) $\frac{1}{8} \div \frac{1}{2}$

21. A tape lasts $\frac{3}{4}$ hour. How many tapes will be needed for 6 hours' music?

22. Give the answers to the following in their lowest terms:
    (a) $\frac{3}{5} \times \frac{10}{21}$, (c) $\frac{7}{8} - \frac{2}{3}$
    (b) $\frac{5}{8} \div 2\frac{3}{4}$ (d) $1\frac{1}{3} + 2\frac{3}{4}$

23. (a) Calculate
       (i) $2\frac{5}{8} - 1\frac{1}{3}$
       (ii) $4\frac{3}{5} \div 1\frac{1}{10}$
       (iii) $\frac{2}{3}$ of $(1\frac{1}{2} + \frac{9}{16})$
    (b) A girl takes $\frac{1}{3}$ of the sweets from a full box and then a boy takes $\frac{1}{4}$ of those still remaining.
       What fraction of the full box is now left?

24. What is the value of 10^{-2} expressed as a fraction?

25. What fraction is equal to 1%?

26. (a) Which **two** of the following fractions are equal?

    $\frac{63}{90}$ $\frac{45}{65}$ $\frac{75}{105}$ $\frac{54}{78}$

    (b) If * means 'divide the first number by 3 and then subtract the second number', find the value of $\frac{1}{2} * \frac{1}{8}$.
    (c) At a football match $\frac{4}{15}$ of the spectators were in the enclosure, $\frac{2}{5}$ were on the terracing and the remaining 12 200 were in the stand. Calculate the total number of spectators at the match.
    (d) The petrol tank of a car can hold 45 litres and petrol consumption is 14 km per litre. What fraction of the tank still contains petrol after a journey of 168 km if the tank was $\frac{4}{5}$ full before starting the journey?

Decimals

A figure's place in a number tells us its value.

←... ——————————————whole number part→ ←decimal fraction part——————————————————...→

thousands	hundreds	tens	units	·	tenths	hundredths	thousandths	ten thousandths
100	100	10	1	·	$\frac{1}{10}$	$\frac{1}{100}$	$\frac{1}{1000}$	$\frac{1}{10\,000}$
3	7	5		·	2	9	6	4

↑
decimal point separates units from tenths

The number in the table is $375.2964 = 300 + 70 + 5 + \frac{2}{10} + \frac{9}{100} + \frac{6}{1000} + \frac{4}{10000}$

Addition and subtraction
1. Set them down with decimal points under each other.
2. Put decimal point in the answer.
3. Work it out like 'ordinary numbers'.

e.g.

```
  129.350  ← put 0s
   52.613    in blank
+  76.000  ← spaces
  257.963
```

Multiplication
× 10, move figures one place left
× 100, move figures two places left
and so on.

```
      0.521
```
e.g. $0.521 \times 10 = 5.21$
e.g. $0.521 \times 100 = 52.1$

The 'quick way'
1. Count number of decimal places (d.p.).
2. Forget the points and multiply.
3. Use number of decimal places to put in point.
4. Check with an approximate answer.

e.g.
```
  0.291 ← 3 d.p. ⎞  total 5 d.p.
× 1.07  ← 2 d.p. ⎠
  2037
 29100
```
0.31137   5 d.p. in answer   right size!

Check: $0.291 \times 1.07 \approx 0.3 \times 1 = 0.3$

Division
÷ 10, move figures one place right.
÷ 100, move figures two places right.
and so on.

```
      0.521
```
e.g. $0.521 \div 10 = 0.0521$
$0.521 \div 100 = 0.00521$

Dividing by a whole number: 1. set it down like a 'long division', e.g. $23\overline{)123.73}$
                                            2. put decimal points in line.

Dividing by a decimal: 1. write division as a fraction
                                2. multiply top and bottom by the same number (10,100, ...) to make the bottom a whole number.
                                3. now you can work it out.

e.g. $10.4 \div 0.25 = \dfrac{10.4}{0.25}$

$= \dfrac{10.4 \times 100}{0.25 \times 100} = \dfrac{1040}{25}$

Decimal → fraction
Look at the last figure.
Its column heading tells you the kind of fraction.

e.g. $0.173 = \frac{173}{1000}$

thousandths

Fraction → decimal
Denominator 10,100, ... That tells you the column for the last figure. e.g. $\frac{9}{100} = 0.09$
Other denominators: write the fraction as a division, then work it out.

1. Write as fractions in their lowest terms:
   (a) 0.7   (b) 0.48   (c) 0.375

2. Express these as fractions. Cancel if you can:
   (a) 0.3   (b) 0.75   (c) 0.284

3. (a) $1.682 + 7.25 + 0.023 + 15$
   (b) $5.32 - 2.93$
   (c) 0.3×0.2
   (d) $1.4 \div 0.07$

4. Find the values of:
   (a) $4.35 - 3.45$ (b) 0.6×0.4

5. Find the exact value of $9.36 \div 1.8$.

6. $1.7 \div 0.4$.

7. Calculate $(6.5^2 - 3.5^2)$.

8. Work out:
   (a) $5.5 + 0.55$ (c) $\frac{1}{3}$ of £69.60
   (b) 0.8×0.8

9. (a) $7.36 + 8.08$ (c) 2.58×9
   (b) $£5 - £2.31$ (d) $17.85 \div 5$

10. Work out
    (a) 73.8×100 (c) one-quarter of 3.236
    (b) $25.83 + 167.5$

11. Calculate the *exact* value of $17.4 \div 2.9$.

12. What is 0.25×0.5?

13. How many pieces of string, each 6 cm long, can be cut from a piece of string 3.6 m long?

14. Work out $3 + 0.36 - 0.17$.

15. Find the value of $\dfrac{1}{0.2} - \dfrac{1}{0.25}$

16. You are given that $19 \times 37 = 703$.
    Find the values of:
    (a) 19×3.7 (d) 190×0.37
    (b) 1.9×3.7 (e) $703 \div 37$
    (c) 0.19×0.037

17. Write $\frac{5}{8}$ as a decimal.

18. Express 0.35 as a fraction in its lowest terms.

19. (a) Convert the fraction $\frac{4}{5}$ into a decimal.
    (b) Convert the fraction $\frac{9}{20}$ into a decimal.
    (c) Convert the fraction $\frac{3}{16}$ into a decimal.

20. Write 0.73 as a fraction.

21. Write the fraction '27 thousandths' in decimal form.

22. Express $\frac{3}{8}$ as a decimal.

23. (a) Change 0.55 into a fraction in its lowest terms.
    (b) Change $\frac{3}{8}$ into a decimal.

24. Simplify the expression $\dfrac{2 \times 2^2 \times 2^3}{10 \times 10 \times 10}$
    giving your answer as a decimal.

25. Use this list of numbers to answer the following questions:
    0.06 0.6 6 600 60 000 60 000 000
    (a) Which of these numbers is most likely to represent the total number of children in a secondary school?
    (b) Which of these numbers is most likely to represent the number of children at a birthday party?
    (c) Which of these numbers is nearest to the total population of the British Isles?
    (d) Which of these numbers is nearest to the area of a page of this book when the area is given in square metres?

Number

Approximations $\approx$ means 'approximately equals'.

Rounding off	**Decimal places** (d.p.)	**Significant figures** (s.f.)

– use to find approximate

answers.

9.572

1st d.p.   2nd d.p.   3rd d.p.

'1st figure'

59.3   0.00047

To round off to the nearest:

   unit : look at tenths,

   ten : look at units,

hundred : look at tens,

   and so on ...

To correct to:

  1 d.p. : look at 2nd d.p.,

  2 d.p. : look at 3rd d.p.,

  3 d.p. : look at 4th d.p.,

  and so on ...

To correct to:

  1 s.f. : look at '2nd figure',

  2 s.f. : look at '3rd figure',

  3 s.f. : look at '4th figure',

  and so on ...

If the number you look at is: less than 5 – forget it,

                       5 or more – add 1 to the figure in front of it.

Standard form

Any number can be written in standard form like this:

$$A \times 10^n$$

number between 1 and 10 $\longrightarrow$ $\longleftarrow$ power of 10

Numbers bigger than 10 have $^+$powers.

e.g. $25\,100 = 2.51 \times 10^4$

Numbers less than 1 have $^-$powers.

e.g. $0.000\,0379 = 3.79 \times 10^{-5}$

Logs

Logarithms are powers. The log of 10^n is n.

To find the log of a number between 1 and 10:
– look it up in log tables.

e.g.

no.	log
1.27	0.104

To find the log of a number bigger than 10:
1. write it in standard form,
2. then use log tables.

e.g.

no.	standard form	log
1270	1.27×10^3	3.104

from tables

To find a number from a log:
– use log tables 'backwards'.

e.g.

no.	standard form	log
12\,700	1.27×10^4	4.104

from tables

To multiply numbers, add their logs.

e.g.

no.	standard form	log
2750	2.75×10^3	3.439
$\times$ 63.4	6.34×10^1	1.802 $^+$
174\,000	1.74×10^5	5.241

To divide numbers, subtract their logs.

e.g.

no.	standard form	log
48\,000	4.8×10^4	4.681
$\div$ 235	2.35×10^2	2.371 $^-$
204	2.04×10^2	2.310

Always check with approximate answers.

1. (a) Add 2.97, 0.643 and 42.065.
   (b) Write the number 627.0583:

      (i) correct to 2 decimal places,
      (ii) correct to 2 significant figures.

2. Round off to the nearest whole number:
   (a) $7\frac{11}{16}$ (b) 100.09   (c) 17.912

3. (a) Estimate your height in metres.
   (b) Estimate, to one significant figure,
      $79\,562 \div 197$.

4. (a) Write the number 5487 correct to two
      significant figures.
   (b) Write the number $5\,260\,000$ in
      standard form, that is $A \times 10^n$ where
      A is a number between 1 and 10 and
      n is a whole number.

5. A recent football match between two local
   sides attracted 49 456 spectators. Express
   this attendance correct to three significant
   figures.

6. (a) Express $9\,532\,678$ to the nearest
      million.
   (b) Express 0.057 metres in millimetres.
   (c) Express 23.405 86 correct to:

      (i) two decimal places
      (ii) three significant figures.

7. (a) Approximations to the nearest whole
      number for 3.175, 12.48 and 7.613
      are 3, 12 and 8 respectively. Use these
      suggestions to obtain an approximate
      result for

      $$\frac{3.175 \times 12.48}{7.613}$$

   (b) Applying the same method as in (a),
      obtain an approximate result for

      $$\frac{9.616 \times 12.16}{17.71}$$

8. Write down the number 1892 correct to
   two significant figures.

9. Estimate the value of $\dfrac{42.1}{7.9}$ correct to
   the nearest whole number.

10. Write 0.02846 correct to three significant
    figures.

11. Express 0.0488:
    (a) correct to two decimal places,
    (b) correct to two significant figures,
    (c) in standard form.

12. Write $290\,000$ in standard form.

13. Write 397 in standard form.

14. Write in standard form (a) 2134
                          (b) 0.3115

15. What is the value of n when the number
    $93\,000\,000$ is expressed in the form
    9.3×10^n?

16. Multiply 3.2×10^6 by 4×10^{-3},
    giving your answer in standard form.

17. (a) Write each of the following numbers
       in standard form:
       (i) 8460   (ii) 0.846
    (b) Evaluate $8460 \div 0.846$ giving your
       answer in standard form.

18. Find the logs of these numbers:
    (a) 2.73   (b) 635   (c) 57.9

19. Find the numbers these logs come from:
    (a) 0.776   (b) 1.072   (c) 4.522

20. Given log 5.87 $= 0.769$, write down the
    value of:
    (a) log 58.7   (b) 5870

21. Use logarithms to calculate:
    (a) 1.36×4.64 (c) $490 \div 18.5$
    (b) 37.7×479 (d) $6.34 \div 1.24$

Algebra

Collecting like terms – putting the same letters together.

e.g. $4a + 3b + a + 2c - b - 5c = \underbrace{4a + a}_{} + \underbrace{3b - b}_{} + \underbrace{2c - 5c}_{}$
$= \quad 5a \quad + \quad 2b \quad - \quad 3c$

Substitution – replacing letters by numbers.

e.g. If $a = 5$, $b = {}^-1$ and $c = 2$ then $\quad 3a \quad + \quad 2b \quad + \quad 7c$
$= 3 \times 5 + 2 \times {}^-1 + 7 \times 2$
$= \quad 15 \quad - \quad 2 \quad + \quad 14$
$= \underline{27}$

Removing brackets – multiply everything inside the bracket by the number outside.

e.g. $3 \ (x - 5) = \boxed{3 \times x} - \boxed{3 \times 5}$
$= \quad 3x \quad - \quad 15$

Making expressions – use flow diagrams.

e.g.

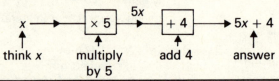

$x \longrightarrow \boxed{\times 5} \xrightarrow{\;5x\;} \boxed{+ 4} \longrightarrow 5x + 4$

think x multiply   add 4   answer
by 5

Inverses – opposites.

Following something by its inverse   e.g.
gets you back to the start.

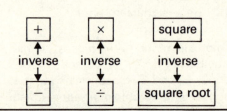

$\boxed{+}$ $\boxed{\times}$ $\boxed{\text{square}}$

inverse   inverse   inverse

$\boxed{-}$ $\boxed{\div}$ $\boxed{\text{square root}}$

Rearranging formulas – making another letter the subject of a formula.

1. Start with the new subject.
2. Draw the flow diagram.
3. Draw the inverse diagram.

e.g. Make a the subject of $P = 2a + 3b$.

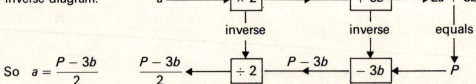

$a \longrightarrow \boxed{\times 2} \xrightarrow{\;2a\;} \boxed{+ 3b} \longrightarrow 2a + 3b$

inverse   inverse   equals

So $a = \dfrac{P - 3b}{2}$

$\dfrac{P - 3b}{2} \longleftarrow \boxed{\div 2} \xleftarrow{\;P - 3b\;} \boxed{- 3b} \longleftarrow P$

Power – tells us how many times the base is multiplied by itself.

n^4 (power, base) e.g. $n^4 = n \times n \times n \times n$ We say 'n to the power 4'.

Any base to the power 0 is 1. e.g. $n^0 = 1$, $a^0 = 1$, $x^0 = 1$.

Negative powers can be rewritten using positive powers. e.g. $n^{-4} = \dfrac{1}{n^4}$

To multiply numbers with the same base, add the powers.

e.g. $a^4 \times a^3 = a^{4+3} = a^7$

To divide numbers with the same base, subtract the powers.

e.g. $c^9 \div c^5 = c^{9-5} = c^4$

Solving equations – finding the unknown (usually x)

Simple equations

e.g. Solve $15 - 2x = 7$

use a □ $15 - \boxed{2x} = 7$

$15 - □ = 7$

find □ $15 - \boxed{8} = 7$

So $\boxed{2x} = \boxed{8}$

find x $x = 4$

Check: $15 - 2 \times 4 = 15 - 8 = 7$

Equations with brackets
1. Remove the brackets.
2. Collect any like terms.
3. Solve the equation as usual.
4. Check.

Simultaneous equations – solving two equations together.

e.g. Solve $2x - y = 5$ We choose to get rid of the y.
  and $3x + 2y = 4$ So we want $2y$ in each equation.

$2x - y = 5$ $\xrightarrow{\times 2}$ $4x - 2y = 10$
$3x + 2y = 4$ $\xrightarrow{\times 1}$ $3x + 2y = 4$

Add the new equations: $\boxed{4x + 3x} + \boxed{^-2y + 2y} = 10 + 4$

$7x \quad + \quad 0 \quad = \quad 14$

So $x = \underline{2}$

Substitute $x = 2$ in one equation to find $y = \underline{^-1}$

page **187**

1. Simplify $3x + x + 2x$.

2. Write in simplest form:
   $5x - 2x - y - 4x + 3y$

3. From $5x + 17$ take $2x - 9$.

4. If $A = 3.1 R^2$, calculate A when $R = 4$.

5. If $A = 750$ and $B = 10$, work out the value of $A \div B$.

6. $S = t(u + 2v)$. Find S if $u = 6$, $v = 2$ and $t = 3$.

7. If $x = 5$ and $y = 1$, find the value of:
   (a) $3x - 7y$ (b) $2(x + y)$ (c) $x^2 + y^2$

8. If $x = 8$ and $y = 3$, work out:
   (a) $5x - 4y$ (c) $\sqrt{2x}$
   (b) $x^2 + y^2$ (d) xy

9. If $a = 2$, $b = {}^-1$ and $c = {}^-2$, work out the value of $a^2 + b^2 - c^2$.

10. If $v^2 = 2as$:
    (a) find s if $v = 8$ and $a = 40$,
    (b) find v if $a = 16$ and $s = 10$.
    (correct to three significant figures)

11. Find the value of $9a^2 + ab - c^2$ when $a = 1$, $b = 2$ and $c = {}^-3$.

12. If $a = 1$, $b = {}^-2$ and $c = 3$, what is the value of $\dfrac{ab - c}{c + ab}$?

13. (a) Calculate the value of $\dfrac{v^2}{xy}$ when $v = 30$, $x = 10$ and $y = 360$.
    (b) Hence use your tables to find the value of angle A if $\tan A = \dfrac{v^2}{xy}$.

14. In the formula $A = P\left(1 + \dfrac{R}{100}\right)^n$, find the value of A if $P = 1000$, $R = 20$ and $n = 3$.

15. Simplify $x(3x - y) - x(x - y)$.

16. A boy said 'If you add 3 to my age and double the answer you will get 26'.

    Calling his age x, write this sentence as an equation.

17. If $y = mx + c$ rewrite the formula in the form $x =$.

18. Rearrange the formula $y = 2x + 3$ to give x in terms of y.

19. (a) $v = \pi r^2 h$.
       Make r the subject of the formula.
    (b) If $s = \frac{1}{2}at^2$, find s when $a = 12.4$ and $t = 2.34$.
       Give your answer to two significant figures.

20. What is the value of 3^4?

21. Express in simplest form:
    (a) $x^2 \times x^3$, (c) $x^9 \div x^3$,
    (b) $(x^2)^3$,   (d) $x^6 \div x^{-2}$.

22. When $2^x = \frac{1}{4}$ what is the value of x?

23. If $2^x = 16$ find the value of x.

24. (a) What is x when $5^x = 25$?
    (b) What is y when $3^4 \times 3^3 = 3^y$?
    (c) What is z when $z^5 \div z^4 = 6$?

25. Solve $x - 3 = 7$.

26. Find x if $3x - 5 = 40$.

27. Solve $2y - 7 = 1$.

28. Solve the equation $2(4x - 3) = 18$.

29. Solve the equation $2(y - 10) = 10$.

30. Solve $4(x - 3) = 12$.

31. When $x + y = 5$, what is the value of $2x + 2y - 10$?

32. When $3(x - 2) = 9$, the value of x is —.

33. Solve the simultaneous equations:
$x + y = 1$
$x - y = 7$

34. Solve the simultaneous equations:
$5x - 2y = 6$
$5x + 3y = {}^-9$

35. $x - 2 = 0$, $y + 2x = 3$, $x + y + z = 4$.
(a) Find the value of x,
(b) then find the values of y and z.

36. $x = \frac{1}{4}$, $y = \frac{1}{3}$, $z = \frac{12}{5}$.
(a) Calculate the value of xyz, giving your answer as a decimal.
(b) Calculate the value of $(x \div y) + z$, giving your answer as a mixed number.
(c) Calculate x as a percentage of y.

37. (a) (i) If $v = u + at$, find u when $v = 20$, $a = 3$ and $t = 4$.
(ii) If $v^2 = u^2 + 2as$, find s when $v = 6$, $u = 10$ and $a = {}^-2$.
(b) To find the value of a number z from two given numbers x and y, you are to double x, add y, and square the result. Write a formula for z in terms of x and y.
(c) If $y = \frac{1}{2}(x + 3)$ copy and complete this flow diagram for finding the value of y from a value of x:

$x \longrightarrow \boxed{} \longrightarrow \boxed{} \longrightarrow y$

Write a similar flow diagram to show how you would find the value of x from a value of y and use it to write a formula for x in terms of y.

38. A recommended time, T, in minutes, to roast a piece of meat of weight W pounds is 30 minutes plus 25 minutes per pound and is given by $T = 25W + 30$.
(a) Using this formula calculate how long it would take to roast a piece of meat weighing 3 pounds.

(b) What is the largest piece of meat which could be roasted in the recommended time of 3 hours?

39. (a) A simple formula used in mechanics is $v = u + at$.
(i) Find the value of v when $u = 10$, $a = \frac{1}{2}$ and $t = 8$.
(ii) Rearrange the formula to make t the subject.
(iii) Find the value of t when $v = 25$, $u = 10$ and $a = 3$.
(b) Two sizes of ice-cream cornet differ in price by 6 pence. A girl buys three large cornets and four small cornets for £2.04.
Write down two equations to represent the details in these sentences. Use x for cost, in pence, of a large cornet and y for the cost, in pence, of a small cornet.
Solve the equations to find the cost of a large cornet.

40. Given, that $L = \dfrac{C}{D^2}$, change the subject of the formula to:
(a) C, (b) D.

41. (a) Solve: $3(p - 4) - 2(p - 3) = 0$.
(b) Solve the simultaneous equations:
$3x + y = 14$
$x - 2y = 0$

42. (a) For a particular school concert 120 tickets were sold. The tickets were 40p and 60p each.
(i) If x tickets at 60p were sold, express in terms of x the number of 40p tickets sold.
(ii) Form an equation in x and solve it to find the number of 40p and 60p tickets sold, given that the total amount received from the sale of tickets was £56.40.
(b) Solve the simultaneous equations:
$3x + 2y = 8$
$2x + 3y = 2$

Percentages

% or 'per cent' means 'per 100'.

A percentage is a fraction with denominator 100.

e.g. $1\% = \dfrac{1}{100}$ $50\% = \dfrac{50}{100}$

100% is a whole one: $100\% = \dfrac{100}{100} = 1$

To find 10% of a quantity:

$100\% \longrightarrow \boxed{\div 10} \longrightarrow 10\%$

e.g. $3.8\,m \longrightarrow \boxed{\div 10} \longrightarrow 0.38\,m$

To find 1% of a quantity:

$100\% \longrightarrow \boxed{\div 10} \longrightarrow 10\% \longrightarrow \boxed{\div 10} \longrightarrow 1\%$

e.g. $4\,kg \longrightarrow \boxed{\div 10} \longrightarrow 0.4\,kg \longrightarrow \boxed{\div 10} \longrightarrow 0.04\,kg$

To find any percentage of a quantity: use 10% and 1%.

e.g. 47% $40\% \longrightarrow 4 \times 10\%$
           $7\% \longrightarrow 7 \times 1\%$

To change a fraction to a percentage: multiply by 100%.

e.g. $\dfrac{2}{5} = \dfrac{2}{\cancel{5}_1} \times \cancel{100}^{20}\% = 40\%$

To write any quantity as a percentage of another:

e.g.   100 g as a percentage of 5 kg.

1. Same unit: $5\,kg \rightarrow \begin{array}{c} 100\,g \\ 5000\,g \end{array}$

2. Write as a fraction: $\dfrac{100}{5000}$

3. Multiply by 100%: $\dfrac{\cancel{100}}{\cancel{5000}_{50}} \times \cancel{100}^{1}\% = 2\%$ (with 2 over 100)

Measures

Length

metre	m	1 km = 1000 m
kilometre	km	1 m = 100 cm
centimetre	cm	= 1000 mm
millimetre	mm	1 cm = 10 mm

Capacity

litre	l	1 l = 1000 ml
millilitre	ml	

Mass

gram	g	1 kg = 1000 g
kilogram	kg	1 t = 1000 kg
tonne	t	

Time

60 s = 1 min	1 year = 52 weeks
60 min = 1 h	= 365 days
24 h = 1 day	(366 in a leap year)

a.m. – morning,   p.m. – afternoon

24 hour times: 4 figures

$$17 \,.\, 35$$

hours after midnight   minutes past the hour

Differences between two times:

Times in the same hour: work out
   minutes from 1st to 2nd time.

Times in different hours: work out
   minutes from 1st time to next hour
   + time from next hour to 2nd time.

Average speed

$$\text{average speed} = \dfrac{\text{distance travelled}}{\text{time taken}}$$

Common units: km/h,   m/s

$$\text{distance} = \text{average speed} \times \text{time taken}$$

$$\text{time taken} = \dfrac{\text{distance}}{\text{average speed}}$$

1. Find 8% of £50.

2. Find 30% of £160.

3. What is 8% of £25 000?

4. What is 15% of £250?

5. What is $9\frac{1}{2}$% of £200?

6. Calculate 40% of 80.

7. What is 5% of £35.80?

8. A fat man must lose 20% in weight. If he weighs 140 kg now, how many kg must he lose?

9. (a) Work out 10% of £60.
   (b) The price of a refrigerator is increased by 10%. The price before the increase was £60. What is the new price?

10. (a) In a school of 300 children 7% are absent. How many children are absent?
    (b) Reduce 400 by 5%.

11. In a school of 1260 pupils, 1050 pupils are present.
    (a) How many pupils are absent?
    (b) What percentage of the pupils is absent?

12. Express $\frac{3}{8}$ as a percentage.

13. What percentage is 4 cm of 2 m?

14. If 25% of a number is 26, what is the number?

15. (a) In England during 1980 there were 6600 road deaths. 40% of this total involved pedestrians and cyclists. Calculate the number of cyclists and pedestrians killed in 1980.
    (b) Of the 80 000 people who were seriously injured, 23 200 were pedestrians and cyclists. Express this number as a percentage of the total injured.

16. How many cm³ make 1 litre?

17. How many:
    (a) millimetres in 1 metre?
    (b) square centimetres in 1 square metre?
    (c) pence in £6.49?
    (d) litres in 4300 millimetres?
    (e) milligrams in 3.4 grams?

18. The following is an extract from a railway timetable for three trains A, B, C.

Train	Birmingham (Depart)	Solihull (Depart)	Leamington Spa (Arrive)
A	09 28	09 44	10 02
B	12 18	12 34	12 53
C	19 25	19 41	19 58

    (a) If it runs to time, how long does train A take to travel from Solihull to Leamington Spa?
    (b) Train B is 2 minutes late leaving Birmingham but it arrives at Leamington Spa 3 minutes early. How long does train B actually take to travel from Birmingham to Leamington Spa?
    (c) Owing to signals failure, train C is 26 minutes late leaving Solihull and 35 minutes late arriving at Leamington Spa. How long does train C actually take to travel to Leamington Spa?

19. A car travels 140 km in 2 h 20 min. What is its average speed in km/h?

20. If a man walks 1500 m in 20 minutes, how many km will he have walked in 60 minutes if he keeps going at the same rate?

21. The distance from Leicester to Edinburgh is 455 km.
    (a) How long will it take a motorist to make the journey if he travels at an average speed of 70 km/h?
    (b) At what average speed must he drive to complete the journey in 7 hours?

Money

Two ways to write our money correctly: £ sign only or p sign only

£2.51½ or 251½ p

Do *not* mix the two!

Foreign currency

A country's money is its currency. Sterling is Britain's currency.

Exchange rates tell you how much of each currency you get for £1.

To change sterling to foreign currency: multiply by the exchange rate.

To change foreign currency to sterling: use exchange rate to find out how much sterling you get for 1 unit first.

Best buy

To compare sizes: either find the cost of 1 unit (e.g. 1 oz or 100 g) for each size, or find out how much a penny buys.

Rates

– tax on property, paid to local councils. Water rates are worked out the same way.

rates due = rateable value × rate in the £

council's total rates = total rateable value × rate in the £

rate in the £ = amount needed ÷ total rateable value

'Home bills'

Electricity, gas and telephone bills are sent quarterly (every 3 months).

You pay: a standing charge (or rental) + (number of units × cost per unit).

On some bills (e.g. telephone) you pay VAT (Value Added Tax). This is a percentage of the total.

Profit or loss

– difference between selling price and cost price.

$$\text{percentage profit (or loss)} = \frac{\text{profit (or loss)}}{\text{cost price}} \times 100\%$$

Simple Interest

Simple Interest is paid or withdrawn each year (annually).

The rate of interest tells you the percentage of the investment paid each year.

To find Simple Interest: work out the interest for 1 year, then multiply by the number of years.

1. Write in figures the amount: 'Thirteen pounds, seven and a half pence'.

2. Add £3.57, £38.06, £2.17 and £1.15.

3. Find the value of £27.02 − £14.27.

4. Calculate the cost of 17 articles at 43p each.

5. (a) Find the total cost of postage for 3 parcels at 76p each and 12 letters at $13\frac{1}{2}$p each.
   (b) How much change is there out of £5?

6. A record player can be bought for a deposit of £12.75 and 5 monthly payments of £3.25. What is the total amount paid if it is bought this way?

7. A packet of crisps costs 12p. What is the total cost of two dozen packets?

8. Calculate the total cost of six garden chairs at £8.75 each and two reclining chairs at £29.95 each.

9. Time and a half is £2.25 an hour. What is the basic rate per hour?

10. Eggs are 60p a dozen. How much will 5 eggs cost?

11. What is the maximum number of 8p stamps which can be bought for £2.50?

12. When a family sells a car for £450 they lose £150 on what they paid for it. How much did it cost them?

13. A travel allowance of 12.7p per km is paid to a teacher. How much does he get for a journey of 7 km? (Answer to the nearest whole p.)

14. Rates are 75p in the £1. A house has a rateable value of £300.
    (a) How much does the householder pay in rates each year?
    (b) 60% of the rates are spent on education.
    How much does the householder pay towards the cost of education?

15. As a result of selling a carpet for £22.50, I suffered a loss of £2.75. How much did I pay for the carpet?

16. The price of a meal is £3.00 + 15% VAT. What is the total cost?

17. A record player is marked in a shop at £108.
    (a) This price includes Value Added Tax (VAT) at $12\frac{1}{2}$% of the basic price. Calculate the amount of VAT paid on this record player.
    (b) For cash, the shopkeeper allows a discount of 10% of the marked price. Calculate the price paid for the record player for a cash sale.

18. Find, in its simplest term, what fraction 40p is of £1.

19. Express £1.85 as a percentage of £2.50.

20. Calculate $28\frac{1}{2}$% of £600.

21. A spindrier which cost £48 was sold for £18. Calculate the percentage loss.

22. (a) An article costs a shopkeeper 80p. He sells it to make a profit of 30% on his cost price. What is his selling price?
    (b) The shopkeeper then takes 4p off his selling price. What is his percentage profit now?

23. If you borrow money using an Access Card you pay interest at the rate of 2% per month. How much interest would you pay if you borrowed £15 for 1 month?

24. Find the Simple Interest on £240 for 3 years at 12%.

25. A salesman was paid a basic wage of £25 a week plus a commission of 15% on all sales above £30.
Find:
   (a) his commission in a week when his sales were £270,
   (b) his wage in a week when his sales were £420,
   (c) his sales in a week when his wage was £127.

26. A man normally works 38 hours per week and is paid at the basic rate of £2.60 per hour. For any overtime that he works he is paid one and a half times the basic hourly rate. How much does he earn in a week, if he works
   (a) a normal 38 hours,
   (b) 42 hours in the week?

27. The exchange rate in Paris is 8.91 francs to the £ and in Frankfurt it is 3.81 marks to the £.
   (a) A man changes £200 into francs in Paris. How many francs does he get?
   (b) After spending all his francs, he changes £136 into marks in Frankfurt. How many marks does he get? Give your answer to the nearest mark.
   (c) He spends 250 marks and then changes the rest back into pounds. How many pounds does he get? Give your answer to the nearest pound.

28. (a) The selling price (excluding VAT) of a freezer of capacity 0.5 m³ is £100, and of a freezer of capacity 0.8 m³ is £140.
      (i) Work out the cost per 0.1 m³ capacity of each freezer. State which is the 'better buy'.
      (ii) Add VAT at 15% to each price, to find the total cost of each freezer.
   (b) A family decides to buy a freezer on Hire Purchase. The cash price is £116.48. They pay a deposit of $12\frac{1}{2}$% of the cash price, and then 12 monthly instalments of £9.70.
      Work out:
      (i) the total Hire Purchase price,

   (ii) the difference between the Hire Purchase price and the cash price.

29. In a certain Borough in 1978 the rates were 55p in the £.
   (a) What rates were paid by a householder whose house had a rateable value of £240?
   (b) What was the rateable value of a house for which the rates payable were £165?
   The total rateable value of the Borough is £1 500 000. For 1979 it was estimated that an extra £180 000 would be needed from the rates to meet increased expenditure on local services.
   (c) By how much in the £ were rates increased to raise this extra amount?

30. (a) Below is an extract from an electricity bill. Meter 2 is for night storage heaters.

	Readings		Units used	Pence per unit	Amount (nearest p)
	Present	Previous			
Meter 1	28497	27126		4.20	
Meter 2		20619		2.03	£2.84
Quarterly standing charge £..........					£9.70

   Calculate:
   (i) the number of units used on each meter during this quarter (answer to the nearest whole unit).
   (ii) the present reading on Meter 2 (answer to the nearest whole unit).
   (iii) the total charge for the quarter (answer to the nearest p).
   (b) The total for a gas bill is £30.25. The first 52 units used cost 21.9p each. All units used after the first 52 cost 19.3p each. There is a standing charge of £4. Calculate the total number of units used. Give your answer to the nearest whole unit.

Angles

Angle

– an amount of turn.

Measured in degrees (°)

1 turn 360°	$\frac{1}{4}$ turn 90°	$\frac{1}{2}$ turn 180°	$\frac{3}{4}$ turn 270°
4 right angles	1 right angle	2 right angles	3 right angles

clockwise ↻   anticlockwise ↺

Names of angles

acute

smaller than 90°

right

90°

obtuse

bigger than 90°,
smaller than 180°.

reflex

bigger than 180°,
smaller than 360°.

Related angles

straight line 180°

$a + b = 180°$

full turn 360°

$c + d = 360°$

right angle 90°

$e + f = 90°$

opposite angles equal

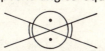

Angles and parallels

When parallel lines are cut by another line,
then:

1. Corresponding angles
   are equal
   (look for the F shape).

2. Alternate angles
   are equal
   (look for the Z shape).

Navigating

Bearing:

Measured: in degrees,
   from North,
   turning clockwise.

It must have 3 figures.

Compass directions:

NW N NE
W ——— E
SW S SE

A course gives: a bearing
   and a distance.

To do a scale drawing of a course:

1. Do rough sketch first.
2. Choose suitable scale (if not a given).
3. For each stage of course:
   (a) draw N line,
   (b) draw 'bearing angle' with protractor,
   (c) work out 'plan length' using scale,
   (d) measure length along drawn direction.

Angles in circles

Angles in the same
segment are equal.

An angle in a semicircle
is a right angle.

The angle at the centre
is twice the angle
at the circumference.

Cyclic quadrilateral – four vertices
on the same circle.

Opposite angles of a
cyclic quadrilateral
add up to 180°.

$\angle A + \angle C = 180°$ $\angle B + \angle D = 180°$

1. (a) When a clock shows a time of 5 o'clock, how many degrees are there between the minute hand and the hour hand?

   (b) If the hour hand of a clock has turned 270° how much time has elapsed?

2. (a) Calculate the size, in degrees, of
   (i) the *larger* angle between the hands of a clock at 10 am
   (ii) the *smaller* angle between the bearings 060° and 270°.

   (b) ABC is a straight line; the size of ∠ABD is greater than the size of ∠CBD by 90°.
   Calculate the size of ∠CBD.

3. When the minute hand of a clock turns through 240°, through what angle does the hour hand turn?

4. The time is 5 past 4. What will it be when the minute hand of the clock has turned through a further 90°?

5.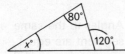

   From the diagram above, calculate the value of *x*.

6. This is a square.
   How big is the marked angle?

7. AB is a straight line. Calculate the value of *x*.

   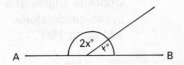

8. If ∠AOB = 125°, ∠BOC = 150°, calculate the size of ∠AOC.

9.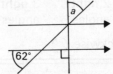

   In the diagram above, ABC is a straight line. Calculate the value of *x*.

10.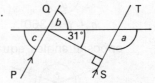

   From the diagram, calculate the size of the angle marked *a*.

11.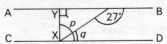

   In the figure, lines PQ and ST are parallel. Calculate the sizes of angles *a*, *b* and *c*.

12. In this figure AB is parallel to CD and XY is perpendicular to AB.

   Calculate the angles marked *p* and *q*.

13. North

   What is the bearing of A from B?

14.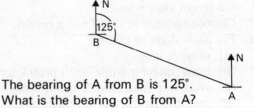

   The bearing of A from B is 125°.
   What is the bearing of B from A?

15. If the bearing of X from Y is 140°, write down the bearing of Y from X.

16.

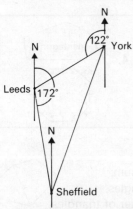

The sketch map above shows the relative positions of York, Sheffield and Leeds. Using the information given on the diagram calculate:
(a) the bearing of Leeds from York,
(b) the bearing of Leeds from Sheffield.

17. (This Question may be done either by calculation or scale drawing using 1 cm to 1 km.)
A man walks 6 km from A in a direction of 045°. He then changes his direction, and walks 8 km in a direction of 135°. How far is he now from A?

18. PQRS is a cyclic quadrilateral. Angle P = 75°. Calculate the value of angle R.

19. From the diagram calculate:
(a) the size of angle x,
(b) the size of angle y.

20. P, Q and R are points on the circumference of a circle with centre O. Calculate the size of angle POR.

21. Find the sizes of the angles shown by the letters p, q, r, s in the following diagrams.
(a)

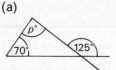

(b)

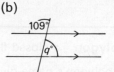

(c)

(d)

O is the centre of the circle.

22.

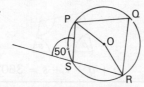

In the figure, O is the centre of the circle and angle PST = 50°.
Find: (a) angle PSR,
(b) angle PQR,
(c) reflex angle POR.

23.

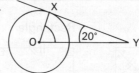

In the above diagram XY is a tangent to the circle centre O. If angle XYO = 20° find the size, in degrees, of the angle XOY.

24.

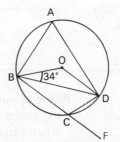

O is the centre of the circle ABCD, and angle OBD = 34°. Calculate the size of:
(a) angle BOD,
(b) angle BAD,
(c) angle DCF.

Shapes

Polygon – a closed flat shape made from straight lines.

A polygon's name gives its number of sides (or angles): tri – 3, quad – 4, pent – 5, hex – 6, hept – 7, oct – 8, non – 9, dec – 10, poly – many.

Regular polygon – all its angles the same size and all its sides the same length.

pentagon

Angles in polygons

Triangle
angle sum: 180°

Quadrilateral
angle sum: 360°

Any polygon
To find the angle sum:
1. split it into triangles,
2. count the number of triangles,
3. use the angle sum of a triangle.

$a + b + c = 180°$ $p + q + r + s = 360°$

Triangles

Equilateral

3 equal sides
3 equal angles
(60°)

Isosceles

2 equal sides
opposite
2 equal angles

Right-angled

1 angle
= 90°

Quadrilaterals

Square

Rectangle

Parallelogram

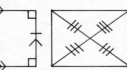
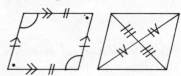

Rhombus

Trapezium

Kite

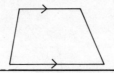
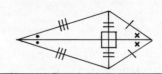

Symmetry
Axis of symmetry
– divides a shape into two
  balanced halves.
  Each half is a mirror
  image of the other

Point symmetry
– the shape looks the same
  when rotated half a turn
  (180°).

Rotational symmetry
– shape looks the same in
  several different positions when
  rotated 1 turn (360°).

Order: number of times
shape fits onto itself in
1 turn.

axis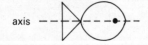

top

do↑

1. In the diagram below, triangle ABC is isosceles and AB = AC. Calculate the size of angle ABC.

2.

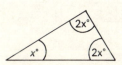

What is the value of *x*?

3. Calculate the size of the angle marked *q* in the diagram below.

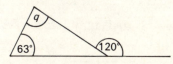

4. (a) ABC is a triangle. CAD is a straight line. Calculate the size of angle ABC.

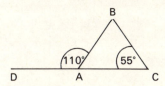

(b) The two base angles of an isosceles triangle are each 65°. What is the size of the third angle?

5.

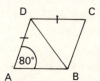

ABCD is a parallelogram in which AD = DC, angle BAD = 80°. Find the sizes of
(a) ∠DCB, (b) ∠ABD, (c) ∠ADC.

6. Each interior angle of a regular polygon is 135°.
How many sides does the polygon have?

7. What is the size of each interior angle of a regular five-sided polygon?

8. Two angles of a triangle are 35° and 40°. What is the size of the third angle?

9. (a) Four angles of a pentagon are 120°, 50°, 150° and 150°. Calculate the size of the fifth angle.
   (b) A regular polygon has an exterior angle of 10°.
      (i) Determine the size of an interior angle.
      (ii) Find the number of sides of the polygon.
   (c) How many tiles, each 50 cm by 50 cm are needed to completely cover a floor of size 5 m by 4 m?

10.

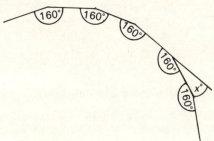

The diagram shows six sides of a regular polygon, each angle of which is 160°. One of its exterior angles is marked *x*°.
(a) Find *x*.
(b) Find the number of sides of the polygon.
(c) Can polygons of this shape be used to tessellate a surface?

11.

SWEBH

In which of the above letters:
(a) is there just one axis of symmetry?
(b) are there two axes of symmetry?
(c) is there rotational symmetry of order 2?

12. Draw all the lines of symmetry in the two diagrams below.

13. This rectangle has two axes of symmetry.
    (a) Mark them on the diagram.
    (b) If another rectangle is found to have four axes of symmetry, what more exact name can it be given?

14. (a) How many lines of symmetry has the rectangle PQRS?

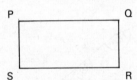

    (b) What is the order of rotational symmetry of the figure ABCD?

15. Draw a quadrilateral which has only one line of symmetry. Indicate the line of symmetry as a broken (dotted) line.

16.

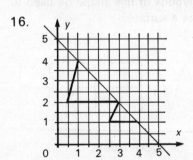

Complete the figure above so that it is symmetrical about the line $x + y = 5$.

17.

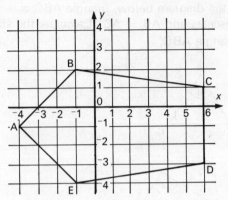

The diagram above represents a pentagon ABCDE.
(a) Draw a dotted line on the diagram to show the axis of symmetry.
(b) What is the equation of the line which you have drawn in part (a)?
(c) Calculate the gradient of the line AE.

18.

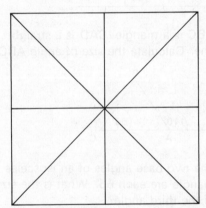

Copy the above grid three times onto your paper and shade four triangles in each of your copies so that the resultant figures have:
(a) two lines of symmetry and order of rotational symmetry 2,
(b) no line symmetry and order of rotational symmetry 4,
(c) one line of symmetry and order of rotational symmetry 1.

Right angled triangles

Pythagoras' Theorem

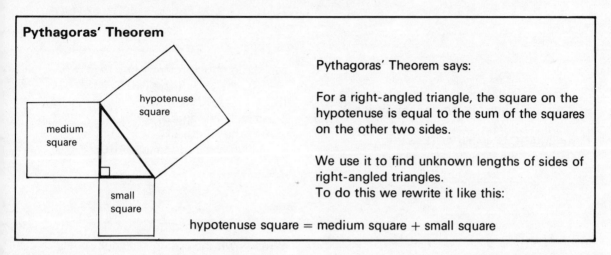

Pythagoras' Theorem says:

For a right-angled triangle, the square on the hypotenuse is equal to the sum of the squares on the other two sides.

We use it to find unknown lengths of sides of right-angled triangles.
To do this we rewrite it like this:

hypotenuse square = medium square + small square

Tangent (tan)

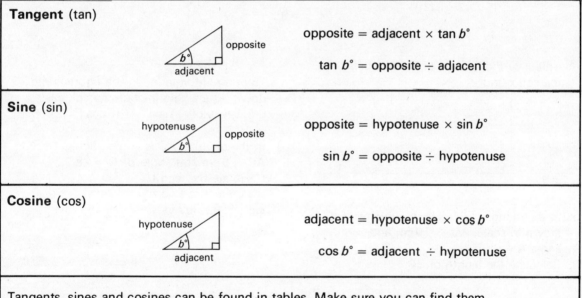

opposite = adjacent × tan $b°$

tan $b°$ = opposite ÷ adjacent

Sine (sin)

opposite = hypotenuse × sin $b°$

sin $b°$ = opposite ÷ hypotenuse

Cosine (cos)

adjacent = hypotenuse × cos $b°$

cos $b°$ = adjacent ÷ hypotenuse

Tangents, sines and cosines can be found in tables. Make sure you can find them.
If you know the tangent, sine or cosine of an angle, you can find the angle.
'Angles from tables' (pages 58–59) shows you how.

Solving problems
1. Draw a clear diagram.
2. Pick out the right-angled triangle you are going to use.
   Label the sides: 'hypotenuse', 'opposite', 'adjacent'.
3. Decide whether you are going to use tan, sin or cos.
4. Write the chosen formula.
5. Work it out.

Angles of elevation and depression

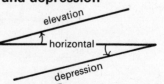

1. Find the length of the side marked R in centimetres.

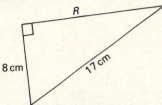

2. A rectangle has sides of length 6 cm and 8 cm. Calculate the length of a diagonal.

3. Angle ABC = angle ACD = 90°. Calculate the lengths AC and CD.

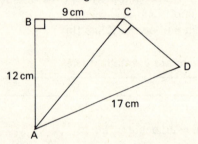

4. Calculate the lengths of the two sides marked x and y.

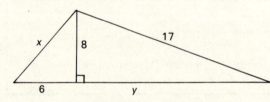

5. In the triangle ABC below, which is not drawn to scale, AC = 10 cm and angle A = 30°.
Calculate the length of CB.

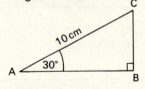

6. Use tables to find the size of the angle marked x.

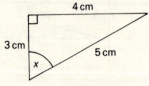

7. The figure shows a right-angled triangle ABC. Angle BAC is 38° and angle ACB is 90°.

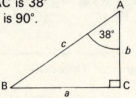

(a) Write down in terms of a, b, c:
(i) cos 38°, (ii) sin 38°.
(b) If $c = 13$ cm, calculate correct to 2 significant figures:
(i) the length BC,
(ii) the area of triangle ABC.

8.

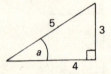

Write down the cosine of angle a.

9.

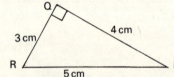

From the information in the figure, write down, as a single fraction in each case, the values of (a) sin P, (b) cos P, (c) tan R.

10. In the diagram AC is perpendicular to BC. AC = 8 cm and angle BAC = 28°. Calculate the length BC correct to two significant figures.

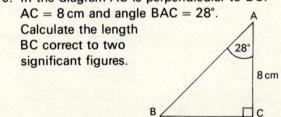

11. Work out the lengths marked x and y:

(a)   (b)

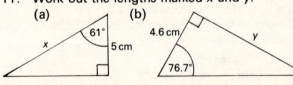

12.

Calculate the length of the missing side of this triangle.

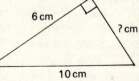

13.

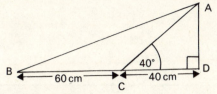

In the figure, BC = 60 cm, CD = 40 cm and angle ACD = 40°. Calculate:
(a) the length of AD,
(b) the angle ABD.

14.

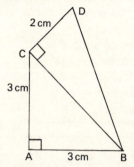

In the diagram shown the lengths are as marked. Calculate:
(a) the size of angle CBA,
(b) the length of CB,
(c) the size of angle DBC.

15.

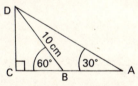

In the figure, angle CBD = 60°, angle CAD = 30°, angle DCB is a right angle and length BD = 10 cm. Calculate:
(a) angle BDA,
(b) length CD correct to 2 significant figures,
(c) length AC correct to 2 significant figures.

16. ABCD is a rectangle BE and DF are perpendicular to AC. AB is 12 cm. AD is 7 cm. Calculate:
(a) the size of angle ACD,
(b) the length of DF,
(c) the length of AE.

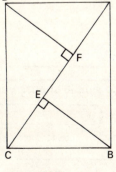

17.

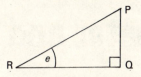

In the above diagram angle *e* is the angle of elevation from R to P. If *e* = 55° what will be the angle of depression from P to R?

18.

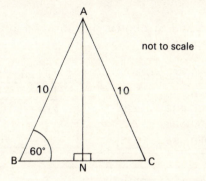

not to scale

In the triangle ABC, AB = AC = 10 cm, angle ABC = 60° and AN is perpendicular to BC. Calculate:
(a) angle BAC,
(b) the length of BC,
(c) the length of AN.

19.

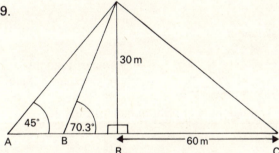

In the above diagram (which is not drawn to scale), AC is a horizontal straight line at ground level. TR is a vertical tower 30 metres high; RC = 60 metres. From a point A the angle of elevation of T is 45°. At a point B the angle of elevation is 70° 18′ (70.3°). Calculate:
 (i) angle ATR,
 (ii) the length of AR in metres,
(iii) angle BTR,
(iv) the length of BR in metres,
 (v) the angle of elevation of T from C.

Perimeter and area

Perimeter
– 'total distance round'.

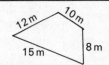

When adding lengths, they must be in the same unit.

Units of length

metre	m
kilometre	km
centimetre	cm
millimetre	mm

Conversion table

1 km = 1000 m
1 m = 100 cm
= 1000 mm
1 cm = 10 mm

Area
– 'surface covered'.

When calculating areas, all the measurements must be in the same unit.

Area is measured in square units:
square millimetres	mm^2
square centimetres	cm^2
square metres	m^2
square kilometres	km^2

Areas of simple shapes

Rectangle

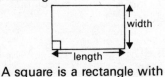

area of rectangle
= length × width

A square is a rectangle with length and width the same

Parallelogram

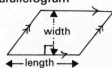

area of parallelogram
= length × width

The width is at right angles to the length.

Triangle

area of triangle
= $\frac{1}{2}$ × base × height

The height is at right angles to the base.

Trapezium

area of trapezium
= area of triangle A
+ area of triangle B

Circle

Circumference (c)
$c = \pi d$ or $c = 2\pi r$
Rearranged:
$d = c \div \pi$ or $r = c \div 2\pi$

Area (A)
$A = \pi r^2$
Rearranged:
$r = \sqrt{A \div \pi}$

Approximations for π are 3.14 (to 2 d.p.) or $3\frac{1}{7} = \frac{22}{7}$.

Areas of other shapes – if you can, split them into simple shapes you know.

e.g.
4 rectangles

rectangles
'hole'
'whole – hole'

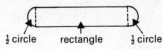

$\frac{1}{2}$ circle   rectangle $\frac{1}{2}$ circle

circles

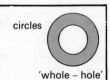

'whole – hole'

1. A square has an area of 81 cm². Calculate its perimeter.

2. The area of a square is 144 cm². What is its perimeter in cm?

3. (a)

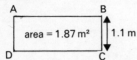

   If the area of the rectangle ABCD is 1.87 m² and the width BC is 1.1 m, what is the length AB?
   (b) Express the area 1.87 m² in cm².

4. Calculate the perimeter of this parallelogram.

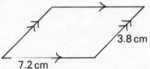

5. Express in their simplest form in terms of a and b:
   (i) the perimeter of the figure,
   (ii) the area of the figure.

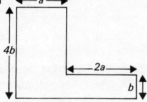

6. In triangle ABC, $AB = (2x - 1)$ cm, $BC = (x - 2)$ cm and $AC = 2BC$. Find:
   (a) the length of AC in terms of x,
   (b) the perimeter of triangle ABC in terms of x. (Answer in simplest form),
   (c) the value of x if the perimeter of triangle ABC is 33 cm.

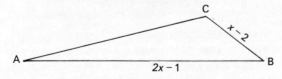

7. Calculate the area of this triangle:

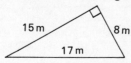

8. Calculate the areas of the following:
   (a) a rectangular sheet of paper 29.7 cm by 21.0 cm,
   (b) a circle with radius 4 cm (use $\pi = 3.14$),
   (c) this triangle:

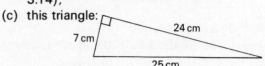

9. A rectangular piece of cardboard 10 cm by 6 cm has equal squares of side 2 cm cut out at two corners. The final shape is shown in the diagram.
   Calculate:
   (a) the perimeter of the shape,
   (b) the area of the shape.

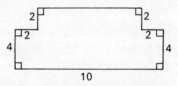

10. Calculate the areas of the following shapes:
    (a) triangle
    (b) parallelogram
    (c) trapezium

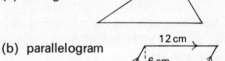
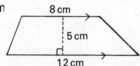

11. A square PQRS is drawn inside a square ABCD of side 7 cm as shown. Calculate:
    (a) the area of the square ABCD, (b) the perimeter of the square PQRS, (c) the length of the line PR, correct to one decimal place.

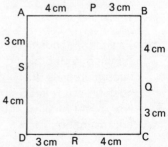

12.

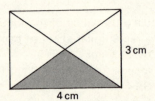

3 cm

4 cm

This is a rectangle.
Calculate the area of the shaded triangle.

13.

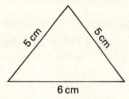

5 cm   5 cm

6 cm

What is the area of the given isosceles triangle in cm²?

14. Calculate the area of an isosceles triangle with two equal sides of length 5 cm and the third side of length 8 cm.

15. Taking π as approximately 3, what is the approximate circumference of a circle whose diameter is 25 cm?

16. I have a circular lawn in my garden which has a radius of $3\frac{1}{2}$ metres. What is its area? (Take $\pi = \frac{22}{7}$)

17.

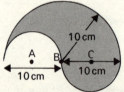

A   B   C
10 cm   10 cm

10 cm

A, B and C are the centres of the semicircles shown in the diagram.
For the shaded region calculate:
(a) the perimeter,
(b) the area.
(Take $\pi = 3.14$.)

18. Five circular cushion covers are to be trimmed with braiding around their circumferences. If the diameter of each cushion cover is 35 cm, calculate the length of braiding required. Use $\frac{22}{7}$ as an approximation for π.

19. A circle has a diameter of 100 cm. If its diameter is increased by 2 cm, by what length has its circumference increased? Use 3.14 as an approximation for π.

20.

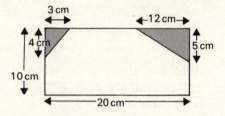

3 cm   ←12 cm→

4 cm   5 cm

10 cm

20 cm

The shaded pieces are cut away from a rectangular piece of card 20 cm by 10 cm. Find the perimeter of the shape that is left.

21.

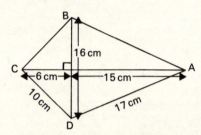

B

16 cm

C   A
6 cm   15 cm

10 cm   17 cm

D

Calculate the area of the kite ABCD.

22. $\pi = 3.14$ **must** be used in this question.
A circle has a circumference of 100 cm.
(a) Calculate its area. Answer to the nearest whole cm².
(b) Calculate the circumference of a second circle whose area is four times that of the first circle. Answer to nearest whole cm.

23. The diagram, **not** drawn to scale, represents a metal plate in the form of a rectangle of sides 40 cm by 68 cm, and a semicircle of diameter 40 cm.
Calculate
(i) the perimeter,
(ii) the area of the plate.
(Take π to be 3.14.)

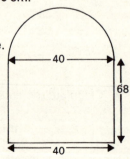

40

68

40

Solids

Volume
– 'space occupied'.

Measured in cubic units:
e.g.   cubic millimetres (mm^3),
        cubic centimetres (cm^3),
        cubic metres (m^3).

When calculating volumes, all the measurements must be in the same unit.

Surface area
– total area of the outside.

Measured in square units:
e.g. mm^2, cm^2, m^2, km^2.
When calculating areas, all the measurements must be in the same unit.

Easily worked out if a net of the solid is drawn.

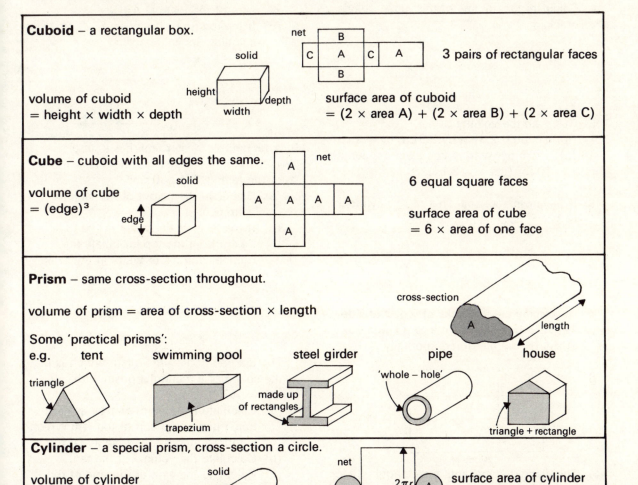

Cuboid – a rectangular box.

net

3 pairs of rectangular faces

solid

height / depth / width

volume of cuboid
= height × width × depth

surface area of cuboid
= (2 × area A) + (2 × area B) + (2 × area C)

Cube – cuboid with all edges the same.

net

volume of cube
= (edge)³

solid

edge

6 equal square faces

surface area of cube
= 6 × area of one face

Prism – same cross-section throughout.

volume of prism = area of cross-section × length

Some 'practical prisms':
e.g.   tent   swimming pool   steel girder   pipe   house

triangle

trapezium

made up
of rectangles

'whole – hole'

cross-section

A

length

triangle + rectangle

Cylinder – a special prism, cross-section a circle.

volume of cylinder
= area of circle × length

solid

A

length

$A = \pi r^2$

net

A $2\pi r$ A

←length→

surface area of cylinder
= area of 2 circles
    + area of rectangle

1. (a) How many faces has a cube?
   The total surface area of a certain cube is 150 cm². Find:
   (b) the length of an edge of the cube,
   (c) how many such cubes can fit into a box 5 m × 2 m × 1½ m.

2. A box (with a lid) is made of wood 1 cm thick. The outside measurements are 10 cm by 12 cm by 14 cm. What is the volume of the *inside* of the box?

3. Find the volume of a matchbox which measures 5 cm by 2 cm by 1½ cm.

4. Calculate the volume of this rectangular block.

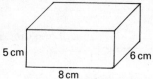

5. Calculate the volume of:
   (a) a cuboid 2.5 cm by 3.9 cm by 4 cm,
   (b) a cylinder with radius 3 cm and length 10 cm (use π = 3.14).

6. If the cross-sectional area of this cylinder is 3 cm², calculate its volume.

7. How many cubic blocks of wood of side 2 cm can be made to fit into a cubic box of side 10 cm measured internally?

8.

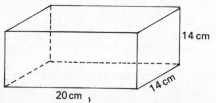

The diagram represents a rectangular block of wood, 20 cm long, with a square end of side 14 cm. Find, in cm³, the volume of the largest solid cylinder which can be cut from this block. ($\pi = \frac{22}{7}$.)

9. (a) Find the length of a side of a square which has the same area as a rectangle 75 cm long and 48 cm wide.
   (b) The figure shows a solid cylinder which is 40 cm long, its uniform cross-section being a circle of diameter 20 cm. Taking π as 3.14, find the volume of the cylinder.

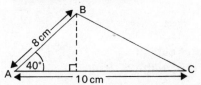

10. A prism has a triangular cross-section as shown.
    (a) Calculate the perpendicular height and area of the triangle ABC.
    (b) If the length of the prism is 24 cm, calculate its volume.

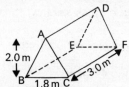

11. A rectangular water tank has a base 1.20 m long and 95 cm wide. The volume of the tank is 855 000 cm³.
    (a) Calculate the height of the tank in centimetres.
    (b) If the level of the water in the tank is 24 cm from the top, calculate the number of litres of water in the tank.

12.

The diagram represents a tent which is in the shape of a triangular prism with AB = AC.
    (a) Calculate the area of canvas used in constructing the end of the tent which is represented by the triangle DEF.
    (b) Calculate the volume of the tent.
    (c) Calculate the area of the side of the tent which is represented by the rectangle ADFC.
    Give your answer correct to the nearest 0.1 m².

13. Alloy rods at a factory were cast from a molten ingot in the shape of the cuboid shown below.

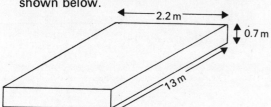

(a) Calculate the volume of the ingot.
(b) Where 1 m³ of alloy weighs 250 kg, find the weight of the above ingot.
(c) Rods cast from the ingot are cylindrical, with diameter 14 cm and length 130 cm. Find the volume of one such rod. (Use $\pi = \frac{22}{7}$.)

14. The diagram shows a pile of wooden fencing posts each with a rectangular cross-section and of length 2 metres.

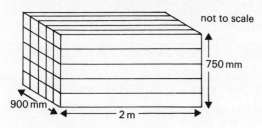

not to scale

(a) Calculate the total length of all the posts.
(b) Calculate the area of the cross-section of each post. Give your answer in mm².
(c) Calculate the volume of the pile in m³.

15. (a) A cuboid is 9 cm long, 6.5 cm wide, and 4 cm high.
   Work out:
   (i) the total length of all twelve edges,
   (ii) the total area of all six faces,
   (iii) the volume.

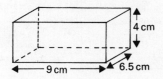

(b)

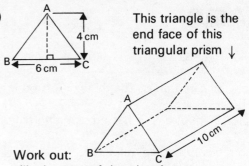

This triangle is the end face of this triangular prism ↓

Work out:
(i) the area of the triangle,
(ii) the volume of the prism.

16. The diagram below represents a steel bar which has the same cross-section throughout its length. All the measurements given are in mm.

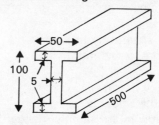

Calculate:
(a) the area of cross-section, leaving your answer in mm²,
(b) the volume of the steel bar, leaving your answer in mm³.

17. The diagram shows a closed box of uniform cross-section with the given dimensions.
AB = 10 cm,   CD = 8 cm,   ED = 26 cm,
AE = 20 cm,   DF = 40 cm.
(a) Calculate the area ABCDE.
(b) Calculate the volume of the box in cubic centimetres.
(c) Calculate the length BC.
(d) Calculate the total surface area of the box in square centimetres.

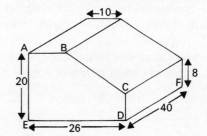

Ratio

Ratios compare things. The things must be in the same units: e.g. 20 m : 15 m

Simplest form of a ratio has no common factors except 1: e.g. 4 : 3

Using ratios to find an unknown:
   (a) start with the ratio you know:

                                      10 : 15

                                        ÷ 5

   (b) change to its simplest form: 2 : 3

                                                $3 \times ? = 24$

   (c) change to the ratio you want: ? : 24

To divide an amount in a given ratio, work out:
   (a) the total number of 'shares' (or parts)
        from the ratio,
   (b) what one 'share' (or part) is,
   (c) the amounts for the ratio.

To alter a recipe or mixture:
   (a) work out the amounts for one,
   (b) then multiply by the number needed.

Similar shapes and solids

Two shapes (or solids) are similar if one is an enlargement (or reduction) of the other.

To enlarge (or reduce) a shape, multiply all its lengths by the scale factor.

$$\text{scale factor} = \frac{\text{length on enlargement}}{\text{matching length on original}}$$

Areas of similar shapes:
            area factor = (scale factor)^2
    area of enlargement = area factor × area of original

Volumes of similar solids:
          volume factor = (scale factor)^3
   volume of enlargement = volume factor × volume of original

A scale model is similar to the real object.
Scales can be written in different ways: e.g. 1 cm represents 500 cm ← same units
                             or $\frac{1}{500}$ or 1 : 500 or 1 to 500
                             or 1 cm represents 5 m ← different units

1. Express each as a ratio in its simplest form:
   (a) 20 to 35,
   (b) 18 mm to 36 cm.

2. On a plan drawn to a scale of 1 : 25, a corridor is 24 cm long. What is the length of the corridor in metres?

3. £56 is shared in the ratio 3 : 5. How much is the larger share?

4. An amount of £8.40 is divided into two parts in the ratio 4 : 3. By how much does the larger part exceed the smaller?

5. A rally car carries 112 litres of petrol distributed in two tanks in the ratio 3 : 4. Find the amount of petrol in the larger tank.

6. (a) Divide £10 between two men, in the ratio 1 : 3.
   (b) If five pencils cost $22\frac{1}{2}$p, work out the cost of (i) one pencil (ii) twelve pencils.

7. A sum of money was divided between Julie and Joanne. Julie received £3.20 and Joanne received £4. In what ratio was the money divided? Express your answer in the simplest possible form.

8. (a) Share £350 in the ratio 3 : 4.
   (b) In a sale, a washing machine marked at £160 is sold at a discount of 20%. What is the sale price?

9. A certain machine can produce 240 identical articles every hour.
   (a) How many such articles can be produced by 5 of these machines in 4 hours?
   (b) How many of these machines are needed to produce 1440 of these articles in 20 minutes?

10. The votes cast for three candidates in an election were in the ratio 8 : 4 : 3. The winner obtained 28 000 votes.

(a) What was the total number of votes cast for all the candidates?
(b) If the information is represented on a pie chart, what is the angle at the centre of the circle for the candidate who came second?
(c) What percentage of the total vote was obtained by the bottom candidate?

11.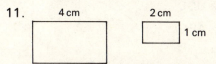

These rectangles are similar. Find the area of the larger rectangle.

12. These two triangles are similar. Calculate the length of the side marked with a question mark.

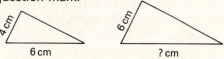

13.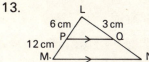

Using the diagram, calculate
(a) the length of LN,
(b) the area of triangle LPQ when the area of triangle LMN is 18 cm².

14. The area of a rectangle is 10 cm². If the length and breadth are each trebled, what would be the area of the new rectangle?

15. In the diagram ABCD, LMNP are squares. LM = 3AB.
   (a) How many times greater is the perimeter of LMNP than the perimeter of ABCD?
   (b) How many times greater is the area of LMNP than the area of ABCD?
   (c) If the area of triangle AOB is 4.2 cm² what is the area of triangle LOM?

16. In the diagram, angle OBA = angle OCD = 90° and OB = BC.
Write down the value of each of the following fractions:

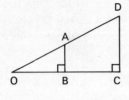

(a) $\dfrac{AB}{DC}$

(b) $\dfrac{\text{area OBA}}{\text{area OCD}}$

(c) $\dfrac{\text{area ABCD}}{\text{area OCD}}$

17.

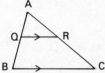

In triangle ABC, QR is parallel to BC.
If AQ:AB = 1:3, complete the following ratios:

(i) QR:BC =

(ii) $\dfrac{\text{area of triangle AQR}}{\text{area of triangle ABC}} =$

18.

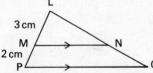

In the triangle LPQ, MN is parallel to PQ, LM = 3 cm and MP = 2 cm.
Write down the value of the following ratios:

(a) $\dfrac{LP}{LM},$

(b) $\dfrac{\text{area of triangle LPQ}}{\text{area of triangle LMN}}.$

19. By using similar triangles, calculate the height of the tree.

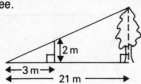

20. A flagpole of height 12 m casts a shadow on the ground of length 8 m. What is the height of a television mast if it casts a shadow 40 m long at the same time?

21. A photograph is enlarged, increasing the length from 6.5 cm to 19.5 cm.
    (a) What is the ratio of the original length to the new length?
    (b) A line is 5.4 cm long in the original photograph. What is the length of this line in the enlarged photograph?
    (c) If the area of the original photograph is 34.7 cm², what is the area of the enlarged photograph?

22.

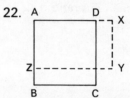

ABCD is a square of side 100 cm. Side AD is increased by 20%, and side AB is reduced by 20% to form rectangle AZYX.
    (a) Calculate: (i) area of square ABCD,
    (ii) area of rectangle AZYX.
    (b) By what percentage has the area of the square been reduced?

23.

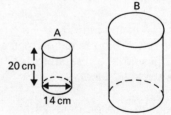

The two cylinders A and B above are similar. The length ratio A:B = 1:2. A has a base radius 14 cm and height 20 cm.
(Take $\pi = \frac{22}{7}$)
    (a) Calculate the volume of cylinder A.
    (b) Hence, or otherwise, determine the volume of cylinder B.
    (c) A third cylinder, C, is similar to cylinder A. Calculate the area of the base of cylinder C if the length ratio A:C = 2:5.

Graphs

Drawing graphs

1. Find the points to be plotted.

2. Choose a suitable scale (it may be given).
   Graph should almost fill the page.
   Scale: what lengths on axes represent,
   e.g. 1 cm represents 5 units.

3. Draw two lines (axes) at right angles.
   Like this
   if all +values:

   Like this
   if some −values:

4. Label the axes.
   Number them from 0.

5. Plot the points.

   e.g. (−3, 2)

   along   up
   x-coordinate y-coordinate

   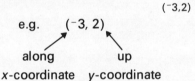

6. Draw the straight line or curve.

Gradient or slope

—— Flat has no slope, so gradient 0.

Gradients need a sign and a size.

Sign:

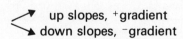

up slopes, +gradient
down slopes, −gradient

Size:

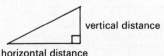

vertical distance

horizontal distance

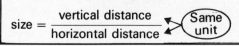

$$\text{size} = \frac{\text{vertical distance}}{\text{horizontal distance}}$$

Same unit

Graphs from data

Data in a table: use to write down ordered pairs.

e.g.

v	0	1	2	3	4
t	0	5	10	15	20

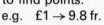

Conversion graphs: used to change units.
Use exchange rate
(or conversion rate)
to find points.
e.g. £1 → 9.8 fr.

Travel graphs: show journeys.
Plot distance against time.
The steeper the slope,
the greater the speed.

Graphs from equations

Lines parallel to axes:

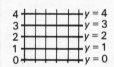

Other straight lines:
1. Put $x = 0$ in equation to find y.
2. Put $y = 0$ in equation to find x.
3. Plot $(0, y)$ and $(x, 0)$ – the 2 points.

Crossing lines:
The crossing point lies on both lines.
Coordinates give solution of both equations.

Drawing curves:
1. Make a table for given values of x.
2. Work out y values using equation.
3. Write down ordered pairs (x, y).

To solve an equation, e.g. $2x^2 - 3x - 1 = 0$,
with a graph:
1. Draw graph of $y = 2x^2 - 3x - 1$.
2. Find where curve cuts x axis (i.e. $y = 0$).
   These two values of x are the solutions.

1.

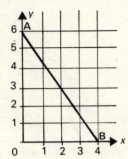

From the above graph find the gradient of the straight line AB.

2. In the diagram the equation of the line AB is $x + y = 6$. N is the point (3, 0) and PN is perpendicular to OB.
   (a) Find the coordinates of P.
   (b) Calculate:
       (i) AO,
       (ii) area APNO.

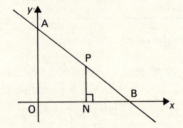

3. The graph shows the curve of $y = x^2 - a$.
   (a) What is the value of a?
   (b) What is the equation of the line of symmetry?
   (c) What is the minimum value of y?

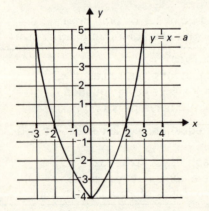

4. The diagram shows a sketch of the graph of $y = 5x - 7$.
   Calculate the coordinates of
   (a) M
   (b) N.

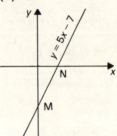

5. The diagram shows the line passing through A and B, whose equation is $y = \frac{1}{2}x + 6$.
   (a) Write down the coordinates of the point A.
   (b) Write down the coordinates of the point B.
   (c) Calculate angle BAO.

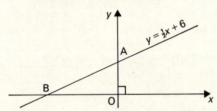

6. Jack sets off from home and walks at a constant velocity of 6 km/h to his friend's house which is 3 km away. He stays for $1\frac{1}{2}$ hours and then borrows his friend's bicycle to return home. The return journey takes 15 minutes. Using the axes given below draw a graph to illustrate the above information.

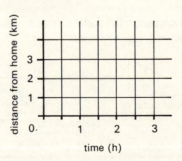

7. (a) Using the axes given below, draw the graph of $2x + y = 6$.

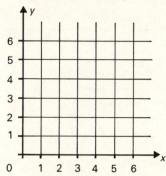

(b) What is the gradient of the straight line $2x + y = 6$ which you have drawn?

8.

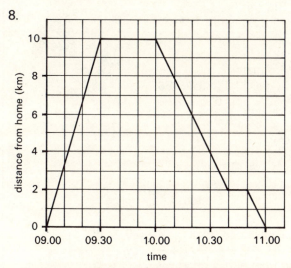

A boy cycled from home to a friend's house at a steady speed. He stayed for a time and then cycled home, but was delayed by a puncture on the return journey. Use the given graph which represents this information to answer the following questions.

(a) (i) How far was his friend's house from his home?

(ii) How many minutes did the journey from home to his friend's house take?

(iii) How many minutes did he stay at his friend's house?

(iv) At what time did he leave his friend's house?

(b) (i) How far had he cycled from his friend's house when the puncture happened?

(ii) For how many minutes was he delayed by the puncture?

(c) (i) What was his average speed in kilometres per hour for the journey to his friend's house?

(ii) What was his average speed in kilometres per hour for the first part of his journey on the way home?

9. Two motorists A and B set out to meet each other on the road between two towns 464 kilometres apart. Motorist A started at 7.30 a.m. and travelled at a steady speed of 80 km/hour. Motorist B started his journey at 10.45 a.m. and travelled at a steady speed until they met at 12.15 p.m.

(a) How long had A been travelling when they met?

(b) What distance had A travelled when they met?

(c) At what speed did B travel on his journey to meet A?

10. Copy and complete the following table for values of $y = x^2 + x - 1$ from $x = {}^-3$ to $x = 2$.

x	$^-3$	$^-2$	$^-1$	0	1	2
x^2		4			1	
$y = x^2 + x - 1$		1			1	

Using scales of 2 cm to represent one unit on both axes, draw the graph of $y = x^2 + x - 1$ from $x = {}^-3$ to $x = 2$. Use the graph to find:

(a) the value of $x^2 + x - 1$ when $x = 1.2$,

(b) the solutions of the equation $x^2 + x - 1 = 0$,

(c) the minimum value of $x^2 + x - 1$.

Statistics

Charts

Tally chart – a tally for each item.

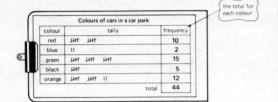

the total for each colour

Colours of cars in a car park		
colour	tally	frequency
red	⊔⊔† ⊔⊔†	10
blue	II	2
green	⊔⊔† ⊔⊔† ⊔⊔†	15
black	⊔⊔†	5
orange	⊔⊔† ⊔⊔† II	12
	total	44

Put the tallies into 5 s:
It makes them easier to count.

Pictogram – pictures show data.

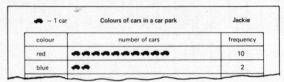

🚗 – 1 car   Colours of cars in a car park   Jackie

colour	number of cars	frequency
red	🚗🚗🚗🚗🚗🚗🚗🚗🚗🚗	10
blue	🚗🚗	2

Choose an easy picture to draw.
Say what it stands for.
Space the pictures evenly.
Use fractions of the picture if needed.

Bar chart – bars show data.

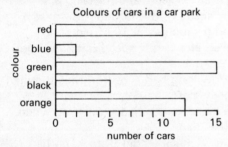

Colours of cars in a car park

Label and number it carefully.
Bars can be upright or sideways.
Bars must be the same width and the
same distance apart.
Lengths of the bars show the frequencies.

Pie chart
– 'slices' show data.

e.g.
For maths:
angle: 110°, total: 360°

fraction: $\dfrac{110}{360}$

For PE:

$$36 \text{ pupils} \rightarrow 360°$$

$$1 \text{ pupil} \rightarrow \frac{360°}{36} = 10°$$

angle: $8 \text{ pupils} \rightarrow 8 \times 10° = \underline{80°}$

Frequency table or distribution – can be made from a tally chart.

It lists values and how often they occur (frequency).

Range – difference between the largest and smallest values
in the data.

length	frequency
10 cm	1
15 cm	7

Grouped data – we group the data when we have a large
range of values. Each group must have
the same range.

scores	frequency
0–19	5
20–39	12

A frequency table can be made using the grouped data.

A histogram can be drawn from the frequency table.

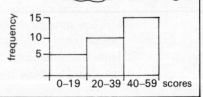

Cumulative frequency

A frequency table can be made into a cumulative frequency table.

scores	frequency
0–19	5
20–39	12

⟶

scores	cumulative frequency
less than 20	5
less than 40	17

} 'running totals'

Plot 'scores' against cumulative frequency to get a cumulative frequency curve or ogive.
If you divide your 'cumulative frequency axis' into four equal parts:
  '$\frac{3}{4}$ way' → Upper quartile 'score' UQ
  '$\frac{1}{2}$ way' → Median 'score' M
  '$\frac{1}{4}$ way' → Lower quartile 'score' LQ.

The curve gives estimates for values:

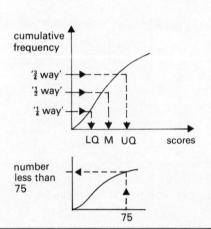

Averages

Mode – the item which occurs most often in a tally.

Modal group – the group with the highest frequency, i.e. with the most values in it.

$$\text{Mean} = \frac{\text{total}}{\text{number of items}}$$

Mean from a frequency table

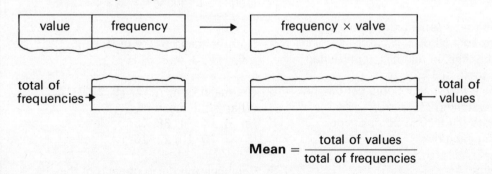

value	frequency

⟶

frequency × valve

total of frequencies →

← total of values

$$\text{Mean} = \frac{\text{total of values}}{\text{total of frequencies}}$$

Median – the middle item when the items are placed in order.
If the number of items is even, find the mean of the two middle items.

1. The number of meals sold in a restaurant on each day of a week is shown in the bar chart.
   (a) How many meals were sold on Tuesday?
   (b) How many meals were sold altogether?
   (c) Work out the mean number of meals sold per day.

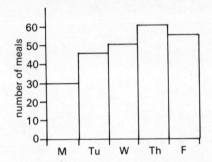

2. The pie chart shows the proportions of the number of members in each of three teams A, B, C. The total number of members in all the teams is 288.
   (a) Calculate the value of x.
   (b) How many members are in team C?
   (c) Write down, in its lowest terms, the ratio of the number of members in team A to the number of members in team B.

3. The pie chart represents a day in the life of a Middlesex schoolboy.
   (a) Find the time, in minutes, represented by an angle of 1°.
   (b) Calculate how many hours per day he spent watching TV.
   (c) Calculate the time in hours spent working each day.

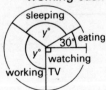

4.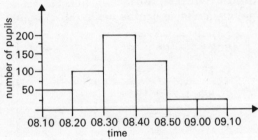

The graph shows the arrival times at school of the pupils. Those arriving after 0850 are late and there are 600 pupils in the school.
   (a) How many pupils arrive before 0840?
   (b) How many pupils are at school that day?
   (c) What is the percentage of pupils absent?
   (d) What is the ratio of the number of late pupils to the number present before 0850? Give your answer in the form $1:n$.

5. The longest word on a page has 14 letters, the shortest has 2 letters. What is the statistical range of the lengths of the words on the page?

6. Copy and complete the following cumulative frequency table for different values of x:

values of x	10	20	30	40
frequency	2	5	6	1
cumulative frequency	2			

7. Find the mean of the numbers:
   0, 1, 2, 3, 4, 8, 9, 10, 11, 12

8. The mean of 4, 7, 17, 19, 23 is 14. What is the mean of
   (a) 8, 14, 34, 38, 46?
   (b) 7, 10, 20, 22, 26?

9. Calculate the mean of each of the following sets of numbers:
   (a) 1, 4, 5, 7, 13,
   (b) 51, 54, 55, 57, 63.

10. If the mean of 3, 4, x is 5, find the value of x.

11. (a) In a mathematics test five pupils scored 81, 31, 47, 49 and 62 respectively. Calculate the mean score.
    (b) Four girls weigh 41.3 kg, 38.2 kg, 40.6 kg and 44.3 kg. When a fifth girl joins them, the mean weight of the five girls is 41.06 kg. Calculate the weight of the fifth girl.

12. Calculate the average age of three children whose ages are 12 years 11 months, 10 years 4 months and 12 years 3 months.

13. 7, 3, 4, 2, 7, 3, 7, 5, 8, 11.
    For the set of numbers find (a) the mode, (b) the median, (c) the mean.

14. (a) The prices of a pound of apples at various shops in town are:
    15p, 12p, 10p, 10p, 14p, 15p, 11p, 17p.
    Work out:
    (i) the median price
    (ii) the mean price.
    (b) The profits of a small local firm have gone up from £10 000 in 1977 to £20 000 in 1981.

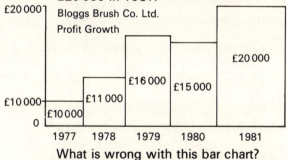

    What is wrong with this bar chart? Draw another bar chart to show the same facts more clearly and fairly.

15. (a) The shoe sizes of a class of children are shown in this table:

size of shoe	4	5	6	7	8	9	10
number of children	2	5	8	5	1	3	1

    (i) How many children are there in the class?
    (ii) Draw a bar chart to illustrate this information, using at least half a page.
    (iii) What is the modal shoe size?
    (b) In a survey, 1800 men were asked how they travelled to work.
    The answers were: Car 200
    Bicycle 400
    Bus 500
    Walk 700
    Draw a pie chart to show this information, using a circle of radius 6 cm. You **must** show how you work out the angles.

16. In a competition organised by the local cricket club 30 cricketers were allowed to bowl 10 balls at a set of three stumps. The number of times the stumps were hit by each bowler is shown below.
    2 0 8 5 7 8 0 2 8 6
    6 2 7 6 4 6 3 1 3 7
    2 3 2 1 8 1 2 3 2 5
    Using these figures complete the following table.

no. of hits	0	1	2	3	4	5	6	7	8	9	10
frequency	2	3									0

    (a) What is the mode of the number of hits?
    (b) What is the median number of hits?
    (c) Calculate the mean number of hits.
    (d) If a pie chart were drawn showing the above information, find the angle which would be required to represent the cricketers hitting the stumps twice.

17. The following table gives the number of years' service by 50 workers in a factory.

26	17	21	18	16	25	26	19	17	18
5	16	1	2	14	8	9	11	2	5
6	10	15	22	15	2	8	21	21	5
7	1	3	6	8	10	2	24	3	4
6	9	3	1	6	9	21	16	9	26

    (a) Construct a frequency distribution using the intervals 0–4, 5–9, 10–14, 15–19, 20–24, 25–30.
    (b) State the modal class of the distribution.
    (c) Calculate the arithmetic mean for the ten workers with more than 20 years service.

Exam paper 1

1. Work out:
   (a) 346×7 (b) $1704 \div 8$

2. Write 18 as the sum of two prime numbers.

3. Find the square root of 169.

4. Calculate:
   (a) $^+3 + ^-7$ (b) $^-4 \times ^-3$

5. Evaluate 9^2.

6. Work out:
   (a) $2\frac{1}{3} - 1\frac{5}{6}$ (b) $\frac{7}{8} \div \frac{3}{4}$.

7. Write $3\frac{7}{100}$ as a decimal.

8. Calculate:
   (a) 1.7×3.23 (b) $97.2 \div 2.7$

9. Express the number 3120 in standard form.

10. Given, $\log 70 = 1.845$, write down the value of $\log 700$.

11. Simplify:
    (a) $5y - 2y$ (b) $5y \times 2y$

12. Solve: $3x - 5 = 7$.

13. Write 76% as a fraction in its lowest terms.

14. Work out 15% of £34.

15. How many grams in 2.3 kg?

16. How many minutes from 08 25 to 09 17?

17. A boy buys two shirts at £6.95 each and pays for them with three £5 notes.
    Find:
    (a) the total cost of the shirts,
    (b) the amount of change he receives.

18. What is the angle between the hands of a clock at 11 00?

19. In the diagram below, AB and CD are parallel lines.

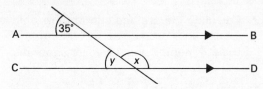

    Find: (a) angle x, (b) angle y.

20. Calculate the size of an interior angle of a regular pentagon.

21. How many axes of symmetry does a square have?

22. ABC is a right-angled triangle.

    Calculate:
    (a) the length AB,
    (b) angle CAB.

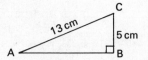

23. Calculate the area of a circle of radius 10 cm.
    Take $\pi = 3.14$.

24. What is the volume of a cuboid which measures 4 cm by 7 cm by 5 cm?

25. In a school of 1170 pupils the ratio of boys to girls is $5:4$.
    Calculate the number of girls in the school.

26. The coordinates of P and Q are $(^-2, ^-2)$ and $(3, 2)$.
    Calculate the gradient of the straight line passing through P and Q.

27. Calculate the mean of the numbers 2, 7, 11, 14, 21.

Exam paper 2

1. (a) A motorist travels 134.7 km, 283.6 km and 428.2 km.
   How much further does he have to travel to complete a journey of 1000 km?
   (b) A person on holiday in France stays 6 days in a hotel which charges 135 francs a day
   plus $12\frac{1}{2}$% service charge.
   What is the total bill in francs? (Answer to the nearest franc).

2. Solve the simultaneous equations:

   $2x + 3y = 7$
   $3x - 2y = 4.$

3. An express bus leaves Nottingham at 09 38 and travels to London, 140 miles away. Another
   bus leaves Nottingham at the same time and travels to Newcastle 157 miles away.
   (a) If the first bus arrives in London at 13 20, how long did the journey take?
   (b) The journey to Newcastle took $4\frac{3}{4}$ hours. At what time did the bus arrive?
   (c) A third bus left Nottingham at 09 48 and travelled to Birmingham 56 miles away at an
   average speed of 48 mph. What time did it arrive in Birmingham?

4. The Rateable Value of a town is £118 576 000 and for the financial year 1982–83 the local
   council charges a general rate of 95p in the £.
   (a) How much will a penny rate raise?
   (b) What will a householder pay in 1982–83, if his house has a Rateable Value of £226?
   (c) Another householder pays £304 in rates. What is the Rateable Value of his property?

5. In the diagram, (not drawn to scale), PQRST is a circle. Some angles are given.
   (a) Calculate the following angles.
       (i) angle PQR,
       (ii) angle PRQ,
       (iii) angle TRS,
       (iv) angle PRS
   (b) What is special about the line PS? Why?

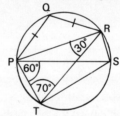

6. The diagrams below show a quadrilateral and a hexagon. (Neither is drawn to scale).

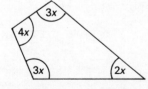 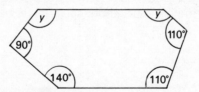

Calculate:
(a) the size of each angle in the quadrilateral,
(b) the size of the two angles marked y in the hexagon.

7. The diagram below is not drawn to scale.

Use it to calculate:
(a) the length AC,
(b) the length AD.

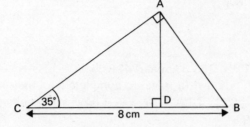

8. Using the triangle ABC in question 7, calculate:
(a) its perimeter,   (b) its area.

9. What is the area of a circle of diameter 14 cm? Use $\pi = 3.14$ and give your answer correct to 1 decimal place.

10. Calculate the volume and surface area of a solid circular cylinder of length 35 cm and diameter 4.5 cm. Use $\pi = 3.14$ and give each answer correct to 4 significant figures.

11. A model is made using a scale of 1:10.
Find:
(a) the actual length if the model length is 9.36 cm,
(b) the surface area of the model, if the actual surface area is 1250 cm²,
(c) the actual volume if the volume of the model is 20.75 cm³.

12. (a) Copy and complete the following table for the curve $y = x^2 - 5x + 1$.

x	⁻1	0	1	2	3	4	5	6
x^2 ⁻5^x +1					 1	 ⁻20 1	25 ⁻25 1	36 ⁻30 1
y							1	7

(b) Draw axes on graph paper for values of x from ⁻1 to 6 (2 cm to 1 unit) and values of y from ⁻5 to 7 (1 cm to 1 unit). Use your table to draw the graph of $y = x^2 - 5x + 1$.
(c) Use your graph to determine:
(i) the values of x when $y = 0$,
(ii) the value of y when $x = 0.5$.
(d) By drawing a straight line on your graph, solve the equation $x^2 - 5x + 1 = 3$.

Answers

Pick your own (pages 6–8)
A. 1 lb
B. strawberries 1 lb, raspberries 2 lb, loganberries 5 lb
C. (a) Raspberries

weight sold	frequency	frequency × weight
1 lb	27	27 lb
2 lb	45	90 lb
3 lb	14	42 lb
4 lb	22	88 lb
5 lb	19	95 lb
	127	342 lb

(b)
Mean weight: 2.7 lb

(a) Loganberries

weight sold	frequency	frequency × weight
1 lb	27	27 lb
2 lb	12	24 lb
3 lb	8	24 lb
4 lb	0	0 lb
5 lb	33	165 lb
	80	240 lb

(b)
Mean weight: 3 lb

Sines and cosines (pages 9–11)
A. (a) hypotenuse (b) opposite (c) adjacent
B. (1) 0.500 (4) 0.940 (7) 0.174
    (2) 0.985 (5) 0.766 (8) 0.342
    (3) 0.766 (6) 0.500

Comparing (pages 12–13)
A. Maths 90%, TD 75%, History 25%, English 68%, Woodwork 70%, RE $33\frac{1}{3}$%, Physics 60%
    Best subject: Maths

B. seeds 6p, shears £2, spade £3, chair £1.50, heater £5.50, mower £18: all profits
C. seeds 15%, shears 25%, spade 25%, chair 10%, heater 25%, mower 4%
D. (1) 30% (3) 20% (5) 40%
    (2) 25% (4) 9% (6) 8.3%

Day trips (pages 14–16)
A. (1) d: departure, a: arrival
    (2) (a) 06.25 (b) 10.15
    (3) Crewe
    (4) Prestatyn, Rhyl, Colwyn Bay, Llandudno
B. (1) 2 hours 59 minutes
    (2) (a) 08.55 (b) 11.45
    (3) Prestatyn 2 hours 28 minutes, Rhyl 2 hours 36 minutes, Colwyn Bay 2 hours 50 minutes, Llandudno 3 hours 18 minutes
C. (1) Wolverhampton, Preston, Blackpool North
    (2) 40 minutes
D. (1) 2 hours 4 minutes
    (2) (a) 1 hour 34 minutes
    (b) 2 hours 27 minutes
    (3) The second train: it's quicker.
E. Oxford: 09.12, 10.25, 11.40, 12.46, 14.00
    Cambridge: 10.30, 11.00, 12.10, 12.31, 13.23

More directed numbers (pages 17–19)
A. (1) 1 (3) 1 (5) 6
    (2) $^-2$ (4) $^-3$ (6) 1
B. (1) 5 (3) $^-3$ (5) $^-6$
    (2) 9 (4) $^-3$ (6) 0
C. (1) $2x + {}^-y$ (6) $p^2 + {}^-2q^2$
    (2) $m + {}^-3n$ (7) $^-2x^2 + {}^-x + 4$
    (3) $x^2 + {}^-2x$ (8) $5x^2 + {}^-3x + {}^-7$
    (4) $1 + {}^-y^2$ (9) $x^2 + 2x + {}^-9$
    (5) $^-3y + {}^-8z$
D. (1) $a + b$ (6) $2m + 3n$
    (2) $4c + d$ (7) $5p^2 + 4p$
    (3) $3p + 4q$ (8) $3p^2 + p + 2$
    (4) $x^2 + x$ (9) $2x^2 + 3x + 1$
    (5) $2y^2 + y$

For charity (pages 20–21)

A.

	1	2	3	4	5	6	7	8	9	10
Adult	40p	80p	£1.20	£1.60	£2	£2.40	£2.80	£3.20	£3.60	£4
Child	25p	50p	75p	£1	£1.25	£1.75	£2	£2.25	£2.50	£2.50

B. (a) 20 hours   (d) 6 hours
   (b) 15 hours   (e) 5 hours
   (c) 12 hours   (f) 4 hours

Well balanced (pages 22–25)

D. The shape of the page is the same
E. On page 22: B 2 and 3, on page 23:
   C 3, 7, 8
F. 6
G. 4, 3, 5, 2
H. On page 22: B 1, on page 23: C 1, 2, 4

(2) (a) $4:1$ (b) $5:2$ (c) $3:7$
     $\times 5$ $\times 6$ $\times 12$
     $5:20$ $30:12$ $36:84$

H. (a) 32 m wide   (b) 49 m long

More shorthand (pages 26–27)

A. (1) $3a$ (3) $-y$ (5) $-8m$
   (2) $-3x$ (4) l (6) $-2b$
B. (1) $a + 4c$ (4) $12f - 2g$
   (2) $4n - m$ (5) $3c + 2d$
   (3) $5x + 3y$ (6) $4s - t - r$
C. (1) $4a - 3b$ (4) $2n - 6m$
   (2) $4p - 4q + r$ (5) $6e - 5f + g$
   (3) $6x - 4y$ (6) $5b + c - 7d$
D. (1) $x^2 + 3x - 3$ (4) $4t$
   (2) $p^2 + 2p + 2$ (5) $y^3 - 3y^2 - y$
   (3) $6a^2 - a - 5$ (6) $n^5 + 9r^2 - 2$

Ratio (pages 28–31)

A. 2 and 1, 4 and 2, 8 and 4, 16 and 8
B. $2:1$, $4:2$, $8:4$, $16:8$
C. (1) (a), (d)
   (2) (a) $4:1$ (b) $4:1$ (c) $1:4$ (d) $1:6$
D. $6:4$, $9:6$, $15:10$, $12:8$
E. (1) (a), (d)
   (2) (a) $5:2$ (b) $4:3$ (c) $7:4$ (d) $6:5$
F. (a) $5:2$ (b) $1:8$ (c) $10:3$ (d) $5:1$
G. (1) 12

Foreign currency (pages 32–34)

A. (1) Dollar   (4) Lira
   (2) Deutsche Mark   (5) Yen
   (3) Peseta
B. (1) 10.10 Fr   (4) $1.825
   (2) 4.03 DM   (5) 425 Y
   (3) 2140 L
C. (1) 353.5 Fr   (4) $109.5
   (2) 100.75 DM   (5) 16150 Y
   (3) 119 840 L   (6) 6900 pta
D. jumper: £8.37, trousers: £16.73, skirt: £21.78,
   slippers: £7.91, shirt: £12.28, tee shirt: £4.38,
   guide book: £4.38, poster: £1.48, bowl: £1,
   post card: 3p
E. £5.13, £5, £3.79, £8.48

Conversion graphs (pages 36–38)

A. (1) 36 fl   (2) (a) 27 fl   (b) 15.75 fl
   (c) 20.7 fl   (d) 44.1 fl   (e) 32.4 fl
B. (1) £2   (2) (a) £4.40   (b) £7.80
   (c) £2.70   (d) 70p   (e) £9.30

Negative powers (pages 40–42)

A. (1) $3 \times 3 \times 3 \times 3 \times 3$
   (2) $2 \times 2 \times 2$
   (3) $7 \times 7 \times 7 \times 7 \times 7 \times 7$

(4) 8×8
(5) $4 \times 4 \times 4 \times 4$
B. (1) 2^4 (2) 7^3 (3) 1 (4) 10^{-5}
C. (1) (a) $10^{-2} = \dfrac{1}{10^2}$ (b) $3^{-4} = \dfrac{1}{3^4}$

(c) $8^{-3} = \dfrac{1}{8^3}$ (d) $5^{-1} = \dfrac{1}{5}$

(2) (a) $\dfrac{1}{10^2}$ (b) $\dfrac{1}{3^4}$ (c) $\dfrac{1}{8^3}$

(d) $\dfrac{1}{5}$

D. (1) 4^2 (2) 6^{-4} (3) 2^{-5} (4) 5
E. (1) 3^6 (2) 5^{-5} (3) 7^{-7} (4) 10
F. (1) $\dfrac{1}{b^3}$ (2) $\dfrac{1}{x^4}$ (3) $\dfrac{1}{p^5}$ (4) $\dfrac{1}{r^8}$ (5) $\dfrac{1}{c^{10}}$
G. (1) a (3) p^{-2} (5) m^{-3} (7) c^{-7}
    (2) x^{-1} (4) r^{-6} (6) y^4 (8) s^{-2}

Fair shares (pages 43–45)
A. (1) £2:£3   (2) £5
B. (a) £140   (b) £210
C. (1) 12   (2) £102.96   (3) £8.58
    (4) Tina's: £17.16, Gary's: £60.06,
    Jackie's: £25.74
D. orange juice: $1\frac{1}{2}$ l, ginger ale: 5 l,
    cranberry juice: 3 l, lemon juice: $\frac{1}{2}$ l

Standard form (pages 46–48)
A. Mercury 5.8×10^7 km,
    Venus 10.8×10^7 km,
    Mars 2.28×10^8 km,
    Jupiter 7.78×10^8 km,
    Saturn 1.427×10^9 km,
    Uranus 2.87×10^9 km,
    Neptune 4.497×10^9 km,
    Pluto 5.95×10^9 km
B. Mercury 4840 km, Venus 12 300 km,
    Mars 6790 km, Jupiter 143 000 km,
    Saturn 119 000 km, Uranus 47 000 km,
    Neptune 51 000 km, Pluto 6000 km.
C. wire 2×10^{-4} m, chromosome 5×10^{-6} m,
    paper 1×10^{-4} m, light 5×10^{-7} m,
    fibre 1×10^{-6} kg
D. shrew 0.0025 kg,
    bacterium 0.000 000 000 000 004 kg,
    sand 0.000 0001 kg,
    atom 0.000 000 000 000 000 000 000 000 4 kg,
    water 0.000 000 000 000 000 000 000 000 03 kg

Two at a time (page 49)
A. (1) $^-21$ (3) $^+6$ (5) $^+42$
    (2) $^+8$ (4) $^-15$ (6) $^-32$
B. (1) $^+30$ (2) $^+24$ (3) $^-48$
    (4) $^+120$

Significant figures (pages 50–51)
A. (1) 3 and 4. At the 4th and 5th
    (2) (a) 40 000, 30 000, 30 000, 30 000,
           20 000
       (b) 36 000, 32 000, 28 000, 25 000,
           20 000
       (c) 36 100, 31 500, 28 300, 25 100,
           20 000
       (d) 36 070, 31 530, 28 310, 25 050,
           19 980
B. (1) 0.000 4930. Look at the 4th figure i.e. 5
    (2) (i) 3   (iv) 6   (vii) 7
       (ii) 5   (v) 8   (viii) 4
       (iii) 2   (vi) 1   (ix) 9
    (3) (a) (i) 0.003   (vi) 0.001
          (ii) 0.05   (vii) 0.7
          (iii) 0.0003   (viii) 0.05
          (iv) 0.06   (ix) 0.001
          (v) 0.8
       (b) (i) 0.0032   (vi) 0.0014
          (ii) 0.052   (vii) 0.73
          (iii) 0.000   (viii) 0.047
          (iv) 0.060   (ix) 0.00096
          (v) 0.81
       (c) (i) 0.003 21   (vi) 0.001 38
          (ii) 0.0517   (vii) 0.727
          (iii) 0.000 282   (viii) 0.0465
          (iv) 0.0602   (ix) 0.000 957
          (v) 0.814

Look alikes (page 53)
A. The drawing on the right has 1 extra apple
    on the tree, 1 extra apple in the basket, 4
    panes in the middle window of the house,
    1 rung missing from the ladder and 1 bird
    missing from the sky.

Bills! Bills! Bills (pages 54–57)
A. (1) 28726 and 30051 (2) 1325
B. (1) £74.33 (2) £6.35 (3) £80.68
C. (1) 09160 and 09917 (2) 757
  (3) 29944 and 30733 (4) 789
D. (1) (a) £44.44 (b) £17.20
  (2) £70.64
E. (1) (a) 5p (b) £46.95 (2) £16.50
F. (1) 15% (2) £62.55
G. (1) £4.88 (2) £3.26 (3) £6.80
  (4) £8.22 (5) £13.68
  Totals payable: £37.38, £25.01, £52.10, £63.04, £104.89

Angles from tables (pages 58–59)
A. (1) 2.8° (2) 25.5° (3) 69.2°
  (4) 37.2° (5) 75°
B. (1) 49.6° (2) 60.3° (3) 54.7°
  (4) 63.6° (5) 61.4°
C. (1) 83.7° (2) 80.5° (3) 75.7°
  (4) 76.1° (5) 89.3°
D. (1) 65.8° (2) 69.6° (3) 71.2°
  (4) 77.3° (5) 72.1°
E. (1) 29.6° (2) 28.3° (3) 31.3°
  (4) 18.3° (5) 12°

Dividing directed numbers (pages 60–61)
A. (1) (a) positive (b) positive
    (c) negative (d) negative
  (2) (a) $^+4$ (b) $^-4$ (c) $^-2$
    (d) $^+2$ (e) $^+7$ (f) $^+3$

Average speed (pages 66–70)
A. 99 km
B. 1 hour
C. Manchester – Sheffield: 61 km/h,
  Edinburgh – Glasgow: 72 km/h,
  Birmingham – Gloucester: 83 km/h,
  Oxford – London: 90 km/h
D. (1) 162 km (2) 2 h
E. (1) 96 km/h (2) 70 km/h (3) 50 km/h
  (4) 79 km/h (5) 89 km/h
F. (1) 72 km/h (2) 112 km/h (3) 87 km/h
  (4) 60 km/h (5) 56 km/h
G. 200 m: 7.7 m/s, 400 m: 6.2 m/s,
  800 m: 5.5 m/s, 1000 m: 4.4 m/s,
  1500 m: 4.3 m/s

H. 100 m: 10.1 m/s, 200 m: 10.1 m/s,
  400 m: 9.1 m/s, 800 m: 7.9 m/s,
  1000 m: 7.6 m/s, 1500 m: 7.1 m/s
I. (1) 10 km (2) 15 km (3) 20 km
  (4) 25 km
J. (1) 14 km (3) 50 km (5) 102 km
  (2) 54 km (4) 15 km (6) 135 km
K. (1) 2 h (2) 3 h (3) 4 h (4) 5 h
L. (1) 4 h (3) 3 h (5) 6 h
  (2) 4 h (4) 6 h (6) $4\frac{3}{4}$ h

Finding lengths (pages 71–74)
A. 1.887 cm
B. 7.232 cm
C. (1) adj.: 0.87 cm (3) adj.: 5.936 m
    opp.: 9.96 cm   opp.: 3.71 m
  (2) adj.: 1.892 m (4) adj.: 1.248 cm
    opp.: 0.652 m   opp.: 5.868 cm
D. (1) AB = 3.76 cm (3) FG = 5.967 cm
    BC = 1.368 cm   GH = 6.741 cm
  (2) PQ 2.94 cm
    QR = 4.045 cm

Pot Black (pages 75–79)
A. (1) Ravis (2) Biggins: 137
  (3) Wobblyneck: 0
B. 137
C. (1) Brake (2) Punk: 139 (3) Bloo: 2
  (4) 137
D. (1)

scores	tally	frequency
0–19	HHT	5
20–39	HHT HHT	10
40–59	HHT HHT HHT II	17
60–79	HHT HHT IIII	14
80–99	HHT HHT	10
100–119	II	2
120–139	II	2

(2) 40–59

More substitution (pages 80–82)
A. (1) $^-4$ (3) 3 (5) $^-6$ (7) $^-8$
  (2) 3 (4) $^-5$ (6) 7 (8) $^-16$

B. (1) ⁻7   (2) 6   (3) ⁻22   (4) 4

C. (1) 25   (2) 625   (3) ⁻500
   (4) ⁻21 875

D. (1) 9   (3) 95   (5) 32
   (2) ⁻83   (4) 28   (6) ⁻29

Travel graphs (pages 83–87)

A. 20 km/h

B. (1) (a) Gary: 20 km,   Tina: 25 km,   Steve: 30 km
     (b) Gary: 2h,   Tina: 1 h,   Steve: $2\frac{1}{2}$ h
     (c) Gary: 10 km/h, Tina: 25 km/h, Steve: 12 km/h
   (2) (a) Tina's   (b) Gary's
   (3) (a) Tina's   (b) Gary's
   (4) The steeper the slope the greater the average speed.

C. (1)

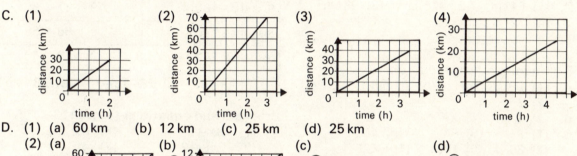

D. (1) (a) 60 km   (b) 12 km   (c) 25 km   (d) 25 km
   (2) (a)

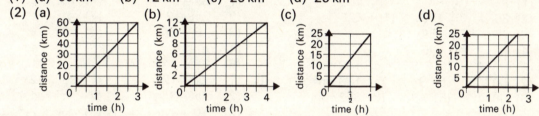

E. (1) (a) 6 h   (b) 2 h   (c) $1\frac{1}{4}$ h   (d) $1\frac{1}{2}$ h
   (2) (a)

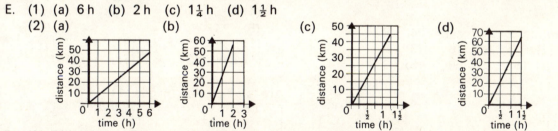

F. (2) $7\frac{1}{2}$ km/h   (3) $\frac{1}{2}$ h   (4) 4 km/h   (5) 25 km   (6) 5 h   (7) 5 km/h

G. (1) 10 km   (2) (a) 12.00   (b) 12.50   (3) 12 km/h
   (4) (a) 12.20   (b) 12.45   (5) 24 km/h

H. (1)

town 10
8
distance 6
from home
(km) 4
2
home 0
   12.00   12.30   13.00
         time
Tina   Tina's mum

                    (2) 12.30   (3) 6 km   (4) 4 km

I. (2) 4 km   (3) 40 minutes   (4) 6 km/h   (5) 1 h 40 m   (6) 10 minutes   (7) 24 km/h

Flight plans (pages 91–95)
A. Binbrook: 032°, Kenley: 115°, St Mawgan: 236°, Swanton Morley: 060°, Llanbedr: 311°, St Athan: 249°, Northolt: 096°, Pershore: 000°

Christmas boxes (pages 96–97)
A. (1) 6   (2) squares   (3) all six
B. (1) 150 cm²   (2) 600 cm²
    (3) 864 cm²   (4) 3750 cm²
C. (1) 6   (2) rectangles   (3) same size: Best wishes from . . ., Happy New Year, Merry Christmas
D. (1) 94 cm² (2) 416 cm² (3) 98 cm²
    (4) 722.5 cm²

Enlargements (pages 98–102)
A. (1) (a) 35 mm   (b) 70 mm
    (2) 2
B. (2) 4
C. (1) 9   (5) 64   (9) 400
    (2) 36   (6) 100   (10) 625
    (3) 25   (7) 169
    (4) 1   (8) 225
D. (1) (a) 4   (b) 16   (c) 144 cm²
    (2) (a) 3   (b) 9   (c) 180 cm²
    (3) (a) 7   (b) 49   (c) 882 cm²

Running totals (pages 104–107)
A. (1) 5   (3) 46   (5) 58
    (2) 15   (4) 56   (6) 60
B.

score	cumulative frequency (CF)
less than 20	5
less than 40	$10 + 5 = 15$
less than 60	$17 + 15 = 32$
less than 80	$14 + 32 = 46$
less than 100	$10 + 46 = 56$
less than 120	$2 + 56 = 58$
less than 140	$2 + 58 = 60$

C. (1) (20, 5), (40, 15), (60, 32), (80, 46), (100, 56), (120, 58), (140, 60)
    (4) (a) 58   (b) 40   (c) 78
    (5) 36
D. (1)

score	cumulative frequency (CF)
less than 20	9
less than 40	$15 + 9 = 24$
less than 60	$11 + 24 = 35$
less than 80	$12 + 35 = 47$
less than 100	$9 + 47 = 56$
less than 120	$2 + 56 = 58$
less than 140	$2 + 58 = 60$

(3) (a) 42   (b) 28   (c) 76   (d) 38

Brackets and equations (pages 108–110)
A. (1) $-3a - 6$ (6) $-8c - 20$
    (2) $-2m - 2$ (7) $-p^2 - p$
    (3) $-15 - 5p$ (8) $-3x - x^2$
    (4) $-q - 4$ (9) $-ab - ac$
    (5) $-21b - 28$
B. (1) $-3x + 12$ (6) $-8 + 12x$
    (2) $-4a + 28$ (7) $-c^2 + c$
    (3) $-10 + 2m$ (8) $-6y + 2y^2$
    (4) $-15 + 5p$ (9) $-pq + 3pn$
    (5) $-14x + 7$
C. (1) $x = 2$ (2) $x = 4$ (3) $x = -1$ (4) $x = -3$
D. (1) $x = 1$ (2) $a = 5$ (3) $y = -1$ (4) $p = -1$

Areas of circles (pages 111–114)
A. 12 cm²
B. (1) 4 cm²
    (2) Area of circle = 3 × area of square.
C. (1) 154 cm²   (5) 50.24 m²
    (2) 346.5 cm²   (6) 314 cm²
    (3) 12 474 mm²   (7) 12.56 km²
    (4) 38.5 m²   (8) 113.04 m²
D. (1) 2.65 cm   (2) 4.18 cm
    (3) 8.77 mm   (4) 15.0 mm

Simple Interest (pages 115–117)
A. (1) £20   (2) £30   (3) £27.50
    (4) £22.50

B. (1) £55   (2) £82.50   (3) £137.50
   (4) £220   (5) £550

Crossed lines (pages 118–119)
B. (1) $y = 2$ (2) $x = 4$ (3) (0, 2), (4, 0)
C. (2, 1)

Prisms (pages 120–123)
A. A triangle.
B. (1) square   (2) rectangular
   (3) circular   (4) hexagonal
C. (1) 24 cm³   (2) 70 m³   (3) 60 mm³
   (4) 28½ m³
D. (1) 77 m³   (2) 20 m³   (3) 115 cm³
E. (1) (a) 5400 cm³   (b) 0.0054 m³
   (2) (a) 75×10^5 cm³   (b) 7.5 m³

Multiplying and dividing in algebra
(pages 127–128)
A. (1) ^-6z (3) ^-3a (5) ^-7b
   (2) ^-20a (4) $36\,m$ (6) $32a$
B. (1) ^-6ab (3) $10xy^3z$ (5) $4p^3q^4$
   (2) $^-8p^2qr$ (4) $^-12r^3s^3$ (6) $^-24c^4d^3$
C. (1) ^-4p (3) $^-6a^2$ (5) $3ab$
   (2) ^-2x (4) $^-4p^2$ (6) $^-4x^2y^2$
D. (1) ^-2p (3) $3a^3$ (5) $^-6r^3$
   (2) $^-5z^2$ (4) ^-6x (6) $25\,n^5$

Cyclic quadrilaterals (pages 130–131)
A. (2) (a) 180°   (b) 180°
   (c) The same, both 180°.
B. (1) $a = 105°$, $b = 100°$ (2) $c = 82°$,
   $d = 126°$ (3) $e = 73°$, $f = 68°$

Cash or credit (pages 132–133)
A. (1) £199   (2) £232, 15%, £197.20
   (3) £223, 5%, £211.85   (4) Dandy's
B. (1) 20%
   (2) (a) £222.75   (b) £235.92
   (c) £258.30   (d) £285.60
   (3) (a) £267.35   (b) £280.52
   (c) £302.90
   (d) £330.20
   (4) (a) £55.50   (b) £68.67
   (c) £91.05   (d) £118.35
   (5) Pay cash at Dandy's. It is the cheapest.

Finding angles (pages 134–136)
A. $\sin b° = \dfrac{\text{opposite}}{\text{hypotenuse}}$, $\cos b° = \dfrac{\text{adjacent}}{\text{hypotenuse}}$
B. (3) (a) (i)   opposite and adjacent
           (ii)   opposite and hypotenuse
           (iii) adjacent and hypotenuse
           (iv)   opposite and adjacent
           (v)   adjacent and hypotenuse
           (vi)   opposite and hypotenuse
           (vii) opposite and hypotenuse
           (viii) adjacent and hypotenuse
       (b) (i) tan   (ii) sin   (iii) cos
           (iv) tan   v) cos   (vi) sin
           (vii) sin   (viii) cos
C. (i) 42.6°   (ii) 49.5°   (iii) 65.7°
   (iv) 80.3°   (v) 71.6°   (vi) 58.7°
   (vii) 86.8°   (viii) 87.2°

Similar solids (pages 138–141)
A. Natasha
B. 2 cm and 4 cm.
C. 8 cm³, 64 cm³
D. (1) 3   (2) 8 cm³ and 216 cm³   (3) 27
   (4) volume factor = (scale factor)³
E. (1) (a) 8   (b) 512   (c) 512 cm³
   (2) (a) 6   (b) 216   (c) 8640 cm³

Drawing flight plans (pages 142–145)
C. (2) 31.5 km on 108°   (3) 288°
D. 9.2 km, 297°

Rates (pages 146–149)
B. (1) £174   (2) 142p
C. £247.08
D. (a) £121.04   (b) £20.17
E. (1) £106   (2) £150.52   (3) £2.89
F. Gary's: £60.90, Jackie's: £37.10, Exercise 1
   properties: £43.40, £48.30, £92.05,
   £114.45
G. £26 715 000
H. 152p

Solving problems (pages 150–153)
A. (1) 8.04 m   (2) 11.46 m   (3) 5.562 m
   (4) 12.66 m
B. You must **never** look at the sun. It could
   blind you.
C. 1100:31°, 1200:36.9°, 1300:31.8°,
   1400:25.1°, 1500:18.4°
D. 6 m

Simultaneous equations (pages 154–156)

A. (4, 1)
C. (1) $x = 2, y = 1$ (2) $x = 5, y = {}^-2$
    (3) $x = 4\frac{1}{2}, y = 6\frac{1}{2}$
E. (1) $m = 1, n = {}^-2$ (4) $p = 3, q = 1$
    (2) $x = 2, y = {}^-4$ (5) $x = {}^-3, y = 6$
    (3) $r = {}^-1, s = {}^-1$ (6) $a = 2, b = \frac{1}{3}$
G. (1) $x = 2, y = 2$ (2) $r = 1, s = {}^-2$
    (3) $x = 7, y = 10$

Angles in circles (pages 157–160)

A. (2) (a) They are all the same size.
       (b) They are all in the same segment.
B. (1) b, c (2) e, f (3) h, j
C. 2 (b) Angle O is twice angle A.
D. (1) c (2) h (3) k
E. They are all right angles.
F. (1) a, e (2) g, h (3) n, l

Drawing curves (pages 161–165)

A. (1)

x	$^-4$	$^-3$	$^-2$	$^-1$	0	1	2	3	4
$y = x^2$	16	9	4	1	0	1	4	9	16

    (2) $(^-4, 16)$, $(^-3, 9)$, $(^-2, 4)$, $(^-1, 1)$,
    $(0, 0)$, $(1, 1)$, $(2, 4)$, $(3, 9)$, $(4, 16)$
B. (1) 12.3   (2) 2.3   (3) 0.3   (4) 6.3
C. (1) $^-1.4, 1.4$ (2) $^-3.7, 3.7$
    (3) $^-2.2, 2.2$ (4) $^-2.7, 2.7$

Packages (page 166)

A. (1) 495 cm²   (2) 198 cm²   (3) 132 cm²
    (4) 220 cm²   (5) 484 cm²
B. (a) $38\frac{1}{2}$ cm²   (b) 308 cm²   (c) 385 cm²

Party Planners (pages 168–169)

A.

sausages	600 g	60 g	960 g
potatoes	1.2 kg	0.12 kg	1.92 kg
butter	65 g	6.5 g	104 g
cheese	80 g	8 g	128 g
baked beans	550 g	55 g	880 g

B. (1) 32   (2) 48

Topic classification

Each entry is the first page number of a topic.
Entries in italics indicate major subsidiary mathematical areas included in the topic.

Sections	1	2	3	4	5	Revision	Questions
Number and approximation	17	40, 46, 49, 50, 60				178, 184	177, 179, 185
Fractions and decimals	*12*					180, 182	181, 183
Algebra	17, 26	40	80	108, 118, 127	154, 161	186	188
Percentages	12	*54*		115, 132		190	191
Measure	*12, 14, 21, 28*	*36, 43, 46*	66, 83		*168*	190	191
Money	*12, 20, 32*	*36, 43, 54*		115, 132	146	192	193
Angle and shape	22	*39*, 53	91	130	*142*, 157, 167	195, 198	196, 199
Constructions		62	88	124	142		
Trigonometry	9	39, 58	71	134	150	201	202
Area and volume			96, 98	111, 120	138, 166	204, 207	205, 208
Ratio and proportion	20, 28	43	*91*, 98		138, *142*, 168	210	211
Graphs		36	83	118	161	213	214
Statistics	6		75	104		216	218
Calculators	5	52	90	129	170		
Recaps	35	65	103	137	171		
Sidetracks	11, 19		74, 82, 89, 95	110, 119, 136	172, 173		

Hutchinson & Co. (Publishers) Ltd
An imprint of the Hutchinson Publishing Group
17–21 Conway Street, London W1P 6JD

Hutchinson Group (Australia) Pty Ltd
30–32 Cremorne Street, Richmond South, Victoria 3121
PO Box 151, Broadway, New South Wales 2007

Hutchinson Group (NZ) Ltd
32–34 View Road, PO Box 40-086, Glenfield, Auckland 10

Hutchinson Group (SA) (Pty) Ltd
PO Box 337, Bergvlei 2012, South Africa

First published 1983

© Duncan and Christine Graham 1983
Illustrations © Hutchinson & Co. (Publishers) Ltd 1983

Designed by SGS Education, 8 New Row, London WC2N 4LH

Cartoon illustrations by Martin Williams

Printed in Great Britain by The Anchor Press Ltd and
bound by Wm Brendon & Son Ltd both of Tiptree, Essex

ISBN 0 09 141051 7